Biologists

In the Field

Stories, Tales, and Anecdotes
from 150 Years of Field Biology

editors

Michael R. Jeffords
Susan L. Post
Charles Warwick

Design and layout by Carolyn Peet Nixon

Illinois Natural History Survey
Institute for Natural Resources Sustainability
University of Illinois at Urbana-Champaign
August 2008

Illinois Natural History Survey

Since 1858 the Illinois Natural History Survey (INHS) has been the guardian and recorder of the biological resources of Illinois—the state's biological memory. With a staff of over 200 scientists and technicians, it is recognized as one of the premier natural history surveys in the nation. Over the years, its mission has remained fairly constant: to investigate the diversity, life histories, and ecology of the plants and animals of the state; to publish research results so that those resources can be managed wisely; and to provide information to the public in order to foster an understanding and appreciation of our natural heritage.

Stephen Forbes was the first director of the INHS, and to him the word "survey" meant more than a censusing of organisms or publishing lists showing their distribution. Forbes felt that any study should define the relationships among living organisms and their environment—an ecological survey. This theory prevailed in his work and underlined the early research done at the Natural History Survey. In 1880 Forbes stated, "The first indispensable requisite is a thorough knowledge of the natural order—an intelligently conducted natural history survey. Without the general knowledge which such a survey would give us, all our measures must be empirical, temporary, uncertain, and often dangerous." Many components make up the INHS. Its research, collections, publications, long-term studies, field stations, and educational outreach have not only made the Illinois Natural History Survey the largest, but also the most successful state biological survey in the country.

In 1878 Forbes would write, "Without this class of workers [field biologists], devoted to science for its own sake, no solid and valuable progress in science is possible. From them comes the initiative, the incitement. They are the root of the tree by which the raw elements of the natural world have been in ages drawn together and made ready for the nourishment of the organism." Scientific research is the nucleus of the Illinois Natural History Survey. It is the organization's central and most important function that sustains it and its scientists. *Biologists in the Field* documents some of these research moments—good or bad—yet always at the forefront of the scientist's mind is gathering the information.

Contents

Foreword   May Berenbaum vii
Introduction ix
Letters of Stephen A. Forbes to Clara Forbes xii
Chapter 1—Doing the Work 1
   First Responder   Ed Heske 2
   The Summer of Our Discontent   Cathy Eastman and Susan Post 5
   A Net Full of Bats and More!   Joyce Hofmann 8
   The Do's and Don'ts of Research   Don Webb 9
   You Got a Dead One?   David L. Thomas 10
   Adventures in Nighttime Electroshocking   Jeremy Tiemann 12
   The Disappearing Boat   Luke Freeman 13
   Newton Lake   Diane Szafoni 15
   Where Are the Ducks?   Stephen P. Havera and Michelle M. Horath 17
   High Security Bird Surveys   Dan Wenny 22
   Context Dependent Behavior   David A. Enstrom 25
   Life with Bailey   Steve Bailey 27
   Thermal Agriculture   Ed Armbrust 35
   Getting High with the Beetles   Joseph Spencer 36
   Getting Started in the Business   Don Webb 38
   Canned Salamanders   Jen Mui 39
Chapter 2—Blast from the Past 41
   In the Field with Alfred Gross   Tom Rice 42
   Voyages of the *Anax*   William McClain, with Katie Roat and Tom Lerczak ... 45
   Gleaning from Gleason   Susan Post 48
   Robert Evers—Botanist Extraordinaire   Susan Post 53
   The Grabers   Susan Post (with Karen Frailey) 55
   Night Flight with a Thrush   Richard R. Graber (former INHS researcher) 58
   I Remember Bill   Homer Buck 66
   RestauranTouring Illinois (Eateries in Time)   Mark J. Wetzel 68
Chapter 3—Work Abroad 73
   An Electrifying Experience   as told to Susan Post 75
   Across Europe: Bathrooms, Bedbugs, and Bedlam
      Michael R. Jeffords 76
   Brain Borer   Rob Wiedenmann 81
   Stuck on the Border with Bugs   Lee Solter 84
   Cultural (and Biological) Learnings of Kyrgyzstan   Chris Dietrich 87
   International Kindness   Don Webb 101
Chapter 4—Odd Perceptions: Interacting with the Public 103
   Naked Turtles?   Randy Nyboer 104
   Looking Before We Leap: All in a Day's Work at INHS
      Charlie Warwick 106
   Field Talk   Joseph Spencer 108
   Close Encounters of the Constabulary Kind   Don Webb 110
   Small Town Police   Joyce Hofmann 111

To Serve and Protect?   John B. Taft 112
Top 10 Lists of Things We've Learned from the Illinois Natural
History Survey Traveling Science Center
Heather Grotefend and Jen Mui 113
Learning to Trust Our Instincts   Jen Mui and Heather Grotefend 118
Potential Discovery of New Bat Species: *Lasiurus hominidus bicyclius*
Jacquelyn Potter 121
Chasing Frogs Across the "Great Corn Desert" of Illinois   Jen Mui .. 123
Frog and Toad Surveys   Chris Phillips 126
Mouse at DQ   Joyce Hofmann 127
Fieldwork is a Peach of a Job   Don Webb 128
Nightly Knights in Shining Armor   Don Webb 129
To Be a Field Biologist for a Day—IWIN   Susan Post 130
Directions   Michael Jeffords 135

Chapter 5—Ah, the Weather! 137
The Field Botanist's Mantra   Steve Hill 139
A Trip to Illinois' Sinkhole Plain: In which Nature Hints,
Warns, and then Speaks   Steven J. Taylor 140
#12   Michael Jeffords and Charles Helm 146
Winter Sampling Blues   David Thomas 148
All in A Day's Fieldwork   Diane Szafoni 150
Red Oak Backpack Trail   Susan Post 152
Job of My Dreams: A Night on Bath Chute   Kevin S. Irons 155

Chapter 6—Field Mishaps 157
The Electric Canoe   Charlie Warwick 158
Up to My Ass !   Anne Bartlett 163
Collecting Alfalfa Weevils and Other Critters   Ed Armbrust 165
A Halloween Adventure   Matt O'Neal as told to Susan Post 166
A Rattlesnake Tale   Kenneth R. Robertson 169
Entering the Retch Zone   John B. Taft 172
Fragrant Fields   Michael R. Jeffords 175

Chapter 7—To Be a Biologist 177
Journal of Susan Post 178
Goose Killer   David A. Enstrom 179
A Close Encounter   Susan Post 181
Sixty-Minute Cruise   Susan Post 183
A Fox Goes to Work   Joseph Spencer 185
Capturing Mystery   Michael R. Jeffords 187

Chapter 8—Personal Introspection 189
Images from the Field—Field Work   Connie Cunningham 191
Why Do This?   Michael R. Jeffords 192
The Fawn   Ben O'Neal 194
Stalking the Fox   Joe Spencer 195
Finding My Calling   Gail Kampmeier 197
Dissection Haiku   Joseph Spencer 200
Reflections on a Quadrat   Jamie Ellis 201

Comparative Cognition or A World Divided   Jim Sechrest 204
The Black Sheep   Greg G. Sass 208
The Illinois River . . .   Thad Cook 212

Foreword

In 1984, environmental historian Donald Worster famously lamented, "There is little history in the study of nature, and there is little nature in the study of history." This book, *Biologists in the Field: Stories, Tales and Anecdotes from 150 Years of Field Biology*, is a splendid exception to the prevailing trend. This collection of essays offers a glimpse of the range of triumphs and tribulations experienced by field biologists of the Illinois Natural History Survey over the course of its 150-year existence and in doing so offers insights into a scientific enterprise of which the general public is for the most part blissfully unaware. Today, the word "scientist" for most people likely conjures up the image of an individual (generally of the male persuasion) in a white lab coat, bent over a microscope or holding some sort of test tube or odd-shaped flask aloft. Indeed, laboratory science has tended to grab most of the headlines over the past century and a half. But all wise biologists—even those who have never worked with any part of an organism larger than a single cell—recognize that, as powerful as laboratory science is, it is hopelessly inadequate for investigating most aspects of how organisms interact with each other and with their physical environment.

The principal advantage of working in a laboratory is that investigators can carefully control most or all variables and thus, in theory, exclude confusing factors that might make interpretation of results ambiguous. However, it is an inescapable fact that the natural world is inherently complex and that to understand how it functions necessitates actively seeking out and embracing variability, complexity, and unpredictability. Stephen A. Forbes, the first Chief of the Illinois Natural History Survey, described the importance of field biology in his Presidential Address to the Ecological Society of America delivered December 28, 1921:

"We have had in the service of the Natural History Survey of Illinois an ecologist and an entomologist engaged...upon the same economic problem—that of the life history of the codling-moth as affected by...varying meteorological conditions...The entomologist has operated by the method of direct observation, with the aid of field laboratories equipped with apparatus for making continuous records of open-air temperatures, rainfall, humidity, and rate of evaporation; while the ecologist has used the experimental method in a laboratory provided with means of accurately controlling degrees of heat, light, moisture, air movement, and evaporation, thus studying separately the effect of various degrees and rates of change in each of the elements which enter into the complex of conditions that make up the weather...a complex which the field entomologist was compelled to take as a whole without distinction or separation of its parts...Each has contributed the common product important elements...which could not possibly have been arrived out by either one alone."

Field research remains as utterly essential today for understanding the natural world as it was when the Illinois Natural History Survey was founded; although the equipment and technology for working in the field have grown substantially more sophisticated since Forbes delivered his address, the natural world hasn't grown any more predictable or any less variable. Thus, being a successful field biologist requires certain personality attributes. A love of nature is a given—but working in the field also demands resourcefulness, flexibility, and unflappability. When something goes wrong, field biologists can't just go downstairs to talk with tech support; they're effectively left to their own devices. Thus, it's not enough to be well-versed in one's subdiscipline of biology and conversant with hypothesis-testing and experimental methods. As the anecdotes in this collection illustrate so engagingly, field biologists on the job are not just entomologists, botanists, ichthyologists, mammalogists, or ecologists. They're also mechanics, medics, navigators, meteorologists, psychologists, sociologists, and diplomats, when and if the need arises. No one can really anticipate the skill sets that will be useful in the field—few curricula include, for example, communicating in Kyrgyz or cardiopulmonary resuscitation for nonresponsive gray squirrels.

Although I don't know everyone who has contributed to this volume—indeed, some of the essays were written before I was born—I do feel a sense of kinship with the authors; this kinship is probably shared by all biologists who have worked in the field at some point during their careers. My anxiety about driving and predisposition for getting lost have limited most of my own field experiences to roadsides and waste places not more than a quarter-mile from a street sign. However, I've experienced the variability, complexity, and uncertainty even in these postage-sized parcels of seemingly degraded nature, as well as the thrill of discovering new species, describing novel interactions, or even detailing new dimensions of an otherwise thoroughly documented phenomenon. As urbanization and development divide and conquer much of what remains of our natural heritage, field biology becomes more important than ever. These essays showcase the challenges and the rewards of this vital but little-heralded enterprise; I know they will entertain readers but I hope they will also inspire and maybe recruit a few to the cause.

May R. Berenbaum
Head, Department of Entomology
University of Illinois at Urbana-Champaign

Introduction

Does the word "scientist" conjur images of someone dressed in a clean white lab coat, using a variety of glassware full of colorful, bubbling liquids? While that may have been an accurate description of perhaps one-third of survey scientists 30+ years ago, the scientist of today is more likely to wear jeans and some sort of nice nature theme T-shirt during the days in the office. Field attire is usually field pants that dry quickly, an old nature theme T-shirt covered with a long-sleeved shirt, and a hat. Most of our jobs require that we actually be in the field. Perhaps Indiana Jones-type figures come to mind?

Ah, the field. To the Illinois Natural History Survey office staff or other colleagues that never get to experience "the field," the term must seem a magical place where we disappear with tape measures, nets, plant presses, jars, bags, traps, PVC measuring squares, and a variety of other implements to collect data. They see us leaving with smiles, most always laughing and joking. When we return our clothes reek of insect repellent and sunscreen, there is usually a trail of dirt through the clean hallways of our buildings, and our data pages are smudged with stains or warped from the humidity, but we still are laughing and joking. A colleague once quipped "the best day in the office is far worse than the worst day in the field."

To be a field biologist is, well, special. We are an interesting lot, capable of incredible stubbornness in the face of adversity and always willing to do whatever it takes to collect "the data." Ah, the data, always first and foremost in our minds.

In reality, though, we are living our dreams, and how many people actually get to do that? As children many of us chased butterflies, fished, hunted with Dad, or just explored the out-of-doors. We are still outside, but now answering important questions. What organisms occur along a certain corridor? How do we increase certain organisms' population sizes? What is causing a species to decline? How many ducks migrate through Illinois? What is the best way to restore land to its "original" state? How do we get rid of unwanted invasive species? The days in the field may be long, uncomfortable, and full of tedium, but we are still out there, alone or in small groups, having fun in places where we have never lost our passion for discovery.

In scanning the few field journals available while attempting to pull this project together, we [the editors, two of whom are field biologists] discovered several things about our colleagues.

- Collectively, we are not great journalers, as our entries go more toward the mundane; most of our field experiences have taken the form of stories, best extracted over a few beers at a local pub.
- We can all write "to our market," i.e., technical reports and scientific journal articles in our various fields. Even incredibly detailed, convoluted grant proposals are in our verbal repertoire.
- We, with some exceptions, are not well-versed in writing for the popular market. In most cases, scientists simply don't do it.

Thus, this project has proved to be more difficult to implement than we imagined. But having listened to the tales, trials, and tribulations of field scientists for many years—and experienced some of our own—we thought a volume written for the general public, about what it's actually like to spend a frigid night in an open boat shocking fish, crawl through wet, dark cave passages as the sound of thunder rolls through the blackness, stare numbly in the hot, close forest at that last quarter-meter transect of the day, summit remote mountain passes in central Asia with nothing between you and disaster but a cranky, aging truck, or do field work in Illinois in the 1870s, would help citizens understand what we do, and perhaps why we do it. We have attempted to keep scientific jargon out of the narratives and have defined most technical terms in the text.

For *Biologists in the Field* we have sought to humanize biological field science on this, the 150th Anniversary of the Illinois Natural History Survey, to showcase what the life of a field biologist is like, and perhaps give a sense of the passion we exhibiton a daily basis. This volume is by no means a complete treatise on the subject, but rather repesents materials we were able to collect over several months. Many scientists were simply not interested in participating, as this volume is not a "peer-reviewed publication," the intellectual capital of our trade. A goodly number, however, stepped into the breech and contributed materials, while for others we delved deeply into Survey archives and historical documents. For some, a simple interview teased out events and happenings that were well-known, even legendary, tales that inevitably surfaced at any Survey social event involving a modicum of beer. The majority, however, had never been put to paper. An example of this process (sans beer) occurred in Urbana, IL, April 23, 2007.

"I'm sitting in the backyard of a retired aquatic biologist and his wife— R. Weldon Larimore and Glennie—facing a somewhat unkept thicket of a yard, one certainly not likely to be on any garden tour, but one that admirably fulfills its purpose. We're surrounded by life at arm's length— White-throated Sparrows, Mourning Doves, Cardinals, squirrels; even a Broad-winged Hawk flies over. A story about a shrew at their small garden pond from years past contributes to the animal cavalcade. Somehow this all seems appropriate, the correct setting, and the stories come forth, snippet by snippet— names emerging from the dim and not-so-dim past, like the complex, dendritic branches of an ancient oak, slowly appearing from an evening fog. Some stories seem appropriate, others not, most are just random observations from past experiences that certainly breathe life into what makes a biologist a biologist.

- *Female "field" biologists were not allowed to go in the field until the late 1960s. It was thought not to be safe or proper.*
- *Alison Brigham once slipped carrying a large channel catfish and impaled her breast with its spine and had to go to the hospital for treatment.*

• *At Havana in the late 1940s, Frank Bellrose employed old fishermen to man the nets and service the Anax, an early INHS research boat. Once on Lake Chautauqua, crusty fisherman Jake Lim heard a Prothonotary Warbler singing on a buttonbush and uttered, "sing you little son-of-a-bitch, I like to hear you sing."*
• *"Doc" Thompson would disappear from the boat as it approached towns and would invariably reappear with a local female companion for the evening.*
• *We always seemed to have annual parties, but on a weekly schedule.*

It seems that biologists are no different from anyone else, except for the added passion of an intense love for nature. Glennie exemplifies this when she recounts "many's the night I let Larry back into bed, reeking of dead fish, returning after a long night of sampling."

We hope you enjoy the world of the field biologist and perhaps take note the next time you see that mysterious vehicle parked along a deserted roadside. It may be one of us, diligently working away to help keep Illinois a biologically diverse state into the next millennium.

Field biology—it's all about gathering "the data."

Letters of Stephen A. Forbes to Clara Forbes
Stephen Alfred Forbes Collection, Illinois Historical Survey Library, University of Illinois at Urbana-Champaign.

Compiled and edited by Daniel W. Schneider

Stephen Alfred Forbes

One of the first field biologists of the Illinois Natural History Survey (and the "Father" of the institution) was Stephen A. Forbes. His pioneering work in the areas of entomology, aquatic ecology, and biology as a whole, provided the fledgling institution with a firm grounding in science. Many of his scientific writings are timeless and we still draw on them today. But what about the personal side of Forbes as a field biologist and as a man? Forbes was a prolific writer and penned many letters to his beloved wife Clara about his adventures doing field work across Illinois and the country at a time when those activities were far more difficult than today. Rather than a litany of Forbes' entire letters, we have chosen to excerpt from them throughout *Biologists In the Field* to provide a historical context, a setting, even a perception, of what it was like "in the good old days."

Each chapter is introduced by one of Forbes' letters to his wife, Clara.

Chapter 1

Doing the Work

Havana, IL November 1, 1877

Up at 6, all over town before seven for boxes, paper, nails, sawdust, ice, a boat and a fisherman, and off down the river at eight, pulling an oar against a sturdy follower of St. Antony. Weather cold, no woman knows the misery of standing around in a cutting wind with a drop of half-frozen water at the tip of one's nose and the general situation as comfortless as possible. Sitting on a dry-goods box in a fisherman's boat, I measured the bodies and head and eyes and fins of buffaloes and counted their fin rays and scales and entered the notes in my book for over two hours. Then followed decapitation and evisceration and labeling and bottling and noting down again and then, worst of all, dinner. A fine table beside which your kitchen sink is cleanliness itself, a dish of boiled beef that even my fisherman's appetite found impracticable, coffee in bowls, with brown sugar and without milk, grey heavy bread and very good butter. The sugar was in a cigarbox, the butter in a tin can. But that will do for to-night, I think. This evening I rowed up to town alone, four miles up stream, in a little less than hour. The sun had just gone down, the river facing me was one long stream of sunsets, a pale star was just visible before me, the islands and the shores were glorious with autumn color and the strain of rapid rowing together with the frosty air, keyed me up to just the point for the intense enjoyment of the sight of the eye and the hearing of the ear. So I came in with my hands smarting, my arms half paralyzed, my feet wet—but full once more of the old enthusiasm that never is found in museum rooms, nor even in my lady's chamber.

Adaptive first aid—pushing the envelope!

First Responder
Ed Heske

As a field biologist, I have spent considerable time traveling to remote areas of the world, particularly in my youth. Before settling down in Illinois, I worked or traveled at various times on all continents except Antarctica, in habitats ranging from Arctic tundra to tropical forests to hot deserts. Even while working in the U.S., I sometimes have camped and worked far from sources of help should an accident happen, and cell phones are a fairly recent development. Sometimes I have had student field technicians working with me. Consequently, I have taken courses in first aid when they were offered and tried to keep up on my CPR training. Just in case . . .

Mostly, I have been quite lucky, given some of the situations I found myself in. However, they say most accidents happen close to home, and it was not in central Asia, or South Africa, or Australia, or the Galapagos Islands where my first responder skills were put to the test—not even Central America, or the southwestern deserts, or even the Shawnee Hills of southern Illinois. It was right here in Champaign-Urbana.

I was helping with a project comparing body condition, parasite loads, and exposure to wildlife diseases in gray squirrels living in town and in the country. Although I had helped to design the project and get it started, the real work was being done as an honors project by two undergraduate female students, under the watchful guidance of another INHS scientist with degrees in veterinary medicine and epidemiology. In winter, spring, and summer, gray squirrels were captured, weighed and measured, groomed for ectoparasites (ticks, fleas, mites, lice), and a small blood sample was drawn for later testing before the squirrels were released at their capture sites. As this episode unfolded, it happened to be winter.

My INHS colleague had other commitments one afternoon; however, the undergraduates were seasoned veterans at this point. We had captured a half-dozen gray squirrels from a wooded area outside of town and brought them back to a pole barn on campus to process them in a sheltered area. My job was to get each squirrel out of the live trap (small, cagelike boxes made of strong wire mesh), restrain it in a handling cone made of flexible chicken wire, sedate it with an injection of ketamine and xylazine, and then pass it to the undergrads after it was unconscious. The undergrads carefully measured and groomed the squirrels and drew the blood samples, following approved university protocols, while I looked on to make sure everything was done properly and safely. I then returned the squirrel to a cage for holding until it was fully awake and active again. We would take the recovered squirrels back to their homes and release them after all the captures for that day were processed. Things were going quite well, but those winter days are short and we had a lot of squirrels to work on that afternoon.

One adult female squirrel proved troublesome late in the day. Sometimes it's just difficult to locate the artery in the leg from which to draw blood, and we just couldn't seem to successfully get a blood sample from this one. Soon, the squirrel began to show signs of arousing from the sedatives. I decided to give her another small dose of the drugs to knock her out until we finished taking the blood sample.

We finally finished for the day. Some of the squirrels were still wobbly on their feet, but most were coming around quickly and looked OK. Time to take them back to the woods. It was already dark. But one squirrel (the troublesome one) was still unresponsive, out cold.

I couldn't just leave her in the woods, unconscious on a cold winter night, and the pole barn was cold and drafty as well, and not particularly secure. We did not have a lab to house her for the night, but I wanted to keep an eye on her during her recovery anyway. So I broke with protocol and took her home, planning to let her recover on the floor in my kitchen. I put some food and water in the cage, and covered the top and two sides with a black trash bag to keep it dark, leaving the front and back ends uncovered for circulation of air. I expected she would be fine by morning and I would deliver her to her woodland home on my way to work.

When I checked on her a bit later that evening, I noticed she had stopped breathing. In a panic, I took her out of the cage and laid her on my kitchen table. Now, I'm not exactly a bleeding-heart type. I'm not a vegan, enjoy fishing, and think hunting is a fine outdoors activity (although I've only been hunting once myself). However, like most biologists, I was drawn to my profession because I like animals. I try to make my recreational activities

A squirrel in need of CPR!

low-impact. Although I have trapped and handled hundreds (thousands!) of animals in my lifetime, I am never careless of their welfare. Even though this was "just a squirrel," I expect she valued her life in her own way. I did not want this squirrel to die needlessly. Besides, what would I tell the undergrads in the morning? There was only one thing to do: I began CPR.

I laid her on her back, placed my fingers on her chest, and there! I felt a faint heartbeat. She wasn't breathing, but she wasn't dead yet. I tapped her chest gently, but firmly, about 15 times. Then I tipped her head back, like we practiced in CPR training . . . How do you give mouth-to-mouth to a squirrel? How can you pinch that little nose and exhale into that little mouth? You can't. I had to stick her whole face in my mouth and exhale gently, blowing her up like a little balloon, watching to make sure her chest rose, but not too much, then gently depress her chest again. I gave her two breaths, then leaned back. Was this crazy? (Don't answer that.) But then, she seemed to shudder a bit, and took one breath of her own. And stopped again. I waited, but nothing else happened, no more breathing, no further response. I repeated the breath of life, this time using my handkerchief as a makeshift barrier.

It took about a half hour, but finally she started to breath again on her own. Slowly, haltingly, often failing to persist for more than a few attempts, but eventually succeeding. I returned her to her cage, then headed for the Listerine. By morning she had recovered and I released her back into the woodlot where she had been captured, and she sprinted for the nearest tree, not looking back. She looked fine, but of course, any possible psychological trauma is impossible to determine.

Ground squirrels 3, entomologists 0 . . .

The Summer of Our Discontent
Cathy Eastman and Susan Post

The 1993 field research campaign began in an orderly, methodical manner. Our project goal was straightforward: to determine how grasses and grassy weeds might serve as virus reservoirs for the transmission of Barley Yellow Dwarf viruses by aphids into cereal crops in the Midwest. Barley Yellow Dwarf Disease is a problem for cereal crops and pasture grasses worldwide. Armed with good intentions and determination, we embraced this challenge enthusiastically, without a shred of foreboding of what was to come.

Our strategy took shape during several intense breakfast-meeting discussions with our main collaborators, Illinois Natural History Survey (INHS) entomologist Gail Kampmeier and U.S. Department of Agriculture plant pathologist Adrianna Hewings. Teacups and biscuits in hand, we planned a two-pronged approach to the field research. First, we would establish small plots (5 feet by 10 feet) at South Farms on the University of Illinois campus to determine if the unique isolate of a Barley Yellow Dwarf Virus strain we had identified could be moved by aphids in two scenarios: a) from spring oats to susceptible grasses (Oats-to-Grass trial) and, b) from the grasses to winter wheat (Grass-to-Wheat trial). In the Oats-to-Grass trial, oats to be used as virus sources would be planted first in a center row of hills and the test grasses planted later alongside the oats. In separate plots for the Grass-to-Wheat trial, test grasses to be used as virus sources would be planted first in center strips with wheat planted later next to the grass strips. The grasses and cereals to be tested were perennial ryegrass, tall fescue, Kentucky bluegrass, timothy, yellow foxtail, giant foxtail, and sorghum. Border rows of a dwarf variety of soybeans (not susceptible to Barley Yellow Dwarf viruses) would separate the plots. Second, as a Pasture Grass trial we would establish large plots (50 feet by 50 feet) of three pasture grasses (Kentucky bluegrass, perennial ryegrass, and tall fescue) at the "Lost 40" field site in Champaign County. Here, we would use aphids to inoculate plants with our unique virus isolate at sites in the field and then monitor in-field spread of the virus during the summer. By golly, by gum, we had one elegant, *beautiful* field experiment plan!

Trouble soon arrived at our research sites, peering silently over the horizon and stealing in on little cat feet (apologies to Carl Sandburg). A cold, wet spring delayed planting in the Oats-to-Grass trial until May 11. By May 14 only 149 of the 960 oat hills we had planted in the Oats-to-Grass trial remained. Hummmm! What's going on here? A quick search revealed that the South Farm site was "host" to a resident population of thirteen-lined ground squirrels, super hungry after the long winter. Our enthusiasm undiminished, we replanted the oats on May 19, but the low-rider mammal marauders quickly gobbled up all but 100 of the hills in this planting, too. Feeling a bit perturbed at this point, despite our fondness for cute, beady-eyed creatures, we had to try a different approach. Thus, we made a third planting on June 7, this time using oat transplants instead of seeds and leaving an "offering" of sunflower seeds and grain at strategic ground squirrel burrow locations throughout the fields. Success! (But, oh, how fleeting!)

Once the oat transplants were growing well, we infested them with aphids carrying our Barley Yellow Dwarf Virus isolate, then planted the border rows of dwarf soybeans that were to separate the plots from each other. Throughout June we hoed, raked, and weeded to prepare the seedbed for the grass test plants that would surround the virus-infected oats. Flashes of light blinked through the cloud cover. Crack! "Was that lightning, Cathy?" Eight days of rain in June slowed the field progress, but we carried on. By early July the grasses in the oat plots had finally been planted, and we waited to see if aphids would spread virus from the infected oats to the grass test plants. Weeding was attacked with a vengeance. Was that a foxtail seedling (a desirable test plant) or a real "weed?" Crack! Zap!! CrrrrrrrrrrACK!!! "Race you to the van, Sue!" Lightning and another 14 days of rain in July stopped our work in its tracks on many occasions; we had **NOT** included a repetition of Ben Franklin's famous electricity experiments as part of the work plans.

While the field activities continued, so did the record-setting rains. As a result, grassy weeds overran the slower-growing test grasses in some plots, which then had to be replanted. Moss grew in several plots, and the ground was often too muddy for any fieldwork. The excess rain enabled our border rows of "dwarf" soybeans to grow chest-high, shading the experimental grasses and making plot-to-plot access nigh impossible. By early August the plots of timothy and Kentucky bluegrass test grasses were abandoned; although seeded twice, they never established sufficiently to compete with the weeds. Several plots of perennial rye and tall fescue were also overrun. Too bad our ground squirrels didn't seem to like weeds. On August 12 we received 6.3 inches of rain in two hours! (This one rain event, we later learned, caused an estimated $3.8 million in damage to facilities at the University of Illinois.) Even Noah would have dropped his hoe and started building the ark at this point.

With the Oats-to-Grass experiment at least limping along, we turned our weary attention to the Grass-to-Wheat plots. Although the grasses to be tested as virus sources had been planted in June, these plots were now also overrun with weeds. Preparing them required using a machete to hack down the weeds and "dwarf" soybean borders. The plots were then jack-hammered with a spade-fork and hoed to break up the concretelike soil so that we could till them with a portable Rototiller™. To keep down additional weed growth, we covered the newly cleared plots with black plastic until they could be planted. Within two weeks we had salvaged three perennial rye plots from the original June planting and prepared and planted the center strips in another 24 plots with transplants of wheat, sorghum, timothy, and yellow foxtail. But apparently even female scientists are not immune to the old saw "The best-laid plans of mice and men often go awry." Two days after the planting was finished, we found second-generation cutworm caterpillars eating half of the sorghum and yellow foxtail plots, while the ubiquitous ground squirrels were feasting on the wheat and timothy transplants. In addition, areas we had protected with black plastic had become condominiums for families of meadow voles. As a result, we were able to complete only one-quarter of our Grass-to-Wheat experiment. To add insult to injury, we learned we could not obtain additional seed supplies of "Wabash" Kentucky bluegrass, the elite variety we were using in both large- and small-plot trials. And just WHY was that? Because Japan had purchased the entire U.S. production of this variety FOR THE NEXT 10 YEARS for use in their golf courses!

Yes, our high sense of optimism was nearly drowned in the reality of a field season of serial (cereal) disasters. Sometimes one's best efforts are just not good enough. Nevertheless, we Women of Entomology never say die! We sharpened our hoes, stockpiled vast stores of grass/weed seed, and prepared to do battle again next season. But, just in case the Flood of 1993 became the Deluge of 1994, we began planning an alternate research project: whether or not Barley Yellow Dwarf viruses infect AstroTurf™.

It all seemed so simple, so clean, so elegant.

Catching more than you bargained for.

A Net Full of Bats and More!
Joyce Hofmann

One summer night INHS botanist Bill Handel and an intern were helping me mistnet for bats over Yellow Creek in northwestern Illinois. The first time we checked the net we found a couple of bats entangled in it. As I began to remove them, other bats hit the net. More and more bats continued to fly in and soon we had a net full of bats—many more than usual. To complicate the situation, we realized that rain was approaching. The three of us worked to extract the bats from the net as fast as possible—not always an easy task, removing a squirming bat from a nearly invisible net in the dark. As soon as we had removed the last of the bats, we closed the net, lest more be captured. That evening we ended up with a pillowcase bulging with 39 unhappy individuals, a true "bag o' bats." Apparently we had placed the net close to a maternity colony of little brown bats and had managed to catch a significant number of them. We quickly examined and released them all, finishing just as the rain began.

On another night when I checked a mist net set over a creek, I saw that a fish had become entangled at the very bottom of the net. I grabbed the fish to remove it and discovered that a water snake also had hold of it. After a brief tug-of-war to free the fish, I let the snake have its meal.

Because many people are not familiar with the type of biological surveys we do, our intentions are sometimes misunderstood. For example, one day we stopped at a business to ask permission to leave our vehicle in their parking lot to walk across a cornfield to a creek where we wanted to mistnet for bats. When we told the man in the office that we were going to catch bats at Yellow Creek, he said "Bass? There aren't any bass in that creek."

On another night a group of us was netting for bats on the Little Vermilion River. As the three of us walked through the river to check the net, we saw something very large in it. At first I worried that it was an owl, which would be painful to extricate from the net. As we got closer we realized it was a young great blue heron standing in the river with its bill caught in the net. Now, this was ironic because the previous night we had been talking about herons and someone had said that they "go for the eyes" with their big bills. Taking this advice to heart, we approached the bird very cautiously. I immediately grabbed the bill and held it shut. Another person grabbed the body and the third untangled the net from the bill. We then turned 180° in unison, like some bad biological ballet, released the heron, and let it fly away.

Too much diversity!

The Do's and Don'ts of Research
Don Webb

Field research is never as clear cut and precise as you designed in it your office. As part of an on-going research study of the springs of Illinois (SPOIL), my colleague Rick Phillippe and I were involved in determining the animal and plant species of Salt Well Spring (Negro Spring, Salt Wells) in Gallatin County. This salt spring was within The Great Salt Springs site listed on the National Register of Historic Places in 1973, and during the late 1800s was a source of saltwater for the commercial production of salt. The current springhead is four square meters in area and three meters deep and is enclosed by bridge timbers laid half a meter above the surrounding floodplain. Normally, the collection of aquatic organisms was a simple task of sieving a measured amount of bottom material and determining the number of species and biomass (weight of living organisms) per square meter. In July of 1993 this procedure took on a whole new meaning. Upon approaching the saltwell, Rick and I were confronted with a female white-tailed deer (*Odocoileus virginianus*) floating exhausted in the spring. It had apparently jumped over the retaining wall into the enclosed springhead and was unable to extricate itself. This brought up several safety concerns, including the thought of being bitten as we lifted it from the pool or perhaps being eviscerated by its hooves. Still, the animal was exhausted and would eventually drown if we were to leave her there, so gallantry triumphed over personal safety and we lifted her passively from the spring. In time, the young doe rose to her feet and wobbly walked off into the woods. While this was a true victory for nature conservation, it posed a perplexing problem for strict scientific research. Could we legitimately add her name to the species richness of the spring and should we have weighed her and added her to our biomass estimates?

So that's what happened to the Survey's Petermore dredge!

You Got a Dead One?
David L. Thomas

One of the ways science makes advancements is through the development of new scientific equipment and instrumentation. As a young scientist you often end up with the job of testing this equipment to determine how it works and to begin collecting the data needed to meet research objectives.

One of the special treats of working with Illinois Natural History Survey (INHS) scientist R. Weldon Larimore in the 1960s was that he was always thinking of better ways of collecting data. Collecting scientific data in large rivers was a particular challenge, and presented difficulties not encountered in our smaller streams. One of these challenges was to collect benthic macroinvertebrates (bottom-dwelling animals without backbones) from the bottom sediments of the Kaskaskia River. Standard dredges used in lakes just didn't seem to work most of the time, usually because sticks and other debris found on the river bottom kept the dredge from properly closing, and the sediment was lost in retrieval of the dredge.

Dr. Larimore had the idea that if you could put a dredge on poles and manually close them (sort of like a post hole digger), you would have much greater success in obtaining samples. So he modified a more standard Peterson dredge to operate using two five-foot poles that could be used to close the dredge. Because the Kaskaskia often ran significantly deeper than five feet, an additional five-foot extension was added to allow sampling in waters up to nine feet deep. The dredge itself became affectionately known as the Petermore dredge.

I was involved with testing this sampler, along with two other INHS staff (one was Paul Fishman) in the Kaskaskia River below Carlyle Dam (the dam was completed in the summer of 1966, but was not closed off and the lake filled at that time). The water was running fast and the small motor on our boat barely maintained us in the current. The dredge was lowered to the bottom, but as Paul tried to close the dredge the boat lost ground to the current and he finally lost his grip on the dredge, sending the whole unit to the bottom.

We tried to recover the dredge by making free dives to the bottom and feeling blindly in the murky water to see if we could locate it. After each dive we would end up a significant distance downstream because of the current and then have to come back up and try again. I found the handles once and made it to the surface, but as I cried out for assistance the current took me under and I had to let go of the dredge. We finally gave up and went into Carlyle to the police station to see if we could borrow a grappling hook. I remember the Chief of Police asking us if we "had a dead one." We said "no, we lost a piece of equipment that we needed to retrieve."

I don't believe they had what we needed, so we went back to the site and finally two of us were able to grab hold of the handles and drag the dredge into shallow enough water where it could be retrieved by the boat. We certainly didn't want to tell Larimore that we had lost his prized new piece of equipment, but we did lose a whole afternoon trying to retrieve the dredge. Such are the trials and tribulations that come with aquatic fieldwork.

The continuing saga of superhero Shocker Boy!

Adventures in Nighttime Electroshocking
Jeremy Tiemann

Excerpt taken from my diel [daily] fish study field notes:

19 September 2003

So there I was, walking in the creek back to camp for some much needed sleep after finishing my midnight sampling. I was looking forward to a midnight snack and a comfy place to lie down. I was almost back to camp when the pitch-black sky opened and dropped a hideous monster in my path. This creature was enormous and was coming straight for me. In a millisecond, it plunged at me and let out a squawk that would have scared Lucifer himself. I screamed like a movie star, ducked, and nearly fell in the stream. My only thought was, "Holy &%*@!!! That 'thing' was a pterodactyl!" After making sure I didn't mess myself, it dawned on me that the backpack electroshocker was still running, so I could be like a new X-Men character ("Shocker Boy") and fry this colossal beast. But the creature was gone in an instant, I regained my balance and braced myself in a defensive position and waited for the monster to make another pass. Thankfully, I did not have to use my perceived super powers, because the Great Blue Heron that I had startled from its evening repose did not return.

After all, they did evolve from dinosaurs.

Having people, being in charge, it's good, mostly . . .

The Disappearing Boat
Luke Freeman

The mind is a curious beast. At the height of consciousness and awareness of one's surroundings, the inevitable rears its ugly head, and one is reminded no matter how advanced the college degree one possesses or how accomplished one is, field work is an equalizing factor that does not forgive mistakes resulting from absentmindedness.

The summer field sampling season for a fisheries technician is characterized by long, hot sweaty days full of overexposure to UV radiation, muscle strains, and calloused hands. Likewise, it is a great way to get a golden tan, toned muscles, and have an excuse to jump in the lake periodically to cool off. One day, in particular, stands out in my mind as a typical sampling day, but with a twist.

I began working for the Illinois Natural History Survey as an intern in December 2004. I was sort of a greenhorn, with limited experience navigating a boat, much less backing a boat trailer down the boat ramp, but I had a newly acquired biology degree with aspirations of turning the scientific world on its ear. A few weeks of winter remained, and we waited it out, eagerly anticipating the spring sampling season. Upon spring's arrival, the technicians at Sam Parr Biological Station near Kinmundy, Illinois, quickly started showing me the sampling protocol during weekly trips to our designated lakes. I was itching to learn how to control the boat and use the electrofishing equipment and looked forward to the day when I would be the technician. That day came in the summer of 2005 and as a newly appointed technician, I had the opportunity to teach the summer interns the protocol in which I was now well versed. Thus, I was entrusted to take an intern along with me on a sampling trip. This was my big break to prove myself. I obviously had what it takes to prepare the boat and stock the truck with sampling gear. I assumed the guise of a NASA flight engineer, checking, double and triple checking the supply list. I was the Buzz Aldrin of the sampling world, the electrofishing boat was my shuttle.

The day that would soon become a permanent reminder of my human frailties started beautifully. A warm, southerly wind was blowing, visibility was 30 miles, and Forbes Lake in southern Illinois shimmered like a princess-cut diamond; we set out with aspirations of greatness and sampling prowess. Intern Matt and I arrived at the first sampling site that required a single, shoreline seine pass; easy enough. We beached the boat on the shore, threw the anchor, and proceeded to seine. The wind had picked up considerably, but we had seen these conditions before; it was nothing to worry about. After seining (collecting fish by dragging a long net through the water), we proceeded to identify, take length measurements, and count the fishes in the net; the day was shaping up nicely. As many seasoned biologists know, as soon as a nice sampling rhythm is established, something inevitably jams the gears of the proverbial sampling machine. Intern Matt was gathering up the seine, because I felt he needed the "experience." As I was carrying the clipboard back to the boat, or toward the last-known whereabouts of the boat, I noticed a key ingredient missing—the boat. I rubbed my eyes, counted to five, and looked again, but the boat was still gone. I shouted an expletive, as one might in a state of duress, and ran back into the cove, hoping to find a boat, but had no luck. Just then intern Matt yelled, "I found the boat, it's in the middle of the lake!" He stripped down and bounded into the water, Baywatch style.

I scratched my head in confusion, wondering what had gone wrong. The answer quickly came as I thought about previous trips to the lake and painstakingly retraced the steps necessary for a textbook sampling effort. I had forgotten to tie the bow of the boat to a tree as a backup precaution in case the anchor failed, as one might expect on a windy day. As quickly as panic had seized me, a rush of refreshing laughter washed over me. "I'll never make that mistake again," I said to myself. Just then Intern Matt arrived, apologizing right and left for not tying off the boat. "Don't worry about it," I said, "Everybody makes mistakes; you didn't do it on purpose." All the while I knew it was my fault. All was right with the world, and we shared a good laugh, but the story isn't over yet.

Amused at our stupidity, Intern Matt and I cruised to the second sampling site with renewed confidence. This time we beached the boat on a log jutting out from the shore, with complete assurance that history would not repeat itself. The anchor was thrown, seine unloaded, and clipboard removed. Again, we pulled a flawless seine haul, sampled a one-eyed largemouth bass, among other things, and started the recording process. Intern Matt rolled up the seine, I grabbed the clipboard, and we headed back to the nonexistent boat. That is correct, the boat was missing, leaving only two bruised egos in its wake. I yelled yet another expletive that would make a person's grandma blush, and Intern Matt, overcome with outrage, headed down the shoreline, back into the cove, and I ran out to the edge of the shore to gaze across the expanse of Forbes Lake, keeping my eyes peeled for a flat-bottomed boat with a phantom driver. Lo and behold, Intern Matt rolled up a few minutes later, in the runaway watercraft, and this time he was beside himself. I couldn't stop laughing. Poor Intern Matt looked like an abused puppy; he was ready to throw in the towel. Upon seeing my jovial condition, Intern Matt couldn't help but join in the maniacal fit of laughter he was witnessing. I said, "Matt, one day we will both look back on this day with fondness." That is indeed what I am doing today.

Don't be a stick in the mud.

Newton Lake
Diane Szafoni

It was a beautiful summer day in 1991. Technician Carie Nixon and I were out in an army green, flat-bottom johnboat with an old, pull start motor. We were in the restricted arm of Newton Lake in Jasper County, Illinois. In 1985, there had been an oil spill several miles upstream in one of the small rivers that fed the Newton Lake Power Station cooling lake. We were part of a research team studying the rate of recovery of the aquatic life in the lake and had been making weekly trips here since the spring to take dissolved oxygen readings at each of the sampling stations. Each station was marked by a buoy, a white gallon bottle, capped to keep the water out, and tied to a cinder block with a wire cable. We had just finished the morning's work and were at the half-way point. After taking the last reading at buoy number 16, we broke out our lunch pails and leaned back on the sides of the boat to eat our sandwiches, and enjoy the warm, sunny day. As we sat there, an Osprey banked over the lake, then suddenly tucked its wings and dropped to the lake surface. Emerging with a gizzard shad, he shifted it around for a better grip and flew over to the top of the dead tree nearby to join us for a mid-day meal. We smiled and said "We're getting paid to do this."

After lunch, we continued working our way up the arm of the lake, motoring our way from buoy to buoy, cutting the engine, and dropping anchor. I dropped the probe over the side of the boat, holding the cord so that the piece of tape marked "1 foot" rests just at the water line. As I called out the reading, Carie wrote the number on the form; down went the probe to the next tape mark, repeat. I felt the probe hit bottom and backed it off a bit so that it wasn't buried in the lake sediment. "Last one," Carie snapped the metal clipboard shut and pulled the start cord. The motor rumbled to life as I pulled up the anchor. We puttered on to the next buoy to repeat the ritual. When we got to the top end of the lake, we could see our buoy and cinder block exposed on the mud flat. The lake level had dropped since spring. "I'll get it," I said as I grabbed my hip waders. "That will be it for that station." Carie eased the boat as close as she could and I swung my legs over the side. My foot came to rest a few feet down. The silt that washed off the farm fields upstream had traveled down the river, dropping out of suspension when it hit the slower waters of the lake. A nice "delta" of rich black goo spread out from the mouth of the stream. It came up to my knees. I grabbed the top of my waders and pulled my left leg out. Pop, step, slurp, pop, step, slurp, I caught a rhythm as I moved toward the stranded buoy. I stopped to check my progress. At least I stopped my legs. My body still moved forward. I swung my arms out to catch my balance—too late. My trapped legs were useless at breaking my fall. I fell, slow motion backwards, landing on my backside in the black goo. It wasn't all silt; the water table was not far beneath the surface. Carie called out from the boat "Are you all right?" "I'm fine." I yelled. I struggled up, only to fall again. Then I'm laughed so hard I could hardly get up. "Well, I'm this far." I finally managed to say. "I can't get much wetter. I might as well finish getting the buoy." Pop, step, slurp, I finally made it to the buoy and grabbed the cinderblock. I swung it around and headed back to the boat. Carie took the brick as I struggled back into the boat. "Ugh," I said, "There's nothing worse than cold, wet, muddy jeans." I looked around. There was nothing on the shore—just the Prairie Chicken sanctuary on one side and the power plant off in the distance on the other. "There's no one here," I muttered as I peeled off the soaked jeans and tied my jacket around my waist like a skirt. "This will have to do." I said as I wrung my soaked jeans out and spread them out on the floor of the boat to dry. "Yes, we're getting paid to do this . . . "

Flying with our web-footed friends.

Where Are the Ducks?
Stephen P. Havera and Michelle M. Horath

Like magic each fall, when the waves of migratory waterfowl and other avian species begin to appear, the telephone begins to ring at the Illinois Natural History Survey Forbes Biological Station's Frank C. Bellrose Waterfowl Research Center. The station is nestled in a corner of the Chautauqua National Wildlife Refuge, along the Illinois River north of Havana. The callers, most often the public, biologists, and media, invariably ask "Where are the ducks?" Of course, the correct answer would be "wherever they want to be," but that reply is flippant, and, of course, biologically unacceptable. As wildlife biologists, we know the food, habitat, and weather conditions that vary each autumn affect the timing of migration as well as the distribution and numbers of waterfowl species. We also know, pretty much, where they are. It's part of our job. In a very general way, many critical locations, such as Lake Chautauqua, are the focal point of migration, or staging areas, each fall and also in spring. But the people on the phones don't want "general answers" to their very specific question, "Where are the ducks?"

The Pioneers
The mystique of waterfowl migration and the rich waterfowl tradition in the Illinois and Mississippi River valleys, occupying the heart of the flyway, have fostered a deep appreciation of the many, web-footed species since the middle 1800s. Market hunters, sportsmen, and bird enthusiasts have traversed the marshes, lakes, and sloughs of the river floodplains to cultivate in various ways their experiences with waterfowl. This strong interest, and the importance of this international waterfowl resource, led to the Survey's employment of Arthur S. Hawkins and Frank C. Bellrose in 1938, during the embryonic era of wildlife research and management. As the first employees of the Wildlife Section of the Survey, these two waterfowl biologists soon settled in a new field station at Havana, an area where Stephen A. Forbes and other Survey scientists had been studying various ecological aspects of the Illinois River since the 1870s. As such, the Forbes Biological Station is the oldest inland aquatic research station in North America, and the dedicated wildlife program began at the station with Hawkins and Bellrose.

The Program
Located at the center of the waterfowl world, Hawkins and Bellrose realized that one of their first research programs should be to document the numbers and distribution of waterfowl in the Illinois River valley. In the fall of 1938, and in subsequent years, Bellrose traveled by car and boat with binoculars and a spotting scope to record waterfowl numbers from various vantage points in the Illinois River valley. When Bellrose initiated experi-

mental aerial inventories in the fall of 1946, he noted that the time required to inventory the Illinois Valley was reduced from a week to a day, and that a large part of the Mississippi Valley could be included in the one-day flight. "Do I remember the first flight? Indeed I do," Bellrose chuckled. "It was on the Mississippi. I was counting as many decoys as I was ducks."

Aerial inventories of waterfowl date back to the early 1930s, but opportunities became more practical with the availability of aircraft and fuel after World War II. Since 1948, aerial inventories have been conducted by the Illinois Natural History Survey in the Illinois River valley from Spring Valley to Grafton and the Mississippi River valley from Alton to Moline. Various other areas of waterfowl habitat have also been monitored over the years. Periodic inventories during spring migration have been conducted intermittently since 1955. The former Illinois Department of Conservation, now the Illinois Department of Natural Resources has financed most of the cost of the aircraft for the waterfowl inventories since 1956.

The purpose of the aerial inventories conducted by the INHS was *not* to acquire complete counts of waterfowl numbers within specific geographic areas. It was to estimate the number of each species (Mallards, Northern Pintails, Canvasbacks, etc.) in order to document the timing of migration over the years and the distribution of each species throughout the area. Because of the efforts of the INHS, the annual inventory data on numbers and distribution of migratory waterfowl in Illinois are unequaled by any other state. For consistency since the inventories were initiated, only four observers have participated; Bellrose from 1948 through 1970, Robert D. Crompton from 1971 through 1989, Michelle M. Horath from 1990 through 2004, and Aaron P. Yetter from 2005–present. Pilots were retained for several years to ensure that routes were flown in a regular manner and that the observer had the best possible views. We made every attempt to standardize our observations. Comparable flight lines were followed each year; the same areas (mostly open wetlands and deep water habitat) were flown during similar times of day; comparable low flight altitudes and speeds were used with the same type of aircraft; and when possible, the flights were made on the same day of the week and under generally similar weather conditions. Waterfowl observations were made from a single-engine, fixed-wing aircraft flying at an elevation of approximately 200–450 feet at speeds of about 100–150 miles per hour.

An often-asked question is "How does one count ducks from the air?" Bellrose, for example, relied much on his experience. He knew each marsh, backwater lake, and duck-holding pond in Illinois as well as the wisest webfoot guiding the flocks each spring and fall. He explained, "We use the area-density basis: We observe the area a flock covers and the density of the birds on the water at rest." The system is actually rooted in photography. Pictures were taken of various flocks, thin and thick; long and short; broad and narrow. A grid was placed over each photo, and actual numbers counted. Bellrose carried the photos in the plane, on his lap, for comparison.

"In all the comparisons we've made, I'm generally within 10% of what we've actually counted in the photos," he said, admitting "it isn't always that way. You have bad days doing this just like anything else. A fellow has to warm up to the situation and let his mind adjust. The main skill you must learn is identifying the species. The quicker you accomplish this, the easier and faster the job becomes."

"The biggest task," Crompton said, "was to keep your eyes moving. You can't focus on one flock too long. You have to train yourself to scan." Crompton figured his system also to be 90% accurate. "One day over the Mississippi photographs were taken of a flock he estimated at 350,000 birds." By actual count later, the flock numbered 347,000. "Lucky," Crompton noted. But it is more than that. "You use them for reference, but you can see it in your mind's eye. You look for length, width, and density of the flock. Then block 'em off: 1,000; 5,000; 10,000." The most difficult thing Crompton had to learn was not counting, but identifying. "Cans [Canvasbacks] are big, blocky, and white. Buffleheads show white, but are smaller. Mallards look gray but with black backs. The puddlers sit all over in shallow water and the divers sit more in strips—and I don't care how rough the weather is—they tolerate it." Bellrose admitted he could not prove his figures. No one can show they're wrong either. He felt, however, the most important thing about these surveys was the trends they show. "With the same person using the same method week to week, place to place, and year to year, the status of waterfowl food, water conditions, and flyway populations can be determined," he said.

Why systematic inventories?

Our ability to monitor populations and habitat conditions on the breeding, migration, and wintering areas is essential to the management of the waterfowl resource. For example, the numbers of ducks and wetlands inventoried on the breeding grounds in May are critical factors in determining hunting season regulations the following fall. Elsewhere in the flyway, monitoring ducks and their distributions within states are also important for identifying critical areas of waterfowl concentrations and the habitats that support them. With the loss of about 90% of our natural wetlands in Illinois, as well as in some neighboring states, we need to know what areas are essential for waterfowl. Many times the patterns of use by waterfowl identify these areas for us.

Bellrose remarked that, although "enormous strides" had been made in determining the size of North American waterfowl populations since the first aerial survey in 1935, "the results are still less than perfect." However, the inventories on the numbers and distribution of waterfowl in North America provide information that is essential in the management of this valuable international waterfowl resource. For example, the INHS inventories have documented the change in peak populations of Mallards, the most abundant duck species passing through Illinois, during fall in the Illinois and Mississippi River valleys since fall 1948. The inventories have also documented the drastic decline of Lesser Scaup in the Illinois River valley during the 1950s, and the subsequent increase and then ensuing decline in numbers in the Mississippi River valley.

Humor

Sometimes the inventory flights are accused of scaring ducks and affecting the success of nearby hunters. Hunters, of course, are always searching for any excuse to justify their poor success! One of the most interesting anecdotes involved Bellrose. It was late morning in the fall of 1949. Two hunters were crouched in their Illinois River blind near Snicarte, scanning the sky for ducks. A low-flying airplane banked sharply above their marsh, circled, and proceeded downstream. "There goes that damned Bellrose again . . . scarin' all our ducks out," grumbled one of the well-bundled occupants. Unnoticed, a stranger in hip boots pulled through the muck toward the men. "I'm sorry," said the approaching man, "but I can't be two places at once." And he introduced himself as Frank Bellrose of the Illinois Natural History Survey. Two faces lit up with embarrassment. The guy "scarin' their ducks" was somebody else.

Danger

The flights can be exhilarating, tiring, interesting, and dangerous. Any flight can present elements of danger, especially under poor weather conditions, during periods of peak migrations, or elevated bird activity. Although flights have been fired upon by disgruntled duck hunters on at least three occasions without sustaining any plane damage (most duck hunters are poor shots!), the most hazardous situations are caused by bird strikes. Numerous waterfowl have struck the plane in various areas, but on two occasions Mallards actually crashed through the windshield. During one incident, 500 feet in the air, Crompton thought he had "bought the farm." It was 10 a.m. on an overcast day in northeast Illinois during the 1978 mid-winter waterfowl survey, and the pilot put the plane into a tight circle over Goose Lake, Grundy County. Returning late from feeding in cornfields, a flock met the plane head on. In a flurry, there were hundreds of flailing ducks. Wings and webbed feet cascaded around the plane. Unable to dodge the 140 mile-per-hour airplane, one hen Mallard crashed through the windshield, struck the pilot's head, and turned the cockpit into a wind tunnel, with slivers of glass coming off the windshield. "There was blood and guts and feathers and corn all over," Crompton said. "I looked over at the pilot and thought that he was a goner." Luckily, the pilot was conscious and guided the plane to a safe landing at Joliet, 30 miles away.

Another life-threatening situation occurred when Horath was inventorying waterfowl over Banner Marsh Fish and Wildlife Area, south of Peoria, on February 22, 2000. In spring, the flight movements of birds are more unpredictable than during fall, when flocks are usually larger and more concentrated. In this instance, thousands of ducks were feeding on corn in the Spring Lake bottoms and were returning to Banner Marsh across the Illinois River. Suddenly the plane was in the middle of a flock of Mallards, all maneuvering in an attempt to avoid us, and we in the plane attempting to do the same. As the plane pulled up to avoid a group of birds, a lone drake crashed through the windshield on the passenger side, striking Horath in the side of the head before smashing into the rear of the four-seat plane. Horath recalls,

"I remember the pilot asking if I was okay, and I really wasn't sure because I was covered in blood and didn't know if it was the duck's or mine." Any passenger in the seat behind Horath would likely have been severely injured. Fortunately, Horath sustained only minor injuries, and the pilot was able to safely navigate the plane back to the Logan County Airport where the flight originated.

The Future
The information on waterfowl and habitat conditions collected on the aerial inventories becomes more valuable each year, not only for waterfowl, but other species as well. Few databases of this magnitude and longevity exist elsewhere. Consequently, the Frank C. Bellrose Waterfowl Research Center will continue to conduct aerial inventories of waterfowl as an important part of the INHS's research program to benefit waterbirds and their habitats in Illinois, a keystone state of the Mississippi Flyway. And, perhaps most importantly, to continue to answer the now age-old question, "Where are the ducks?"

Bellrose at the "scope" and preparing for flight.

An endless supply of red tape.

High Security Bird Surveys
Dan Wenny

Three strands of barbed wire followed the edge of the roof of the small guard house. An opaque hemisphere (that we assumed covered a surveillance camera) bulged from the wall. Barbed wire also topped the six-foot-high chain link fence. Signs prohibiting private vehicles, maps, notes, photographs, and many other things decorated the fence. With a little fog or mist it would have made the perfect movie set for a cold war spy thriller. But this was Illinois, not Berlin, and we were here to do field work. We passed through the gate and into the ammunition storage area at the Savanna Army Depot.

During the 1940s and 1950s the depot employed several thousand people, some from as far as Freeport, about 50 miles away. Now in 1998 the base was all but abandoned, with only 400 employees. The economic damage to the region caused by downsizing the depot had occurred long before the base was listed for closure. Yet, the fences, warning signs, and guard stations were evidence of the continued buzz of human activity. Now, however, the abandoned weapons manufacturing plants provided only an eerie backdrop for Western Meadowlarks and Grasshopper Sparrows.

We were here to conduct grassland bird surveys, but the morning gauntlet of approvals, permissions, and inspections had effectively turned our day into a scouting mission. Of course, if we followed all the guidelines on the signs we would not be able to do any meaningful field work, because taking notes and photographs was prohibited. But, the base was closing and we were there to collect baseline data in the remnant prairies to develop restoration goals and management guidelines. Our broader goal was to establish a biological field station to facilitate research on sand prairies and the surrounding area.

We spent the morning learning what we could and could not do from Sue Torrison, head of security. Later, we found out one of our volunteer eagle counters had nicknamed her "Sweet Sue" after the dictatorial bandleader in the movie "Some Like it Hot." At the time, however, everything was very serious. We turned in a list of serial numbers of all of our optical equipment. The guards inspected our vehicles and instructed us on the proper use of fire extinguishers. They filed away copies of our drivers' licenses. Surprisingly, fingerprints were not part of the routine.

Finally, with lunchtime nearing, Sue assigned us newly laminated "Camera Authorization" permits and "Limited Area Vehicle passes" and we were free to go. While the remnants of military activities were interesting in a creepy sort of way, the remnant prairies were far more intriguing to a biologist. The Army bought the land in 1917 before the advent of center pivot irrigation. Thus, the majority of the area had not been plowed or cultivated because the windswept, sandy soils were not suitable for row crops. Although the Army constructed many buildings and roads, they spaced them widely to reduce the risk of an explosion in one building setting off ordnance (explosives) in another. Thus, the matrix was remnant sand prairie. At some 5,000 acres, it is perhaps the largest native prairie left in Illinois. Several rare plants occur here and nowhere else in the state. Grassland bird species that can be hard to find elsewhere are abundant here. The biological importance of the site cannot be overstated. The amazing aspect of all this biodiversity is that it was protected by accident because the Army mission required restricting human access to much of the site.

Over the course of the summer we managed to figure out how to navigate the security system with a minimum of hassle and were able to complete two rounds of point counts, during which we count all the birds seen or heard from each of 50 designated points. The bird communities at the former depot (now called Lost Mound Unit) are fantastic and include over 250 species (over 100 species during the breeding season). Large populations of Grasshopper Sparrows, Western and Eastern Meadowlarks, Field Sparrows, and Dickcissels occur in the grasslands surrounding the former ammunition storage area. Smaller, but still sizable, populations of many other grassland and savanna species also occur. Twenty-one state-listed (threatened or endangered) bird species are found at Lost Mound, including Loggerhead Shrike, Upland Sandpiper, and Henslow's Sparrow. Bald Eagles nest in the floodplain forest and hundreds can be found each winter, while several other rare species are found only during migration. The size, variety, and quality of the habitats and their importance as breeding, wintering, and stopover sites earned Lost Mound the designation as an Important Bird Area.

Apparently the guards had been watching us conduct the point counts from a distance, because later that summer one of them said to us, half seriously, "When this place closes I want to work for you guys, because all you do is stand around." While I was tempted to retort that he was more suited for some other (nameless) state agency, I asked instead how many bird songs and calls he knew. Similarly, several depot employees soon to be laid off came to our office asking for jobs: "I like to hunt and fish, so I could work for Illinois Department of Natural Resources." At the time I didn't realize that qualifications of (not to mention respect for) government biologists were thought to be so minimal.

Security gradually waned and eventually disappeared as the ammunition was moved to other sites. Our passes expired and we were not required to obtain new ones. The warning signs remained in place, but many were becoming unreadable or overgrown with vegetation. The main purpose of the fences changed from protecting the ammunition from people to protecting the people from unexploded ordnance and other Army contamination. Yet, no pretense of high security seemed to affect the wildlife. Holes in the fences allowed animals to pass freely in and out. As redevelopment efforts stumbled over themselves and Army activity declined, the prairie began to recover from years of intense grazing. Buildings deteriorated beyond the point of reuse and two-lane roads were reduced to one lane as vegetation encroached. New species colonized the site as the prairie recovered. These new species include both state-endangered or threatened species (very good) and non-native invasive species (not so good). Unfortunately, the latter often get the upper hand and spread rapidly. Conservation by default, which worked for the Army, will not have the same success now. Ironically, the absence of high security makes our new efforts to protect the habitat all the more important.

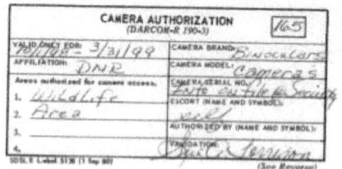
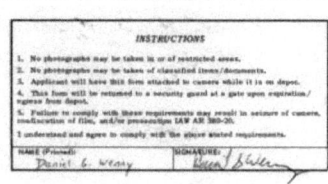

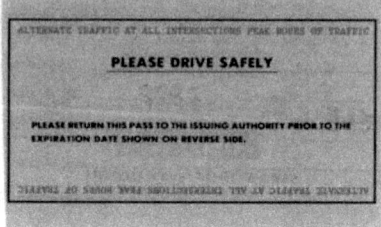

"Red tape."

A Jekyll and Hyde bird.

Context Dependent Behavior
David A. Enstrom

My first job as a biologist was with the National Audubon Society's Project Puffin, whose goal was to reestablish Atlantic Puffins on their former nesting islands off the Maine coast. In my third summer with the project in 1982 I traveled to Gull Island, Newfoundland, to help collect 100 Puffin chicks for transplant to Eastern Egg Rock in Muscongus Bay, Maine. Puffins imprint on their natal island (island of birth) and return from the North Atlantic after about five years to that same island to breed. It's a waste of time moving adult Puffins—they'll just head back home. If you want them to nest where you put them, they must be moved when they're still dependent on their parents for food and before they know where "home" is. Over 2,000 Puffin chicks were collected from huge breeding colonies off the northwest coast of Newfoundland and raised by hand in artificial nests on Eastern Egg Rock by Project Puffin. The project has been a tremendous success. The transplants have thrived and their descendants have been lured to and breed on most of their historic nesting islands in the Gulf of Maine. (For information on *Project Puffin* see http://www.projectpuffin.org/)

During the chick-gathering trip I learned that brooding (caring for young) adult Puffins are incredibly docile, almost inert. We would reach into nesting burrows, which are dug in the shallow island turf, scoop up the brooding adult, set it on the ground next to us, scoop out the chick and, if it was old enough to be moved, place it in a special carrying case for transport back to Maine. When this was done, we would pick up the adult, still in its wakeful stupor, and set it back in the burrow. The experience reinforced my impression that Puffins were extremely passive, almost mechanical birds.

The next year I was sent to the Puffin colony on Machias Seal Island near the U.S./ Canadian border (see http://landscape.acadiau.ca/acwern/) to look for Maine-reared birds. Some of the Maine transplants were approaching breeding age and the project director, Dr. Stephen Kress, was anxious for information about their whereabouts. Machias is an eight-hectare island teeming with seabirds. Thousands of pairs of Puffins nest there, along with Common Eiders, Arctic Terns, Common Terns, Laughing Gulls, Greater Black-backed Gulls, and Herring Gulls, and three other species of Auk, Black Guillemots, Razorbills, and Common Murres. Machias Seal Island is a Canadian lighthouse station and at that time was manned by families of civilians. Several biologists from the Canadian Wildlife Service (CWS) were also stationed on the island during the breeding season. The biologists were my hosts.

Most adult Puffins in a breeding colony do not stay in the nesting burrows at night. Unmated birds and off-duty parents instead roost on the promontories around the colony. For the Puffins of Machias a favored roosting spot was the steep-roofed engine house that provided power to the island. Occasionally an unusually thick fog rolls up on the island during the night and condensation on the engine house causes some of the sleeping Puffins to slide down onto the well-maintained lawn in the interior of the island.

Puffins, like many other water birds, cannot take flight from a flat land surface. A Puffin's wings are a compromise between air flight and underwater "flight," similar to those of penguins. Because their wings cannot generate the necessary lift to get airborne at low speeds, Puffins must jump from a sufficiently high spot, such as a cliff face or an engine house, to gain powered flight. So Puffins on the lawn provided the biologists with a rare and eagerly anticipated opportunity to capture, mark, and measure dozens of birds.

As the sun rose on my third day at Machias I awoke to the sound of the head CWS biologist bellowing, "Puffins on the lawn." When I got to the door I saw two other CWS biologists rounding up Puffins in the short grass. The chased birds had their wings extended fully and flapped wildly while their backward-facing legs pumped as fast as they could. It was an impressive site, 60 or so Puffins scooting about the two-hectare lawn, often turning on a dime to evade capture. My host shouted, "Get after them!," which I did with gusto.

I failed to notice two things. First, the Canadians chasing the Puffins were wearing heavy leather gloves. Second, as soon as I joined the chase, the Canadians stopped their pursuit and watched me. After a couple of minutes I captured my first Puffin, quickly folded its wings, and just as quickly felt the not trivial pain of the Puffin's bite. The bird had clamped down on my left thumb with great force and shook it like a dog killing a small animal.

This behavior was not at all consistent with my previous experience with the famously docile bird. I knew them to be nonreactive, almost catatonic in the hand, and I had no reason to fear handling them. But Puffins are not tiny or weak-billed birds. They weigh about 500 grams and have 45-cm-long, razor-sharp mandibles. Their lower mandible is also lined with backward-facing projections which allow Puffins to collect several fish for their chicks during a single foraging trip. Fish are slippery, and so the Puffin's jaw musculature emphasizes clamping shut, like an alligator.

Caught off guard by this terrierlike behavior I yelped a bit, bled a lot, but brought the bird safely to the banding table. My Canadian friends applauded my efforts and bade me to "Quick! Grab another one!" while weakly suppressing their laughter. I think this is when I noticed their leather gauntlets.

I was the victim of "hazing the rookie" and my being a "Yank" most likely enhanced their pleasure in my initiation. They gave me tape and gauze for my wounds, which they had already laid out, and as I bound my thumb and fingers I blithered on about my previous experience with the enigmatic Puffin. As the chief biologist handed me my very own pair of gloves he said "You have now experienced both aspects of the *context-dependent aggressive behavior* of the Atlantic Puffin. Consider the evolutionary implications." He then patted me on the back, gave me a push toward the lawn and added, "Now do be careful out there, Mate."

Adventures of a field ornithologist.

Life with Bailey
Steve Bailey

Lost and Found

A typical Critical Trends Assessment Program (CTAP) study site trip to Lee County in northwestern Illinois turned into more of an adventure than I had bargained for. It was mid- to late afternoon in mid-May and I had one more site that I wanted to check out before returning to my motel for the evening. The site was reached by a one-lane, pot-holed road, and turned out to be an extremely degraded, but fairly good-sized, young woodlot. Upon arrival, I immediately heard thunder in the distance. The area had obviously been nearly clear-cut within the last several years, but it had a fairly good stand of regenerating trees. The good news was that there was a maze of "trails" crisscrossing the woodlot. The bad news was that what was not a trail was close to impenetrable, with large multi-flora rose bushes and other thorny undergrowth. My first impression was that the site would probably not be acceptable for our study, because our CTAP botanical protocols call for forest sites that have approximately 75% canopy coverage. But my job with CTAP, bird surveys, often requires me to investigate many such botanically unacceptable sites. This particular site had probably less than 50% canopy coverage, but I have learned not to give up on a site too quickly, no matter how negative my initial impression.

Despite the ominous thunder and darkening skies, I was sure I had a few more minutes for investigation, so I headed down one of the overgrown trails. As I tried to access the interior of the site, I continually checked and tried to memorize which direction I was turning every time I ventured onto another path. Naturally, I forgot to bring my compass, but I didn't think I really needed it for such a quick check of the area. After 10 to 15 minutes, and satisfied that this site would not be a suitable one, I was glad I was not too far from my vehicle when the first raindrops began to fall. After three or four trail switches, however, and no sign of daylight or vehicle, I began to jog as the rain got heavier. More time passed before I finally realized that I had no idea where I was, and the woodlot was bigger than I had initially thought. Now I just hoped to find an exit from the maze. As I became soaked in the increasingly heavy thunderstorm and felt a little panicked in the premature darkness, I ran in any direction that looked like it would take me into the safety of the open corn and bean fields and allow me to get my bearings. I hoped to at least be able to see my vehicle after exiting the woods. Such was not the case, as after exiting the woodlot my vehicle was nowhere to be seen. However, I did notice a county road in the distance and decided to make my way there.

The rain turned into a full-fledged deluge and I resigned myself to the fact that at least I couldn't get any more soaked or lost than I already was. After walking a mile or more along the road, a pickup truck finally appeared.

The driver stopped and offered me a ride. Had it not been for the downpour and my sodden, downhearted appearance, this generous person probably wouldn't have stopped because his truck was already stuffed with a variety of junk! He suggested we drop off some of these items at his house, a couple of miles down the road, and come back.

Even though there was almost no room for me to squeeze into the front seat, I was not going to turn down any opportunity to escape the weather. After dropping off the truck's cargo, we retraced our steps to the general area of my misfortune. Because I really couldn't tell him exactly where my vehicle was, I simply described the area with the long lane leading to the spot where it was parked.

As we made our way down the road, the rain reached its crescendo, with the windshield wipers barely able to keep up. Suddenly, the driver slammed on his breaks, just as I saw what he had—a downed utility line laying across the road! Bracing for the shock, we stopped directly over the top of it. Luckily, the line was not live and we continued on. Although the area did not look quite the same, large pools of water having appeared in the surrounding fields, we eventually found the long lane going back to my vehicle. Our adventure, though, was not over. By now, the dirt/sand road itself was full of large, water-filled potholes, making it extremely muddy, and very slippery. At first, my new friend was just going to drop me off where the lane met the road, as he did not have four-wheel drive. He had a last-minute change of heart, however, and agreed to try to make it to my vehicle, at least a half mile down the very muddy lane. What a mistake! In no time the truck became mired in the mud after my acquaintance made an ill-advised decision to turn around and head back. After it became clear that he was not going to make it out, I left his truck and made my way on foot. I really was not looking forward to stopping to help out my new friend under these conditions, but I really had no choice. Eventually, we were able to wrangle both our vehicles out of the muck and back to the main road.

The next morning, I had just signed out of my motel, and as I went out the front door, I was summoned back for a phone call. With all of the excitement of the day before, I was at a loss as to who would be calling. To my surprise and joy, it was my daughter saying that I should get back to Danville as soon as possible to be part of my soon-to-be granddaughter's delivery! Heading south immediately, instead of my planned northward destination, I was able to make the three-plus-hour trip with about a half hour to spare to see my new granddaughter, Kirstiana, enter the world. It had been quite a 24-hour period, but one never to forget for many reasons.

Adventures with Snakes and Such

Many small adventures have enlivened my life during the 19 years of my tenure at the Illinois Natural History Survey. I began working during the summer months on various projects for Dr. Scott Robinson, a noted ornithologist, located in central, northwestern, and southern Illinois, especially in the Shawnee National Forest and Cache River area. Much of my time was spent wandering the wooded hills and swamps, searching for bird nests and conducting avian censuses. Most of my memories naturally revolve around encounters with certain bird and other animal species. However, I will never forget the time I was deep within a large, mature, swamp forest below Wildcat Bluff when a wild thunderstorm broke and poured torrents of water through the trees. A tornado passed within a mile that afternoon, closing off back roads and highways with downed trees and utility lines. The forest that I was trying to escape turned wet and silvery. The sound of large limbs cracking and crashing to the ground had me wondering if the next one was meant for me. It was probably one of the most beautiful, exhilarating, yet eerie and frightening couple of hours that I have ever spent in the woods.

Some of my more memorable experiences are wildlife encounters, such as the spring in which I encountered at least 10 white-tailed deer fawns hiding in tallgrass fields and brushy forested areas. One fawn was almost perfectly camouflaged, curled up next to a bald cypress tree on high ground in a shallow swamp. I noticed each one at the last second, most just before I would have stepped on them. Some bounded off, while others, hoping I would not notice them, lay perfectly still.

On another occasion I found 23 active bird nests in one day, including several hard-to-find warbler species such as Kentucky, Hooded, and American Redstart. Once, my 12-year-old daughter was along with me at Trail-of-Tears State Forest, and we had walked more than a half-mile down into a steep ravine when I realized that I had forgotten my nest-check pole used to monitor bird nests. I told my daughter to wait and that I would be back shortly, after retrieving the nest checker. She simply sat quietly at the base of the ravine, doodling in the dirt and leaves. I was back within 20 minutes or so, having run much of the way. When I returned, she told me of the big cat with the short tail that had quietly crept down the opposite hillside and gotten quite close to her before it looked up and noticed my daughter sitting quietly only meters away. Her excellent description left no doubt that it was her first bobcat sighting! It was gone long before I had gotten back to see what would have been my first bobcat sighting, despite having spent hundreds, if not thousands, of hours in prime bobcat habitat. Nevertheless, I was quite happy that my young daughter now had a unique and rare story to tell her friends in central Illinois.

Although I am an ornithologist, I most vividly recall some of my snake encounters. There was the cool spring when an undergraduate student found a particularly colorful timber rattlesnake coiled on a rocky hillside near the mess hall at camp. Several of us went up the hill for days after to find and photograph it still coiled in the same place. We even put up an orange-flag marker to guide people to this extremely photogenic reptile.

While wandering the woodlands of southern Illinois, I would stop to listen to some songbird or to look more closely at a hard-to-find nest. Sometimes, I would get a strange sensation, an aura if you will, that someone was staring at me. On these occasions, I would often times find that I had stopped right next to a coiled rattlesnake or copperhead. Needless to say, I tried hard not to think too much about poisonous snakes, because I would not have found many bird nests or gotten much accomplished while preoccupied with that next close call.

One evening, coming from the mess hall at our Dutch Creek camp in Union County, I noticed something parting the tall grass near me. My first instinct was to reach down and catch the snake, as southern Illinois is blessed with a variety of colorful and interesting snakes and other reptiles, most non-poisonous. Instead, I retrieved a flashlight from the mess hall and returned with a friend. Lonnie Morse and I were able to get the snake into a cooler and release it in the woods so that nobody accidentally stepped on this beautiful, but poisonous young copperhead.

Late one day I had to check a bird nest a long walk from any trail or road at Trail-of-Tears State Forest. As light began slipping away, my hurried walk turned into a jog, and then a run, through the dense undergrowth. Although the selectively logged woods within Trail-of-Tears State Forest contained the densest population of both rattlesnakes and copperheads of any area I had seen, neither species was currently on my mind. However, as I quickly made my way the last several meters towards the target, two unusual figures arose from the leaf litter just ahead of me, stopping me dead in my tracks. Two long, dark silhouettes were moving in an unusual fashion, and formed a strange shape, almost like one being with two heads. Through my binoculars, I was able to make out the bodies of two large snakes, with a large part of the front portion of their bodies held off the ground. They were writhing and twisting and turning around one another, first clockwise, then counter-clockwise. Back and forth they went. Even though I am not particularly frightened by snakes, including the poisonous species, the shadowy appearance of these large snakes in the darkening forest quickly caused my spine to tingle. I realized they were the largest rattlesnakes I had ever seen! They were at least as big around as my wrist, with the widest sections of their bodies appearing as large as my unflexed bicep. Although certainly eerie, I had never seen such behavior by two snakes, not to mention two poisonous snakes, and the sight held me entranced for some time. They were within meters of the nest I needed to check and posed a slight problem. While attempting to take a more circuitous route toward the nest, the two snakes apparently detected my movement and untwined. I was left with the task of monitoring the nest, but considering abandoning the job before I accidentally stepped on one of those monster reptiles in the gathering darkness. I monitored the nest.

In South Ripple Hollow in Alexander County, I found a small rattlesnake coiled six feet up in cane growth. I rushed back down the trail to tell Todd Fink, a well-known biologist with IDNR at the time. We hurried back to the spot, with Todd seemingly in more disbelief than I that a rattlesnake would be this high off the ground in a plant. Of course, when we got there the snake was gone.

Another time I was using a machete with reckless abandon in giant cane, trying to clear a path to a CTAP study site in Larue Swamp. As I took a brief break, I looked over to see a small cottonmouth sitting between waist-

and shoulder-high in the tangle of tall grasses and forbs. I began to wonder how common an occurrence it is to find this species so high off the ground. I wound up clearing the rest of the path at a much slower speed and with a greater appreciation for that species' climbing aptitude.

At a White-eyed Vireo nest in the Cache River State Natural Area, I once discovered a copperhead coiled with its head and upper body pointed up in the air, directly toward the nest. It was apparently awaiting the return of the adult vireo. I waited some time to see the outcome of this potential encounter, but my patience was neither as good as the snake's, nor the vireo's, and I finally departed with the snake still staring up at the nest.

Another time found me desperately searching for a much-coveted and relatively rare nest of a pair of Hooded Warblers. I had followed the male all over his territory and back to a large brush pile formed by the discarded limbs from a long-ago logging operation in Trail-of-Tears State Forest in Union County. I then heard the chipping of the female Hooded Warbler, which is always a sure sign of a nearby nest. Her calls came from a large pile of dead limbs with various briars growing upon and within the pile. I climbed into the pile and ended up upside down with my head pointed at a fairly steep angle into the pile's center. Only my feet held me and kept me from sliding head first into the brambles at the bottom of the pile. As I scoured every possible place that the warbler could hide a nest, my gaze came to the bottom of the pile where a rather large copperhead was lying, quietly taking in the sight of an upside-down human suspended above it! Trying not to panic, I reviewed the few exit strategies I had from such an unusual position. Originally, I had planned to simply let myself fall somewhere into the center of the pile, then clamber back out when I was done searching for the bird nest. The presence of the snake, however, precluded this strategy. To be honest, I don't remember how I extracted myself from that position, but somehow I did, and it was likely accomplished fairly carefully, yet quickly!

I also had an encounter, not with a poisonous snake, but a none-the-less extremely large, fat-bodied water snake. Not only was this snake several feet long, it was also extremely wide—easily out-measuring the diameter and circumference of my flexed bicep. The circumstances surrounding the encounter, however, were more intimidating to me than the snake's impressive size. I was trying to cross a wide, deep section of the Cache River near Heron Pond. I finally found a log that was big and long enough to allow me to cross without slipping into the river. When I was about a third of the way across the tree I realized that the large, long object ahead of me was not part of the tree, but the very large snake previously described. Many species of water snakes can be nasty-tempered and bite aggressively, and I noticed it was slowly making its way toward me, apparently trying to cross from the opposite end of the log. Unfortunately, it was moving faster toward me than I was able to back away from it. Luckily, the snake stopped when I reached out and tapped it with a branch that I broke from the log. Ultimately, I was able to back off of the tree without further incident, and even managed to take a photo of the snake.

Bird Nest Curiosities

My bird research has had its share of unusual happenings—for example, the time I was following the progress of a Wood Thrush nest in Trail-of-Tears State Forest. The nest was rather high in a tree as Wood Thrush nests go—30–35 feet above ground. Because our checking poles could only reach about 30 feet into the canopy, we were unable to see into the nest to make a head count. About the second or third time that I checked this nest, I could see an adult bird sitting upright in the nest. When I checked the log for this particular nest, I noticed that it was already several days beyond when the young should have left the nest (fledged). Another unusual aspect of this nest was that I had jotted down the short note, "bird's leg hanging outside of nest." I could still see the leg hanging from the nest, a pretty peculiar way for a bird to sit, once, let alone on multiple occassions. When I returned a couple days later, the bird was still sitting upright in the nest, still with one leg hanging over the side. Although it was nesting in a particularly hard tree to climb, curiosity overcame me and I was able to climb high enough into a nearby tree to reach the nest with one of our long, telescoping nest-check poles. Surprisingly, the adult bird did not budge as the pole approached. Something unusual was going on. I tapped the bird with the end of the pole. Still nothing! At this point, I decided that I should do what was necessary to extract the bird from the nest, and when I did, it simply tumbled to the ground! A full set of eggs remained in the nest, and when I made my way to the ground, I retrieved the bird, which had obviously been dead for some time. It is very rare that one finds a bird that has not met its death either through some human-related cause or through a predator-related event. A "natural" death, although presumably a very common event with birds and other creatures, is seldom witnessed or recorded. This bird appeared to have expired while on the nest, trying to bring a few more of her species into this world.

Another nest-checking episode involved one that was 40–45 feet high and in low-light conditions. The usual scenario was to perch myself on the lower limbs of nearby trees and extend my 30-foot telescoping nest-check pole just above the rim of the nest, while trying to attach myself safely to the tree. Each time I checked this nest, which again just happened to be a Wood Thrush, there seemed to be a larger "egg" in there than those of the Wood Thrush. My guess was that it was possibly a Yellow-billed Cuckoo egg, as that species occasionally parasitizes other bird's nests, much like the better known cowbird. The other interesting thing about this nest was that the female was incubating long past the regular incubation period of about 13 days. One day, two of us went to the nest, and I managed, with help, to get further up the tree where the light was a little better. I could now see that the "egg" was actually a hickory nut, which was most likely keeping the other eggs from getting the right amount of heat for proper incubation. The adult continued to incubate the eggs, finally giving up about 10 to 15 days after the time the eggs should have hatched!

On another occasion I was trying to check an Acadian Flycatcher nest about 40 feet up yet another unclimbable tree. The only way that I could see to check this nest was to ascend a nearby tree and, with my telescoping nest-checking pole fully extended, reach over and look inside the nest. Sounds simple enough, right? I am glad nobody with a video camera was filming this escapade. To begin with, the only tree near to the nest tree was much too small for me to attempt climbing. Not to be foiled, however, I climbed the very thin tree about as high as I dared, and had to wait for the small tree to stop swaying under my weight. With one hand holding the 30-foot extended pole and mirror, I reached out as far as I could, then used my other hand to hold and focus my binoculars while holding onto the tree. I began a series of leans toward the nest tree, trying to get the mirror positioned at the right angle to permit proper viewing and identification of the nest contents. The heat and humidity steamed my eyeglasses as my muscles grew weak from trying to hang onto the too-small tree. Finally, I got the tree I was in to sway (read bend) far enough toward the nest tree. But, unfortunately, the swaying tree did not stop bending. I quickly dropped the nest-checking pole and hung on for dear life as the tree bent all the way to ground. All the while I hoped that it would not snap under my weight. Luckily, it bent slowly and actually dropped me relatively lightly on my back. The whole process seemed more like a fall leaf drifting to the surface, rather than a 160-pound human riding a tree, upside-down, to the ground.

In the Pine Hills/LaRue Swamp Ecological Area in Union County, I was again contemplating how to check another Acadian Flycatcher nest hanging high in a very large American beech tree. Shortly, I noticed a dead log leaning against the nest tree, possibly high enough to allow me to reach the first branch of the beech. When I stepped onto the log, my foot broke through. As I pondered another strategy, I found myself swatting (without looking) at some annoying biting insects. The bites soon got my attention when they became more intense and numerous. I looked down to see that I had stuck my foot into a nest of yellowjackets (*Vespula* sp.). By this time they were completely covering my foot and lower leg and starting to sting other parts of my body. I immediately shook my foot and leg furiously, then began running toward the main road, swatting and otherwise waving my arms like a madman. I would have presented quite a sight had any other people been in the area! I stopped once before getting to the road, thinking that I was far enough away from the nest. A quick look back revealed there was still a line of yellowjackets heading in my direction. I made the 50 yards or so out to the road with a few wasps stinging unprotected areas of my body. A little later, after I was satisfied that all of the yellowjackets had been removed from my person, I found a more hospitable area of Pine Hills to look for more bird nests.

One of the few encounters I have had with poisonous spiders also involved a bird nest, or in this case, an old, used bird nest. I was collecting an old Indigo Bunting nest close to a clearing in the forest near Little Black Slough State Natural Area in southern Illinois. When I found the nest, I noticed a spider web inside the nest cup. I simply stuck my finger into the nest and began twirling it around in the web to condense it and evict the spider. Out came a shiny, jet-black spider onto my hand. Immediately, I noticed bright red on her abdomen, and that it formed an hour-glass pattern. I was holding a very poisonous black widow and quickly flung it away. However, after the initial shock subsided, curiosity took over and I went to find the black widow so that I could get several close-up photos with my macro lens. I may be an ornithologist, but most things interest me that I encounter while traipsing over, around, and through the Illinois landscape.

Bailey surveying the "great corn desert."

High tech fire . . .

Thermal Agriculture
Ed Armbrust

I'm an entomologist, an alfalfa pest management specialist, and my scientific career centered around developing strategies to manage insects in alfalfa without the use of massive quantities of pesticide. My technician, Steve Roberts, and I were once given an expensive, fancy piece of equipment that looked a little like a field sprayer. Instead of spraying an insecticide, however, it shot burning propane from its nozzles. During the fall we set up replicated plots in an alfalfa field that was heavily infested with fall-laid alfalfa weevil eggs in the alfalfa stems. Newspaper reporters from St Louis were on hand to view and report the results of this innovative research. Steve made one pass in the field with this contraption and, *whoosh*, the entire field went up in flames. Although singularly impressive, a single match dropped inadvertently by Smokey the Bear would have given the same results.

Up, up, and away!

Getting High with the Beetles
Joseph Spencer

The answers to some scientific questions sometimes require adoption of broad, experimental perspectives. One such suite of questions revolved around the daily and seasonal patterns of between-field flights by western corn rootworm beetles (WCR). For years, Eli Levine (Survey entomologist), Scott Isard (aerobiologist for the University of Illinois), and I had deployed a variety of insect traps to measure patterns of adult WCR abundance at our "Lost 40" field site, northeast of Urbana. One evening after Scott and I wrapped up our collections of WCR beetles flying between corn and soybean fields, Scott made a mad suggestion.

The humid evening was drawing to a close. A distant line of trees had just failed in a good attempt to tangle the sun in their branches and extend the day, and the sun slipped out of sight. I recall how the dew had begun to accumulate on the soybean leaves and the WCR beetles, long before the sun escaped. Once beetles are clothed in dewy cloaks, they do not fly, and it's time to go home.

We were leaning against our vehicles, reviewing what we'd observed, and pausing to regard the brilliant orange fingers of sunset that were rapidly pulling a gun-blue sky over us.

A shared frustration occurred as we noted the many beetles that flew above our heads, sometimes even arcing upward and lifting out of sight and reach—a common complaint at the end of the day.

This evening Scott suggested that we should not put up with that anymore; "Let's build towers." I think I laughed, but asked him what he meant.

"Towers, scaffolding towers that will put us up where the beetles are flying."

"Like a platform?" I asked.

"Yeah, like a tower 10 m above the canopy," Scott responded. Silhouetted against the orange sky, I could see Scott look up and gesture upward with his hand at an alarming angle.

I confess that while this was a very interesting idea, the thought of a tower that one might need to crane your neck to see was not what I had in mind. At that moment, I was not feeling as adventurous as I should have. I questioned how such a thing could ever be built in a cornfield and whether it could ever be safe.

Despite the growing urgency with which we both slapped at the accumulating mosquitoes, Scott took his time to reply. He dug his hands into his pockets and walked a few steps toward the nearby cornfield and then back to his truck, where he leaned over the hood, "We can use sections of construction scaffolding. We'll rent it and assemble it here. I have some money to pay for it."

"Gee, I don't know…" I wanted to be enthusiastic, but this sounded a little "out-there."

Scott punctuated my comments with a resounding slap to his forearm. "These things are eating me alive!…I've gotta get home," he said. "We'll talk in the morning…"

With that, Scott hopped in his truck and started it up. I tossed my insect net into the cab of my truck next to a cooler of samples and hopped inside.

Scott pulled alongside my vehicle and rolled down his window halfway. "See what Eli thinks. I'll make some calls."

With that, he drove away. I watched his taillights glide away down the alleyway and blink out as he turned the corner.

You've got to go where the beetles are.

Biologists in the Field

. . . to be a fly on the wall.

Getting Started in the Business
Don Webb

In 1966, I began my career in the Section of Faunistic Surveys and Insect Identification at the Illinois Natural History Survey. In earnest I started rearing and describing the immature stages of nonbiting midges (chironomids—a family of aquatic flies that are abundant in lakes and streams). This process entailed mounting the larval and pupal skins (exuvia) on a slide in Canada balsam, along with the dissected parts of the adult. Specimens were then identified to species and illustrations made of the diagnostic characters (wings and male genitalia). In time, sufficient information was attained to produce a manuscript describing the larval, pupal, and adult stages of new or revised species. This being the era before Microsoft Word, computerized illustrations, and laser printers, illustrations were hand-drawn in pencil and then outlined in India ink. The manuscript itself was handwritten in pencil and given to a secretary to be typed on a manual Underwood typewriter. At the time, the section possessed only one hand-cranked pencil sharpener outside of the office. Thus, every hour or so, one had to traipse down the hall to sharpen one or two pencils. After doing this for some time, I mustered the courage to speak with Bob Watson, our Administrative Director, about purchasing a separate pencil sharpener for myself, thus being able to increase the time I spent doing research. At that time, the Survey's budget was not exorbitant, but we certainly were not in a state of poverty. Still, this prompted a reply from Bob that it would be impossible for me to purchase a new sharpener, for if he allowed me to have one then soon everyone would want one.

Amphibian parade.

Canned Salamanders
Jen Mui

Many pond-breeding species of amphibians (frogs, toads, salamanders) lend themselves quite nicely to population studies because they migrate to ponds and breed en masse (all together in large numbers). This is particularly true of species in the mole salamander family, Ambystomatidae. One method commonly used to study them involves building a drift fence encircling the breeding pond, with coffee cans sunk into the ground on both sides of the fence. The idea is that the salamanders reach the fence, walk along it, and fall into a can, where they patiently wait to be removed, measured, marked, and released on the opposite side. The drift fence can be used to conduct a population census, collect demographic data, and determine the approximate direction from which each salamander entered or exited the pond.

The first drift fence I built was around a small, artificial pond. As there was no way to get coffee cans into the ground, I left cover boards along the fence, hoping that the newly metamorphosed salamanders would take shelter under. This was very effective with the youngsters, as they were small and not very good at climbing over obstacles.

My next drift fence was built around a large, natural, ephemeral pond with many tree roots and fallen trees. The cans went into the ground easily and a cover-board was placed over each can in order to deter raccoons from treating the traps as a salamander smorgasbord. The raccoons, crafty and intelligent beings that they are, soon learned how to lift the cover boards. It's hard to know if they ate any of the salamanders (unpleasant to the taste) or just gave them a fright, but I still wanted to keep them out. I went searching through the hardware store for something to foil future raccoon attempts and happened upon L-shaped shelf brackets. I thought these might prevent the raccoons from removing the cover boards. I received very strange looks from the cashier and customers when I purchased 58 shelf brackets and nothing else. The brackets worked well, though, and I slept easier at night, knowing my salamanders were safe.

As effective as drift fences are at catching salamanders, some are clever enough to avoid detection. First, mole salamanders are, like their namesake, fossorial (they are good diggers), and despite burying the fence in the ground, inevitably some would dig underneath and avoid being caught. More surprisingly, those salamanders could really climb! One night I arrived at the pond to find an adult salamander sitting on top of one of the fence posts, more than a foot off the ground.

One rainy morning in February 2001, I learned what a mass salamander migration was really like. Until that day, between 1 and 70 salamanders had come to the pond on any given day. The night of February 21, 2001 was warm—50 degrees Fahrenheit—and it rained heavily. My friend and fellow

INHS graduate student Mike Dreslik had been studying reptiles and amphibians for quite some time and wisely asked me if I would like help the next morning when I checked my traps. Not wanting to inconvenience someone, and being incredibly naïve in the ways of herpetology, I declined his kind offer.

When I walked up to the fence that morning, I checked the first trap and found a few salamanders. I smugly thought to myself, "Ha, this isn't too bad!" and continued on to trap two where there were only three salamanders. "What was he talking about?" I thought. Trap 3 had 30 salamanders, and I started to worry, but maybe this was just a fluke, I hoped. Continuing on, the traps had between 1 and 30 salamanders each, until I hit the last 7 traps. In trap 21, I found 45 salamanders, all standing on their tails with their little faces staring at me; same thing at the next trap. The last trap, number 27, had more than 70 salamanders, standing up on their tails like fat toothpicks, with a few lucky individuals crowd-surfing across the upturned faces of their brethren. All told, 501 salamanders made it into the traps that day. They all needed to be measured, marked, and freed on the opposite side of the fence from which they were caught. Dreslik had been correct; I needed help.

There was nothing else to do except load all 500+ beasts into coffee cans and truck them all back to the lab in Champaign. A quick phone call brought a crew of friends and even my advisor and his family. We established an assembly line to anesthetize, measure, mark, and revive the salamanders. Annie, the youngest child of my advisor, was in charge of watching the salamanders in the anesthetizing and reviving tanks. Lindsey, her older sister, used the video camera to document the entire process. The rest of us measured, marked, and made slides of blood from each salamander. After many hours, we were done and I drove back to the site, accompanied by many cans of processed salamanders, all eagerly peering out and happy to be returned safely to their pond, perhaps to be caught again another day.

Salamanders by the pound.

Chapter 2

Blast from the Past

September 16, 1879

The state of Illinois has placed at my disposal (through myself as agent) one of the vessels of her fleet, to convey me to and from the city—in other words, I've bought a skiff, being offered the choice of paying six dollars for the craft or 50 c a day for the use thereof, and the blisters on my hands already attest my zeal if not my skill, as an oarsman. My Kentucky friends with the best intentions, are fast becoming unendurable—but I shall endure them, nevertheless. When you are worried by the blessed babes thank heaven that they are not pigs and drunkards, and vagabonds, and dogs and burs and dirt and flies in the butter and that they don't smell of mingled smoke and bacon grease nor swear nor drink nor chew. Whatever happens to you, console yourself by remembering that you are not in the Kentucky bottoms.

Ah, the good old days . . .

In the Field with Alfred Gross
Tom Rice

"The field work was always interesting and exciting," wrote ornithologist Alfred Gross of his bird studies in Illinois during 1906–1907. "We could never predict what birds we would see and what adventures we might experience. We traveled on foot under all sorts of conditions." Gross had been selected by Stephen A. Forbes, head of the Illinois Natural History Laboratory at the University of Illinois, to compile abundance and density data over a variety of habitats to determine the potential ecological role of birds and their economic effect on agriculture and horticulture. Gross, described as an eager and industrious student, was still only an undergraduate when he began to survey the entire state of Illinois for the project with fellow student Howard Ray. Their first steps in their 3,000-mile journey came in August 1906. The following is from the autobiography of Gross:

> The clothing we wore had to be suitable for all field conditions as well as semi-respectable when seeking accommodations at hotels or private homes wherever we chanced to be at the end of a day's field work. A small trunk containing a limited amount of clothing, books, large 8 x12 journals, taxidermy supplies, bird skins, and miscellaneous materials, was expressed ahead of us to wherever we expected to be at the end of a week. On Sundays I made duplicates of our voluminous field notes, wrote my journals, and attended to official and personal correspondence.
> Throughout the field work we dressed alike. During the winter months we wore heavy durable double-breasted coats and trousers of similar material. We had fur hats which could be adjusted for either cold or warm weather and we wore flannel shirts with black neckties. In both summer and winter we were equipped with high lace boots that were well water proofed for wet conditions of travel. In summer we used lightweight shirts, khaki coats and trousers, and brown felt hats. Each of us was equipped with binocular field glasses, compass, and cameras. Mr. Ray shouldered a canvas knapsack which contained a first aid kit, toilet articles, specimens collected, and miscellaneous materials.
> A 16-gauge shotgun was used in collecting birds for identification and others desired by the Natural History Museum at Urbana. There were about 200 birds collected and preserved and hundreds of photographs taken during the survey to show conditions of vegetation and terrain.
> We could not make reservations at hotels because the distance to be traveled could not be determined because of weather and other conditions to be encountered. There were many days we could not obtain a lunch because there were no restaurants and hotels in the towns we passed. Sometimes we were welcomed by farmers to have dinner with them but more often we had to

go without food or rely on the chocolate bars we carried for such emergencies. There is nothing better than chocolate to appease hunger.

Unusual Experiences

There were times when darkness came before we could reach our planned objective. One summer day when we were very tired we slept in the open with the star studded sky as our only cover. At another time we were comfortably nestled in a huge straw stack remote from any human habitation. It was a delightful experience as throughout the night we were entertained by the singing of Mockingbirds, Yellow-breasted Chats, and Carolina Wrens.

On February 7, 1907, in southern Illinois, we arrived in a small village at sunset hoping to obtain accommodations for the night. It was not possible to sleep in the open because of the cold winter weather. There was one small store where the owner informed us there was absolutely no place for us to stay. Meanwhile a farmer in his dilapidated wagon stopped at the store. After hearing of our predicament he said "Of course you can stay at my house." We gladly accepted. He drove for six miles over a rough country road to his isolated home nestled in a deep valley among the hills. As he approached the house his four children rushed out to greet their father. The father called to his wife: "Mollie, we are going to have company, put on a few more 'taters' for supper." After the supper of potatoes, bread, and tea we all settled down in the one room in front of the glowing fireplace. All of the family were fascinated by our cameras, compass, field glasses, and other equipment, as well as by our stories of experience in the field. Since we were very tired after the hard days journey under difficult conditions I soon asked where we could sleep. Ray and I had great misgivings since there were only two beds for eight people. Without hesitation the man of the house said "There is the bed, fellers. 'Shuck off' any time you like." Ray and I looked at each other in amused and bewildered expressions as the wife and children were still toasting their toes in front of the fire. I finally mustered courage, pulled off my heavy boots and topcoat and got into the bed with the remainder of my clothes. Ray did likewise. Before we fell asleep we saw the four children put crosswise in the other bed. The man and his wife improvised a sleeping place on the floor. The next morning after a breakfast of pancakes I asked the man for his bill. He answered "Oh, nothing at all. We are glad to help you out." Such hospitality had to be rewarded and I insisted he accept the amount we would have had to pay at one of the best first class hotels.

When our day's journey ended at a large city we enjoyed excellent accommodations at the best hotels which were in striking contrast to a morbid experience we had at a hotel in southern Illinois. At the dingy, ill-kept hotel we were obliged to accept the only available room in the town for which, as usual, we paid in advance. Before going to bed we discovered the bed was inhabited by a rich population of bed bugs. Although tired there was no sleep for us that night. Ray had a brilliant idea for amusing ourselves. He captured one of the bugs and pinned it to the wall. Others were treated in a similar manner until we had a long line arranged like a company of soldiers from private to captain.

Suddenly Ray exclaimed with delight that he had captured a huge cockroach which he placed at the head of the company as the general. We were so amused with the ridiculous, repulsive procedure that we forgot our discomfort of losing a night's sleep.

At times, especially in winter and early spring, we were uncomfortable from wet clothing and mud-covered boots. On January 15, 1907 on a trip from Galena southward along the Mississippi bottoms we had to cross a small stream. I broke through the thin ice and was thoroughly soaked to my waist. The only thing I could do was to keep going and after a few miles I was not uncomfortable. It is remarkable that we both kept in good health and able to walk long distances often under adverse conditions.

Early version of "Motel 6" while in the field.

Adventures on a boat named after a dragonfly.

Voyages of the *Anax*
William McClain, with Katie Roat and Tom Lerczak

The caption under the photograph read like an epitaph, *ANAX*: 1931–1959. It was appropriate wording because the old boat depicted was little more than a hulk of weathered, rotting boards when I first saw it back in June 1993. Mud daubers, paper wasps, and field mice had made their homes in it; and a badger had a den under the aging hull.

Yet, something about that boat spoke of a proud and distinguished past, and I wondered why it was perched high on a sand dune far from any water. That question lingered unanswered for eight years until I recently noticed photographs of the same crumbling boat hanging in the Forbes Biological Station of the Illinois Natural History Survey (INHS) at Havana.

The name *Anax* seemed familiar to me, too. At first I thought that it was the first part of the scientific name for the Mallard duck. That seemed logical. After all, I was in the Forbes Biological Station, a research laboratory with a long history of distinguished work on waterfowl. Besides, Frank Bellrose, a waterfowl biologist with more than 60 years of research and experience on the Illinois River, and station director Steve Havera were standing a few feet away. I would soon learn that I was wrong. The Mallard's scientific name is *Anas*. *Anax* is the genus name for a group of dragonflies.

I have admired the flying dragons of the insect world since my early childhood. Their appearance reminds me of a World War II bomber, but with an uncanny ability to hover in flight. They are big, wary, and exceptionally fast predators of other insects. No other insect would chase a dragonfly.

My interest in the old boat named after a dragonfly had been piqued. What can you tell me about it, I asked. Everyone said: "You need to talk to Frank." I walked over and asked, "Do you know the history of the *Anax*?"

"Sure," he said, "I used it a lot when I was doing my survey work. Motels weren't so common in those days, so I would stay on the *Anax*. It didn't cost anything to stay on it. Do you know about it?"

"Not really" was my reply. I only knew that it rests on a sand dune not far from Havana, and I have never been able to figure out how a boat that large got there. For several years, I had thought that it must have been left high and dry after one of those big Illinois River floods, like a boat from a previous great flood but on a smaller scale.

I learned that the *Anax* had operated as an excursion boat on the Rock River in its early years. This would explain the sleekness and elegance that I sensed when I first stood by it. The boat, which was made by Bergendahl and Crawford of Rockford, was crafted almost entirely of wood and was 48 feet long, with a six-cylinder Chrysler Marine engine. It was big, powerful, and fast. Like a dragonfly, nothing chased it.

It was perfect for the fisheries work being done on the Illinois River by the INHS. It was a completely equipped floating laboratory that could accommodate up to 40 passengers. It had microscopes, files, scales, tables, sinks, and other laboratory equipment. Some individuals could stay over-night on four bunk beds that dropped down from the ceiling. They were held in place by chains, and each time a barge came by, the *Anax* would rock and the chains would creak as the bunk beds swung from side to side.

Once the fisheries work had been completed, the *Anax* was used by the wildlife personnel until weather became cold enough to freeze the backwater lakes. During this time of the year, Bellrose often used the *Anax* to protect his duck traps, set for waterfowl-banding studies. Poachers would come out at night, hoping to take the ducks from the traps. When the *Anax* was anchored nearby, they weren't so brave.

The first pilot of the *Anax* was Mike Hunt of Rockford. He soon left to become the chief of fisheries with the Illinois Department of Conservation. Jake Lemm then became the pilot and caretaker. Sometimes, he was even called upon to cook for the passengers. Due to his job on the *Anax*, he received many letters and memos from individuals who worked for the INHS. David "Doc" Thompson (INHS fisheries biologist) once wrote to discuss the colors of paint to be used in the interior of the *Anax*. One shade of green was recommended to replace the four currently in use. Another memo thanked Lemm for the loan of an "undershirt and drawers," which were being returned "disinfected and laundered."

The records indicate that the *Anax* was a very busy boat. In 1935, Theodore H. Frison, INHS Chief, organized the first professional wildlife conference in North America. It was held in Champaign and was named the Midwest Fish and Wildlife Conference. The field trips included a drive to Havana, where an excursion was taken on the *Anax* on Lake Chautauqua to view waterfowl. Several distinguished scientists were on board, including Aldo Leopold, Paul Errington, Miles Pirnie, Ira Gabrielson, J. Clark Salyer, Frederick Lincoln, and Harry Ruhl.

In 1936, the good boat *Anax* stopped at Ottawa on the Illinois River to pick up Bellrose, a biologist recently hired to study waterfowl populations. In July 1937, it was anchored under the Harlem Street Bridge on the Cal-Sag Canal in Chicago, where fisheries personnel were doing a study to determine why the fishing was so poor in Maple Lake. In December 1941, it was moved to Havana for the winter.

The *Anax* took Governor Dwight Green and members of the Illinois Federation of Women's Clubs on an excursion of Lake Chautauqua in April 1942. Later that year, Thompson conducted a study of the fish populations of the Illinois River from Channahon to Grafton. In this study, 34,000 fish were weighed, measured, and examined for abnormalities. It was a classic study, soon emulated by other states.

In the 1940s, radar was installed on the *Anax* to track bird migrations. It was an APS 42 radar system that had been used on a Word War II bomber. The *Anax* continued to be used to install and run duck traps throughout the 1940s. It now had a keen detection system like the eyes of its namesake.

U.S. Senator Everett M. Dirksen and other officials made a one-day trip in August 1945 aboard the *Anax* on the Illinois River to inspect levee districts between Havana and Peoria. In October 1947, the *Anax* was used to conduct a fisheries survey of Lake Chautauqua. In 1950, the *Anax* was docked outside the Forbes Biological Station on Quiver Creek, never to leave on another survey.

By 1959, the hull of the *Anax* was so badly rotted that it was considered a liability. Some suggested that it should be set on fire and burned. Perhaps they even thought of pushing the burning vessel onto the river on some dark night and letting it float slowly downstream, like the practice of the ancients. When Clyde Eaton, a friend of Bellrose, heard of the plans to burn the *Anax*, he would have no part of it: A boat with a history like the *Anax* should never be destroyed. To save it from almost certain destruction, he asked, "Could I buy it?" The offer fell upon receptive ears. After talking to Harlow Mills, INHS chief, Eaton arranged to buy the boat for one dollar, saving the *Anax* from a fiery death—also avoiding any comparisons with one of its namesakes, the comet darner dragonfly.

Saved from the flames, the *Anax* had to be moved from its resting site near the Forbes Biological Station. A company from Lewistown finally agreed to move it to a sand dune on Eaton's property outside Havana. When the move was completed in July 1959, the cost was a staggering $700. The boat gave the site a nautical look, and children climbed onto the pilot's seat and turned the big steering wheel, making their own trips down the river. These imaginary trips on that sand dune proved to be the last voyages of the *Anax*. After a few years, the old boat was left to slowly decay and crumble into the soil, but isn't this the fate of all dragonflies?

William McClain is a retired natural areas stewardship program manager with the Illinois Department of Natural Resources in Springfield. Katie Roat is an associate support scientist for the Illinois Natural History Survey. Tom Lerczak is a natural areas specialist for the Illinois Nature Preserves Commission. Roat and Lerczak are located at the Forbes Biological Station at Havana.

Exploring the sands of time.

Gleaning from Gleason
Susan Post

Robert Evers and Henry Allan Gleason revisiting Devil's Neck.

Henry Allen Gleason, a renowned botanist, is perhaps best known for the *Gleason and Cronquist Manual of Vascular Plants of the Northeastern United States and Adjacent Canada*. His links to the Illinois Natural History Survey and to the Havana area were his Illinois Natural History Survey publications *The Biology of the Sand Areas of Illinois* with Charles Hart (a Survey entomologist), published in 1907, and *The Vegetation of the Inland Sand Deposits of Illinois*, published in 1910. Gleason received his B.S, and M.S. degrees at the University of Illinois in 1901 and 1904, respectively.

Gleason's first trip to the Havana area was on August 11, 1903. He and Charles Hart took the train and were able to get a room at Mrs. Wright's, an old-fashioned rooming house facing the courthouse. Most of their time was spent on the sand dunes, Gleason studying the vegetation and Hart collecting insects, mostly grasshoppers. Gleason described Hart as "not interested in plants, but was the best companion I ever had in the field."

"We found great expanses of sand alternating with some tracts of black soil. Most of the sand had been covered by prairie. Farmers had put part of it into cultivation and raised poor crops of grain and most of the rest of it had been pastured. In either case, when the cover of prairie grasses was destroyed or weakened, the wind began its work and piled up shifting dunes or excavated deep blowouts. Along the river and to some extent inland, were forests of post oak, black jack oak, and pignut hickory, and it was clear that they were succeeding the prairie as rapidly as possible. So I (Gleason) had a fine chance to see successions of various sorts. . . and, to formulate a general picture of the whole vegetational history of the place.

"Of course I found a lot of plants, which were new to me. One of those was the poppy mallow, . . . one of the most beautiful flowers of the state, with red-purple blossoms two inches across. Prickly pear cactus was very abundant and I found at least one species new to the state, *Cristatella jamesii*.

"We covered these sand deposits northeast, east, and south of Havana for several miles, tramping long distances in the hot weather, lugging my heavy camera, chasing grasshoppers, and returning to Mrs. Wright's pretty tired out.

"But our days were not always so hard and we had plenty of time for fun. We went swimming in the Illinois River, we got a boat and rode the waves behind the big steamboats, we explored the great marshes and lakes on the west side of the river, such as Thompson's Lake and Flag Lake, ate ice cream sodas every night, and in general enjoyed ourselves.

"Across the river at West Havana was the terminus of the little Fulton County Narrow Gauge Railway, better known in the country as the Fulton County Narrow Escape. It rambled off across the country as far as Galesburg, heedless of grades and turning corners around the farmer's fields as abruptly as a trolley car on city streets. Hart and I took a ride on it as far as Lewiston, about ten miles, and then walked back. The little train was mostly freight cars, with a little engine in front, and its average speed was not more than ten miles an hour. Several times I jumped off to collect a plant, caught up with the train and climbed back on. It was a beautiful walk back through the picturesque hills of Fulton County, until we reached the bottomlands of the Illinois River.

"Those were pleasant days for both of us, when Hart was still well and strong and never dismayed by distance or heat, fatigue, or mosquitoes. We were both enthusiastic; we were finding new things and learning new facts and getting new ideas every day, and our long walks home were always shortened by the thought of a swim in the river and our daily trip to the soda fountain.

"Hart was an inveterate punster. One especially hot day we were seven miles from town. A thunderstorm was coming up in the west and the air was heavy with the sultriness, which so often precedes a storm. We were legging it for home [Mrs. Wright's] as fast as we could go, until the heat and the fatigue became too much for Hart.

"Then he asked me 'What was that genus you were collecting so much of today?'"

"*Lespedeza*," I replied.

"That's right; let's speed easy!"

"And that is the only complaint I ever heard from Hart.

"Hart's favorite joke was to discuss his proposed monograph of the soda fountains of Illinois. He was extremely fond of ice cream sodas and we rarely missed a night with out one or even two, and he almost invariably discussed all his plans in great detail. On arrival in any new town, he made it our first evening duty to sample every fountain in the place and after that we patronized the one we considered the best. Fortunately, the towns where we worked were never large. We probably stayed in Havana two weeks or a trifle longer."

Gleason's next trip to the area would be a year later. He was met at the train station by Hart and again got a room at Mrs. Wright's.

"We collected at Devil's Hole, in the black-jack timber north of Havana, in the big black jack timber between Bishop and Forest City, at Devil's Neck, and in the blow-outs south-east of Bath. By far the most interesting visit was to the Devil's Neck, a large, wild expanse of blow sand, where we found many interesting things especially unlimited quantities of *Cristatella jamesii* and a few plants of *Lesquerella spathulata* hither-to-known only from northwestern Nebraska and Montana."

The next sentence of his field notes proves that even though he was a serious scientist, he was also a 22-year-old man. "At Bath I ran across a crowd of Havana girls and took a photograph of them." And of course, "We visited the soda fountains every night, as usual, and in general had a very good time for just one week."

"This Havana work of ours was written up and published as a joint article by The State Laboratory of Natural History [institution that became the Illinois Natural History Survey], but did not appear until 1907."

Gleason would visit the area again in August 1908 and July 1910, each time for no more than a few days, noting landscape changes and botanizing. During his 1910 visit, his group started across the big dunes around 1:10, finding *Cristatella* and *Lesquerella*. They ended their botanizing at Quiver Hill, where they rested half an hour or so. "We got a drink at the house just east of there, and returned to Topeka by road. The farther we went, the faster we walked, and we came into Topeka at about a twelve-minute gate. Achert, Vestal and I left town at 4:26 and made the first three miles in 12.5, 13 and 12.5 over the rough gravel ballast. Vestal couldn't keep up and had to run part of the way, and quit at the end of three miles. Achert and I took the next three miles in 12, 12.5, and 12 and I arrived at the tent at 6:01. The time showed very well how hardened I have become during my three weeks of outdoor life here. I ate no supper except a little ice cream and took a good swim to cool off."

Gleason would not visit the sand areas again until July 1962. His companion was Illinois Natural History Survey botanist Robert Evers. "New roads had been built and old roads abandoned, I was soon lost. We stopped at a poor farm-house which Evers knew, walked through the pasture, climbed a sand hill on the blistering hot day, and found ourselves in the great field of sand prairie which I knew as Devil's Neck, where I had botanized in 1904 and 1910. And just a few feet south of the summit of the highest sand hill, exactly where I saw it 58 years before, was still growing *Lesquerella argentea* [name changed] the only known station east of western Nebraska."

Gleason would make one final visit in 1966 (84 years old); again his companion was Evers. "We turned off several miles east of [Havana] and found that road which was so freshly tarred four years ago. A lane had been cut from it through the pine forest and led directly to the top of the Devil's Neck, where Hart and I had collected in 1903. The lane made the work of climbing the dune much easier than it had been in 1962, although the weather was just about as hot as it had been then. I climbed almost to the top, but then turned back. The other three men went to the very top, and sure enough, there was *Lesquerella spathulata* still growing right where I first discovered it more that a half a century ago. That same kind of plant, represented by just a few individuals, had been sticking it out there for so many years . . . We had a nice lunch of corn fritters in a dark Havana restaurant, crossed the river to see a bit of Fulton Country, stopped at a patch of black-jack woods with an island of prairie within it, which I personally did not see, and at a "goat prairie" along a river bluff where a number of prairie plants were still growing."

Shortly after receiving the news that the sand dune area where he first saw the *Lesquerella* in Illinois would be a nature preserve named after him, he wrote to Edmund Thornton, then chairman of the Illinois Nature Preserves Commission. "During my long life I have had many honors, but none that has pleased me more than this. Sixty-seven years have rolled by since my first discovery of *Lesquerella* in Illinois. We had no cars in those days, and my trips entailed a four-mile walk out, another one back, and probably five or six hours work on those bare dunes of sun-burnt sand. But when I was last there, in 1966, *Lesquerella* was still growing on the top of the highest dune as before, and doubtless has been growing since the Xerothermic Period, at least five thousand years ago."

Comments from Gleason about past Illinois Natural History Survey employees:

Charles Hart

Charles Hart:

"I cannot refrain from adding one joke on Hart which took place on some trip when I was not with him. He was at Anna, the seat of the Southern Illinois Insane Asylum, and was spending the evening collecting June beetles under a street lamp. Some one watched him stealing up stealthily on the bugs, and then pouncing on them and clapping them in a Mason jar. That was too much. An alarm was turned in, and in a few minutes a wagon enclosed with iron grating came up, two attendants jumped out, and poor Hart was captured as an escaped lunatic."

"Hart possessed the remarkable ability of inspiring young men to scientific work, without trying to educate them at the same time. Many persons, myself included, owe him a debt of gratitude."

Biologists in the Field

S.A. Forbes:

"S.A. Forbes, professor of zoology at the University, was a great man, who assisted me more than once in my early scientific work. As director of the State Laboratory of Natural History, he built up a fine working organization and an excellent library. He published for me my first sand-dune work in 1910, based on my studies at Havana in 1903 and 1904. Later he contributed my expenses for peat-bog work in northeastern Illinois in 1906. Again in 1908 he advanced one hundred dollars for my sand-dune work of 1908 and published the results not long after. Forbes was an ecologist long before ecology was recognized as a distinct branch of botany and zoology.

"His daughter married my classmate Frank Scott, and for a time they lived in Scarsdale, where Forbes visited them not long before his death. It happened that, on his eighty-third birthday, he was late getting home to a birthday celebration, drove his car too fast and was arrested for speeding, but released when he explained the circumstances. On this last visit to Scarsdale he called on me at my office, introducing himself by saying 'I don't suppose you know who I am.'"

"Yes," I replied, "you are the man who was arrested for speeding on his eighty-third birthday. Which pleased Forbes immensely."

T.H. Frison:

"It seems that I was unwittingly the cause of Frison's interest in entomology. I used to collect insects, during my freshman year, at an arc-light in front of the Frison home, just a block from our house on West Springfield avenue. Little Teddy, then about six years old, thought he would collect bugs, too, and kept up his interest and activity in entomology from that time on."

Theodore Frison on the "Anax."

Acknowledgements

Thank you to Henry A. Gleason's son, Allan, for sharing information about his father.

. . . a timeless traveler.

Robert Evers—Botanist Extraordinaire
Susan Post

Charles Darwin wrote, "A traveler should be a botanist for in all views plants form the chief embellishment." Robert Evers, a botanist with the Survey for 30 years, beginning in 1946, illustrates this quote best as he traveled far and wide across Illinois. Evers' job was to collect plant specimens each year from all 102 counties of the state. Hill prairies were his particular fascination and resulted in the Survey Bulletin, *Hill Prairies of Illinois*, published in 1955. He wrote, "On the sunny, windswept, upper slopes of some of the bluffs along the major Illinois streams are treeless areas distinctive enough to attract the attention of observing travelers. These areas are grassy strips or grassy openings on the otherwise forested slopes of the bluffs' frontispiece. Most of them have been little disturbed by man or domesticated animals. Those that are covered with prairie plants are prairies."

"Prairies are grasslands. To many persons, prairies are flat grasslands. However, it is not topography but vegetation that distinguishes prairies and other plant communities. Forests occur on flat land or on slopes. So do prairies. Grasslands, or prairies, on pronounced slopes are hill prairies."

Evers photographed and kept numerous field notebooks; these bits of the past allow us to view natural landscapes of Illinois—sites and scenes that may no longer be in existence. With the absence of fire most Illinois hill prairies are rapidly becoming forested. The only evidence that remains of their occurrence are the occasional prairie plants and Evers' detailed field notes. Here are a few of his observations. In 1955, he wrote of Windfall Prairie in Vermilion County, "In May, Indian paintbrush clothed the prairie with a scarlet hue. Scattered throughout were stems of blue-eyed grass, downy phlox, stargrass, bastard toadflax, puccoon, and meadow parsnip. In June the few stalks of leadplant showed their dense spike of purple flowers . . . In late summer and early autumn, blazing star, partridge pea, tall tickseed, stiff gentian (not abundant in Illinois), goldenrod, and several species of asters and gerardias added their colors to the bluff. Seven plants of the hill prairie variant of the ladies'-tresses, an orchid, grew in this prairie."

He later wrote of a visit to Cap au Gres Bluff, in Calhoun County, on October 26, 1967—"Because of the heavy rains (and tornado) of Oct. 24, I had to leave the car at the Dixon farmyard and walk the muddy road to the point where I pass through the cornfield and reach the bluff-top. [As usual in stopping at a farm house and then beginning to hike, the dog (Oscar) followed me all the way]. The prairie was a brownish-red color with only the *Lespedeza capitata* [roundheaded bush clover], *Aster* spp., *Eupatorium altissimum* [tall boneset] and a few other plants with green leaves. *Solidago remorelis* [field goldenrod] was still in bloom. The leaves of *Viburnum rufidulum* [southern blackhaw] had fallen and only the blue fruits remained. After taking a few photographs, I left the prairie which on this day, was cold and windy and most unpleasant."

He noted during an earlier visit to Seehorn Cemetery (1955), "Prairie occupied the cemetery," and one on June 9, 1970, "On this visit prairie no longer occupied the cemetery. The cemetery has some large red cedars, a few other large trees and a host of saplings of *Ulmus* [elm], *Quercus muhlenbergii* [yellow chestnut oak], *Carya* sp [hickory], *Morus rubra* [red mulberry], *Fraxinu americana* [white ash] etc. The herb layer was also practically all forest species." Although the cemetery still exists today, the prairie Evers spoke of has been consumed by trees.

Fifty years after *Hill Prairies of Illinois* was published, Evers' photographs and notebooks were used for comparison and to document 50 years of change in the hill prairie community in a book chapter by Survey scientists and colleagues, Mark W. Schwartz, Kenneth R. Robertson, Brian K. Dunphy, Jeffery W. Olson, and Ann Marie Trame entitled *The Biogeography of and Habitat Loss on Hill Prairies in Illinois*.

A few of the 100,000 specimens collected by Evers.

. . . just outside the gate.

The Grabers
Susan Post (with Karen Frailey)

Dick and Jean on the road with Snipe.

Richard Graber was hired by the Illinois Natural History Survey in September 1956, and his wife Jean, also an ornithologist, worked at his side, unpaid, for many, many years. Jean is now retired and lives in Golconda, IL. On June 15, 2007, Karen Frailey, a member of Shawnee Audubon and a good friend of Jean's asked her about the bird census and her life as a field biologist. What follows are excerpts, anecdotes, and memories of those times.

Experiences

In addition to the bird surveys, both she and Dick received a lot of phone calls around the topic "I've got a bird in my yard!" Letters, too, came in and one Jean particularly remembers was from a kid asking if the Survey would send him a bird and an elephant!?

When Dick and Jean would visit the Survey's field station in Havana, the Survey's Chief, Harlow Mills, had the idea that women shouldn't sleep at the Havana field station, as this would cause "talk," so when visiting the station the Grabers would camp just outside the gate.

The Grabers had been on vacation in Mexico or Central America and after they returned home, Dick noticed red streaks running up his leg. When Jean looked closely at the leg, she saw an insect larva embedded in his calf.

She pulled it out and it was six inches long, when stretched, and still attached! Dick swore she was pulling out a tendon! Jean gave the larva to Survey entomologist Lou Stannard to verify her identification—it was a botfly larva, *Dermatobia hominis*. He verified her ID but added, "I wish you'd left it in to develop, we need an adult for the [insect] collection!"

During 1960, Dick bought an old, two-seater Cessna airplane with cloth wings. Jean learned to fly and had her pilot's license before her driver's license. After they'd both learned to fly, one day Dick noticed clouds on the radar and thought they might be insects. They took insect nets and headed skyward. Jean flew the plane and Dick intended to hold the net out the window—he opened the window and the net flew out of his hands! When he tried it again (with another net) he actually caught three gnats! Over the years Dick would continue to study radar and became a leader in using it to detect bird migration.

The 1956–1958 Bird Census

"After driving into a county, we deliberately chose a starting point in an area that seemed to represent the region. From the starting point, we walked a census strip along the perimeter of a square 1.5 to 2 miles on each side and returned ultimately to the starting point. Our rate of coverage, 45–50 minutes per mile, . . ." from A Comparative Study of Bird Populations in Illinois, 1906–1909 and 1956–1958, Richard and Jean Graber, Illinois Natural History Survey Bulletin, Vol. 28, 1963

Richard (Dick) Graber was initially hired by the Illinois Natural History Survey to repeat the bird census done 50 years earlier by Alfred Gross and Howard Ray. Dick's assistant for the census would be his wife Jean. Instead of hiring student workers for the census, Jean worked unpaid. When asked why, she replied, "When conducting a census you worked every good day, from the end of May to the beginning of July. We didn't want to be hindered by a student needing to be back at a certain time." To census the breeding birds the Grabers had to begin after all the migrants that were there before May passed through and before the young have fledged in July.

" We used our personal car. The Natural History Survey had a limited number of vehicles and everyone wanted them. We also could be gone as long as we needed and wouldn't have to have the vehicle back for someone else to use. We stayed at hotels and the Survey reimbursed us for our food and lodging. Southern Illinois, particularly Pope County, was terrible to find places to stay. Restaurants in southern Illinois were far apart and often we would stop at a grocery and buy a loaf of bread, bologna, and pop. We carried a thermos of coffee and some cookies—we would have coffee about 10 a.m., usually stopping on a log. We took another coffee break in the afternoon. We began at 4 a.m. and it would often take an hour to get to the census point. We tried to always be counting birds by 6 a.m. We censused during summer and winter, starting at the southern end of the state and working our way north. We carried 3 x 5 note cards and wrote all the information on them. While we both did the tabulations, Dick did most of the writing, as he was the better writer. Even though the work was hard and hours long, Dick couldn't believe he was paid to do this.

"Our only other companion during the census was our little dog Snipe, short for Guttersnipe. He was a little mongrel—part Schipperke that showed up as a puppy when we were graduate students in Michigan. He was black, weighed about five pounds, and went everywhere with us. Dick would never pass an ice cream stand and would always buy a nickel cone for Snipe."

Jean remembers one time during the census as they were crossing property near Elkville a posse stopped them. Jean wore pants, so she looked like a man and she and Dick were headed across the field into the woods. Three guys with guns came across the field and stopped them; they were looking for escapees. The posse told Dick and Jean that they should leave, as there were escapees in the area. It appeared in the paper the next day that all the posse got were two birdwatchers.

By plane and radio, scientists follow a northbound migrant. A transmitter borne by the bird reveals its 400-mile course and brings new facts on migration.

Night Flight with a Thrush
Richard R. Graber (former INHS researcher)
Reprinted with the kind permission of *Audubon* magazine
from its November-December 1965 issue.

Each of us, at times, must stand in awe of mankind, of what we have become, of what we can do. The space flights, the close-up lunar photographs, the walks in space—all somehow stagger our imaginations. I was thinking about this as I flew south from northern Wisconsin one morning last May, having just witnessed an achievement of another kind by another species.

What I had observed was one of the most common, yet least observed, events in nature. It was the flight of a bird in the course of its night migration. It occurred to me then that only a few people in all the world had come so close to seeing this event as I had in the past several hours.

The observation itself seemed something of a miracle. I was privileged to experience it because of my association with my colleague William R. Cochran, because of his genius in electrical engineering, and because of our hard work. . . with, I hasten to add, the help of a good many other people, including those that represent the National Science Foundation, and our colleagues from the Illinois Natural History Survey.

Among those who helped was the man who sat beside me. He was Jim Taylor, a pilot and good, calm, cheerful man for a tough demanding job. As we sat there in the sky, clipping along over the west shore of Lake Michigan, my thoughts returned to the bird, and then the events of the day came back in their proper sequence. It would always be a day to remember.

By seven o'clock on the morning of May 24, 1965, I had set six mist nets among the shrubs in the University of Illinois orchards just south of Urbana. A mist net is a light, mesh fabric used by scientists for trapping birds. The nets were closely spaced, so that none would be out of my sight for more than a minute or two.

I was not as careless about the nets as I was when I had first started using them. A month before, I had left the nets unguarded for 15 minutes, and had returned to find two juncos hanging lifeless in the mesh. A hungry sharp-shinned hawk had killed the birds and caught himself in the process. The hawk went free, still hungry, and the juncos had died for no good cause.

Those of us who set traps for wild animals, by whatever means, for whatever reasons, have a special obligation to our quarry.

With the nets hung, my day's work was begun, but other essential work had preceded mine, and the whole idea had started long before that. In our countless discussions, Bill Cochran and I had dwelt at length on the problems of birds in migration. With our friends Frank Bellrose and the late Sue Hassler, we had tried various means of study.

We had listened to and recorded the calls of night migrants as they passed over central Illinois; we had watched the migration on radar; and, alas, we had picked up the birds that were killed by the thousands at TV towers in Illinois. Although we learned something, the information always seemed so little. Some of it was decidedly confusing.

Why, for example, did we see the largest number of migrants in the *middle* of the night when we watched radar, but *hear* the largest number of migrant calls at the *end* of the night in the predawn morning hours.

We realized we would not find all the answers, but we finally decided that there was only one logical way to try. We must go right along with the birds—actually make the migration flight to see what the birds did, how long they flew, how fast, how high, what direction, etc., ad infinitum. Though we couldn't see the birds at night, we could stay with them and tell what they were doing if only they would carry a tiny radio transmitter for us.

Caught up by the challenge, Bill designed and tested miniature transmitters to find the combination of parts and circuits that would give us the best range and longevity for the least weight. In time, he developed a small transmitter that performed even better than what we had hoped. It weighed approximately 2.5 grams, about as much as a dime. A lighter transmitter was possible, but the cost was prohibitive. Through more weeks of experimentation, I finally learned how best to attach the transmitter to a bird.

It sounds so simple; in retrospect I wonder why it took so long to decide to glue the transmitter to the bird's dorsal feather tract. We tried the radios on a number of species of birds and watched to see how well the birds behaved. They preened and fed and seemed to carry on in normal fashion. They flew very well, but the question remained: Could a bird migrate carrying a radio, even a tiny one?

With the support of the National Science Foundation and the special help of two young students, James Hughes and George Swenson III, we had already begun to get some answers by the morning of May 24, 1965. The birds were starting to come into our nets: a Canada warbler, a red-eyed vireo, a Wilson's warbler, an ovenbird—one or two at a time. I took them out, banded and released them. The migration had slackened noticeably since May 18th, and I began to wonder if we would get any more chances to fly. Just any migrant would not do. I was looking for a thrush, a Swainson's or gray-cheeked, or a veery.

I had decided to study the thrushes because I knew they definitely were night migrants and strong flyers, and I felt that I knew enough about them to predict the nights they would fly.

I wanted to choose a thrush that was heavy enough to have a fat reserve for energy. A few thrushes came into the nets, but they were not fat enough. They were banded and released.

Finally, at noon, I caught an immature grey-cheeked thrush. Spotted wing coverts indicated that it had been hatched he summer before; it was making the trip north to the breeding grounds for the first time. It seemed to be a strong, healthy bird with full breast muscles and enough fat reserve for a good fuel supply. I touched a spot of glue to the transmitter I'd been carrying and, in turn, touched the radio to the bird's back. In two minutes the glue was dry enough, and the bird was released. The thrush had been captive less than ten minutes. It was the 19th transmitter we had launched.

Would the bird accept the radio? One adult gray-cheeked thrush we had tagged had taken a definite dislike to its radio and had removed the thing along with a few of its back feathers. The immature was tolerant of the transmitter.

This bird's activity fell into a kind of pattern that we had come to expect from the migrants through our work of the preceding weeks. With a special radio receiver mounted in a truck, we checked on the bird periodically throughout the day. At times it was quiet, apparently asleep. Then it would become very active again, foraging through the shrubs and trees. We avoided approaching the bird but could always tell where it was by means of the truck's directional radio antenna, and we could tell whether the bird was active or not.

When the bird moved, the fine wire antenna on the transmitter moved, and this produced fluctuations in the signal that came through our receiver. As other tagged thrushes had, this one stayed all day in the same grove of trees where it had been captured.

For us the long day was a protracted question: Would the bird fly that night? The sky was clear, the midday temperatures were in the 80s, the winds were from the south—all classic signs for spring migration according to W.W. Cooke and other well-versed naturalists. There was also the fact that the migrants seemed impatient to go north. Since mid-May the northern species had not been holding over long at the orchards. Every day seemed to bring in a new group, for the birds I banded one day were not to be found the next.

After the thrush had been tagged, our own activities fell into a kind of pattern, too. First, we called Illini Airport to alert Jim Taylor to the fact that we might need him for a flight that night. He was to be ready by 6 p.m. He, in turn, started checking the terminal forecasts for information on flying weather to the north. He wanted to be able to make the best decision in the event that bad weather should threaten the flight.

Throughout the afternoon Jim Hughes, who had learned from Bill how to build the bird transmitters, was at work on the next transmitter. Each one had to be perfect, and received the attention of a work of art. George Swenson and I were checking on the bird and making sure the receivers were operating properly.

By six o'clock conditions still looked good for a flight, though some thunderstorm activity was erupting well to the northwest. If the bird went, we would track it as far as we could. Jim Taylor and I went up in the plane to tune in the plane receiver. We flew over the orchard. I turned the receiver dial, and the signal came in. The sound, an intermittent cheerp-cheerp-cheerp, was, in pitch and quality, surprisingly suggestive of the monotonous call of some hungry young bird tagging after its harassed parent. When the plane was turned toward the orchard, the signal was loud and clear, but as we banked away, it faded quickly. Everything was working well. We landed to wait out the hour and a half till darkness.

Well before dark the members of the crew were ready at their respective posts. George Swenson and my wife, Jean, were to monitor the bird's take-off from two fixed receiving stations located almost two miles apart in Champaign-Urbana. Both stations had rotatable antennas perched 50 or more feet above ground level. This height greatly extended the tracking range. Now the unidirectional antennas were both pointed toward the orchard.

If the bird departed, the signal received at the two base stations would increase in strength as the bird climbed into the sky. George and Jean would then know that the bird was up and would start to follow the moving radio signal by turning their antennas and keeping the signal at a peak. On the rotor dials by their receivers they could read the direction from which the peak signal was coming.

By seven I was at the airport. Jim Taylor was waiting. The plane sat in the open, ready for a quick take-off. If the bird flew, George would call us by telephone. Once we were in the air, both Jean and George could reach us by radio to give us the bird's direction.

Our plane, a Piper Cherokee 180, which we had leased from Illini Aviation, Inc., had come to be known as the Porcupine because of the rows of antenna whips along its back. The whips, part of the unidirectional antenna which Bill Cochran had designed especially for our work, often were the cause of some wry comments. One onlooker asked if we hung our laundry on them.

For all of us anxiously waiting for the thrush to fly, there was now a period of tension. The thrush, on the other hand, seemed perfectly quiet after a burst of activity in the late afternoon. Even before darkness had settled fully, the bird seemed to take up its night roost. For all we knew, it would sleep until morning. The quiet was deceptive. Jim and I sat in the airport office waiting for the phone to ring. Jim's briefcase was filled with sectional air charts. When you follow a bird you have to be prepared to navigate in any direction.

At 7:56 the phone rang. It was George. Calmly he said: "The bird is in the air. Take-off time was 1955 (7:55 p.m.) Central Standard Time."

The walk to the plane was brisk. A short taxi to the head of the runway, the aircraft "run up," and then we were off. By the time we had reached 100 feet, messages were coming in over the radio. Alternately, George at the Survey building and Jean at our home on Franklin Street filled us in on the bird's progress.

"I have him northeast of here."

"He's southwest of Franklin Street now."

The thrush was crossing town, passing between the two base stations.

More reports were coming in:

"Now north-northeast of the Survey building, and stating to fade slightly."

"He's due west of Franklin Street; signal still good here."

A pause, and then voices again: "The signal now at 0 degrees, and definitely fading."

The bird was now not far from the airport, which lay just two miles north-northeast of town. Jim put the plane into a steep bank, and started a tight circle. As the plane's nose came east, the familiar signal came through our headphones. I radioed back to the two base stations:

"We've got him."

The transition from ground contact to air contact had been made. If all went well, Jim and I would be with the bird until it landed again.

We climbed to 5,500 feet to avoid crowding the bird. We had to give it plenty of room to fly free, and yet not lose it. Visibility was good. Stars were visible on all horizons, but far more prominent than the stars were the lights on the ground. Everywhere there were lights—solitary pin points in the dark expanse of the farmlands, small clusters of lights that marked small towns, and expansive clusters of white and colored lights in larger cities. The distribution of lights was a useful navigation cue for Jim and me, but what could it mean to the bird? The experience was unique. A thrush was guiding us to some unknown destination.

We could judge our proximity to the bird fairly well from the strength of the radio signal. We tried to stay a least a mile from it but periodically closed in from behind and above the bird to get an accurate fix on its location. If we passed directly over the thrush, we could detect a distinct pause in the radio signal. The metal of the plane apparently created a useful sound block in our receiving system, for even in test flight we could not receive a signal from a transmitter directly under the plane. This pause or null was the clue to the precise location of the bird at a given moment. The miles rolled by.

At 8:49 we made a position check on the bird. It was over Thawville, Ill. A check on the map showed that the bird was on about a 10-degree heading from its take-off point, and it was making a ground speed of about 50 miles per hour. Could it really be going that fast?

Jim called the nearest flight service station for data on winds aloft (3,000–5,000 feet). The winds were from the south-southwest at 22 knots. The bird was getting considerable help from the wind. Its own air speed was about 33 m.p.h. Not bad! A few miles southwest of Kankakee, Ill., we noticed that the bird was still flying almost 10 degrees from Champaign, and its ground speed was still just under 50 m.p.h.

Ahead lay Chicago. If the bird held its course, it would fly right over the middle of the city and out over Lake Michigan. I began to worry about what might happen at Chicago. Perhaps all the lights would confuse the bird, or perhaps we would lose contact with it because of all the electrical interference above the city. In tests our air-borne transmitters often had given us a working range of 25 miles or more, but tonight reception was exceedingly poor.

Near the south edge of Chicago we made another good position check. The bird was still holding its heading and speed with almost unbelievable constancy. The ignition noise over the city was terrible; we started to have trouble hearing the signal from the bird. Somewhere near Midway Airport we lost it altogether. It was 10:15.

Marking the course that the thrush had held for the past 50 miles, I extended a line on an air chart. The line intercepted the shore of Lake Michigan just north of Evanston. If the bird did not become confused, if it held its course and speed, it would be just north of Evanston at 10:37. That was the only chance we had of finding our bird again.

Jim flew a fairly direct route to the north of Evanston. There, north of most of the city, the electrical interference seemed to decrease. If the bird came that way, we were sure we could find it. We circled slowly.

At 10:37, just as we had hoped, the signal from the bird came in strongly. It was right on schedule. Over that vast sprawl of lights, the bird had held its unerring course, just as it had in the relative darkness of the farmlands to the south. Now, abruptly, the terrain changed again, and the bird faced the stark, lonely darkness above Lake Michigan.

Perhaps here the bird would change its course. I almost prayed that it would hold to the relative safety of the shore. But no. It reached the shore and flew out over the lake at the same undaunted pace it had kept for the past 140 miles. Seemingly nothing could deter it from that unknown destiny which lay somewhere ahead. We followed the thrush a few miles over the lake. Then, reluctantly, we had to make a decision, and Jim Taylor swung the plane back toward the mainland.

Where that lone, delicate bird went, we could not risk going. In that moment, as the signal faded in the darkness, I felt overwhelming admiration for that bird. Compared to the achievement, the determination, the seeming purposefulness of that small creature in it first year of life, making a journey it had never made before, to a destiny it could not know, all of human technology somehow dimmed to insignificance.

Hoping that its course would carry the thrush across the waters in the shortest possible distance, I looked at the map and extended its course line northward. My hopes sank. The bird was not to cross the lake in the shortest possible way, but in the longest. Opposite Waukegan it would be 10 miles off shore, at Milwaukee more than 20 miles. Unless it changed its course, it would fly virtually the length of Lake Michigan, almost 250 miles over the open water—this in addition to the 140 miles it flew before reaching the lake. Nearly 400 miles and more than 8 hours of flying with no chance of rest.

Near the north end of Lake Michigan, Washington Island would be the bird's first chance for a landing unless it was lucky enough to find one of Mr. J.P. Perkin's floating forests, which he described so well in "17 Flyways Over the Great Lakes," in the September-October 1964 Audubon Magazine. I thought of Mr. Perkins and wished there were more like him.

Thinking of that vast expanse of water made me wonder about the bird's fuel supply. The bird was little more than an ounce of bone and muscle and fat. Was that enough for such a journey? Thinking of the transmitter, I flinched. What right had I to add almost three grams of useless burden to the hardships this delicate creature faced? If only I could take it all back. Let the bird keep its secrets, only let it be safe. That was my fervent wish.

Yet nothing could change what was already started. The chain of events that had begun that morning was not to be wished away. Still, there was a chance the bird would come through safely. There was even an outside chance that we might find it again.

We couldn't keep track of the bird from the shore; the thrush was too far out over the lake. But if it held its course and if it held its speed, the thrush would be near Washington Island sometime around daybreak. Perhaps we could meet it there. Jim reminded me that that was a lot of "if."

He called Chicago radio for winds aloft data. As luck would have it, the winds aloft were almost identical in speed and direction at Chicago, Milwaukee and Green Bay. This was a hopeful sign. There was an ominous note though, for lines of thunderstorms were moving into northern Wisconsin and Michigan, and there were storms over northern reaches of the lake. Even now, clouds were coming in over us to block the stars from sight. Still, there was a chance.

We would refuel the plane at Austin Straubel Field, Green Bay, Wis., and then head toward Sturgeon Bay and Washington Island, trying to reach the shore north of Sturgeon Bay by 2:30 a.m., at the latest. If the bird had come through, it might be within reach of our receiver from that shore by about 2:40.

Flying up the shore north of Milwaukee, we could see the storm over the lake north of us. It looked ominous. Vertical bolts of lightening shot straight down into the lake. Jim was unperturbed. He had the calm sureness of a man who knows his profession well. I knew that he wouldn't let us get into any real danger, but I was worried about the thrush. If it tried to pass through the storm directly in its path, it might become soaked with rain and flutter helplessly into the dark water. I tried to banish the thought because I felt a special kind of communion with that solitary bit of warmth and protoplasm winging its way through the storm-laden sky.

Soon we were landing at Green Bay. Stepping out of the plane, I immediately heard migrant calls of many thrushes and warblers filtering down through the night. Obviously, we had been sharing the sky with tens of thousands of birds, each on its own remarkable journey to some tiny plot of land. How, in all this vast expanse of land and water, did each one find its way to that very special place?

At 2 a.m. we took off again, flying up the Door County Peninsula. The thunderstorms were north of Sturgeon Bay. Moving along the east shore of the peninsula, soon we seemed to be getting extremely close to the storm. Lightning flashed and thunder rumbled over the engine noise. Still short of Washington Island, we at last reached the wall of the storm that held us from our hoped-for rendezvous. Below us, heavy ground fog obliterated the line between the shore and lake. I looked at the map and then measured the distance from our position to the bird's projected flight line. It was about five miles, well within the range of our receiver if the electrical storm didn't cut us out. Surprisingly, except when the lightning crashed, the storm offered less interference than had the Chicago radio traffic earlier in the night.

It was now 2:30 a.m., and there was no sign of the thrush. Hanging there in the sky with that wall of storm so close, the whole thing suddenly seemed hopeless to me: The bird had probably changed its course, or drowned. . . . Then it was 2:40, and still no sign.

"There's no hope, Jim. Let's go back." I finally said what I had been thinking for the past 15 minutes. But Jim still wasn't quitting. We continued our lazy circle, listening. The storm was unrelenting and noisy, but we were quiet.

Suddenly, at 2:48, we simultaneously came alive. We looked at each other, quizzically, hopefully. Had we heard that familiar cadence? Jim wheeled the plane around again. There, about 130 degrees from us, the signal was coming in stronger. We flew toward it until we were absolutely certain, and then turned back to shore.

Neither of us actually spoke aloud, but there was a sigh of relief between us that said, "Thank God! He made it." It had been four hours and nine minutes since our last contact with the thrush. The bird had come 200 miles over water, still holding its speed near 50 miles an hour.

Northward, inexorably, the thrush flew on into the storm, leaving us, as it had before, in safer circumstances. The wall of storm, the dense fog, held us back. More lines of storms were coming from the west. We had waited as long as we could, and now we had to return. On its course, the thrush would come ever closer to land. In 12 minutes it would be just two miles from shore. In 140 minutes it would be over Washington Island, just as daylight was coming on. At last there would be time for rest. True, there was still the storm to bridge, but somehow there is great hopefulness in such determination.

In the 2,500 miles or more the bird had flown from its winter home in northern South America, it must have faced many storms, and now its goals was not far away. Two more long nights of flight might bring it home. If, in the nights to come, the thrush held so steadfastly to its course, it would cross 100 miles over Lake Superior and then the vast river-laced stretches of Ontario to the south shore of Hudson Bay.

Perhaps in some quiet, dark forest is the special place it seeks. *How* and *Why* are Life's eternal questions. The questions will remain. I only know that in that small drab creature there is great hopefulness, grandeur, greatness.

I stand in awe and admiration of it, and I wonder: In each year's cycle how many perils does this noble creature face, how many cold, wide waters must it cross, how many poisoned orchards does it escape? How many poorly managed banders' nets, how many giant towers, how many thoughtless traps and snares can it encounter and survive?

Size does matter.

I Remember Bill
Homer Buck

William F. Childers has been a treasure trove of memories for me for many years, and I want to add a little lore, another legend, concerning this already legendary Survey field scientist. We had many good times together, whether working, fishing, hunting, partying, or maybe just sharing a few yarns over a bottle of bourbon. Above all, Bill was a master storyteller. It was always a special treat for us at the INHS Sam Parr Field Station in Kinmundy, when Bill would come down for a day or two to help with some

The perks of a fisheries biologist.

sampling or collecting data on one of his pet projects. The payoff for us came during coffee break or after work when we got to hear some of Bill's stories. One of the special treats for me was to sit and listen to how he had polished and embellished some of the very stories that he had gotten from me. He could take a story and refine and enrich it to the point that it was unrecognizable. Bill, however, always said that there was never a story or a joke that couldn't be improved, and he usually was a master improver.

Bill could not only deliver stories, he could manufacture them based on his life experiences. I have one special recollection connected with some work that Bill was doing at Kinmundy. He was interested in the relationship of size to the success of spawning fish. For example, could an over-sized male spawn successfully with an undersized female, given their great differences in sizes. To investigate this he set up a little experiment to watch and record some of this information. He brought a graduate student with him, who was to help observe. In one of our 50–60 gallon tanks, about 6 feet long and 30 inches wide, Bill had placed sand and gravel in an artful reproduction of a spawning nest, hoping that the sunfish would use it. In the other end was a standpipe, which controlled the level of water maintained in the tank. So, the fish were placed in the tank, and the grad student was placed in position where he could observe and could give Bill continuous reports on what was happening. Bill was busy across the room, doing some microscope work.

So, the experiment is in motion and went something like this. The fish are there, and Bill says, "Well, what are they doing?" And the grad student would say, "Well, he's trying to coax her into the nest, or down to the nest, but she doesn't seem to want to go. She keeps trying to run by him, and he cuts her off and heads her for the nest. She gets to the nest and then she makes a run for it again."

"Well, what's he doing now?"

"Well, he's got her corralled and he's bringing her back, he's driving her up toward the nest. But there she goes again, and he's after her again. And he's bringing her again, but she always manages to escape." this went on for quite some time. Finally, there was a prolonged silence from the grad student. Once again Bill said, "What's going on? Tell me what's happening!" Another prolonged silence followed, then in a distressed voice the student cried, "HE ATE HER!" So ended the experiment.

Ah, the meals I've had . . .

RestauranTouring Illinois
(Eateries in Time)
Mark J. Wetzel

Many of my colleagues, both in Illinois and elsewhere in the world, have often directed queries regarding places to eat—their own and those of others—to me. I am a gourmand more than a gourmet, expressly focusing for most of my adult life (if such a life stage exists) on 'comestibilia'—all things affiliated with the practice and behavior of eating, and whether or not I was dining solo or blessed with the company of others. Like the old adage of biologists, especially those who have an expertise with a particular group of animals or plants, you can't be a true specialist unless you have eaten one or more representatives of the group with which you work (I work on aquatic worms.). In this light, I have always conveyed a caveat with my recommendations for places to eat—if I hadn't personally eaten at a place, my recommendations were but qualified rumors.

Ma Hale's Restaurant was located in Grand Tower, Illinois, a very small town in southwestern Jackson County, along the Great River Road (Illinois Route 3), and not far from other small, unknown jewels of our state.

Miss Melissa "Ma" Hale opened her boarding house in 1939, primarily for people associated with the river (river boat captains and crews). Although the boarding house part of her enterprise never expanded (accommodations were limited to about six rooms), the kitchen and dining area for the boarders did grow . . . in size to some extent, but most certainly in numbers of satisfied—and returning—customers.

An article written on August 1, 1971 by Robert Goodrich, and published in the Metro East Journal, mentioned the regional fame of Ma Hale's (when Ma Hale was age 79). Customers arrived via riverboast, tow boats, excursion trains, and even helicopters. . . just to dine there. For a while, the number of customers for Sunday dinner ranged from 1,200–1,500! A Presley Tours excursion train once stopped there, and it was rumored that 2,250 customers spilled out for dinner at Ma Hale's. [Please understand that these near-unbelievable numbers of customers for a single meal were conveyed to this writer; therefore—in light of the truth...or "as legend would have it," and with no irrefutable way to confirm these figures—I present this historical accounting with a bit of caveat lector.] This tremendous customer base once convinced Ma Hale to increase the price of each meal, hoping to reduce the persistent customer load; alas, no relief was realized.

During the time that Ma Hale was directly involved, she maintained a guest book for all customers. Once, a customer who signed his name as Peter Rabbit, remarked "salad was delicious."

For decades, Ma Hale's Restaurant served up gut-busting family style breakfasts, lunches, and dinners; later in "her" history, the restaurant more or less limited its fare to week-day lunches and occasional dinners.

I suspect that many a visitor to Ma Hale's happened upon the place purely by accident, on their quest to view Tower Rock, located across the Mississippi River, on the western (Missouri) shoreline. Tower Rock is a story unto itself.

Tower Rock, as it exists today, is a small limestone island, rising 90 feet above the river at normal pool and about one-quarter acre in size, supporting small upland forest stands of oak-pine and oak-hickory-beech trees. Tower Rock was formerly the "cornerstone" of a line of rocks creating a series of falls at this point in the river. As commercial and recreational traffic on the river increased, so did navigational constraints through these rocks during periods of low water. The other rocks were blasted with dynamite, but Tower Rock was spared. It is accessible by boat, and was even accessible by foot from the Missouri side of the river in 1988 when the water level was extremely low. The earliest mention of this island was by Jacques Marquette in 1673; later, Meriwether Lewis mentioned this island in his journals. Magazines often proclaimed (incorrectly) that Tower Rock was the nation's smallest national park; in fact, a statement to this effect appeared in a Ripley's "Believe It or Not" newspaper feature many years ago. Tower Rock was never a national park, nor national monument, and was "withdrawn for public purposes" by President Ulysses S. Grant on 24 February 1871; the island is now part of the Tower Rock Natural Area, managed by the Missouri Department of Conservation. Tower Rock was designated a National Historic Site on 15 November 1972.

Personally, Ma Hale's was far more interesting to me than Tower Rock. The meals at Ma Hale's were served in the family style: large oval plates and dishes, loaded to the edge (and higher in the middle)—regardless of the size of your group (two to eight).

The menu was not lengthy; "regulars" (such as many of us became, proudly wearing an imaginary badge of honor after just one visit), usually ordered sans menus, opting for the family style meal, regardless of what was being offered. The family style meals were exceptional and people returned again and again to enjoy these delicious offerings. The meat dish was often fried chicken, but occasionally included sliced chuck roast, chicken and dumplings, beef and noodles, or shank ham slices. Side dishes included real mashed potatoes and gravy, corn, country-style green beans, succotash (corn and peas, or corn and beans), home-made rolls, then later batter-whipped white Bunny bread, with margarine patties; desert was usually a selection of fruit crisps or cobblers (each matching or exceeding the crisp/cobbler standard set by the long closed Iron Kettle restaurant, formerly located on the east side of Anna, where their moniker on the front screen door read, "If you had beans for lunch, don't come back for dinner." [but I *digest*].

The employees and guests of Ma Hale's were as diverse as any group of unrelated people you might rub elbows with . . . on any given day or at any given venue; one or two of them were dentically challenged, and several may have been family (but I don't remember us ever asking). Regardless, their kindness, and pride in serving us, remained exceptional over the many visits during the earlier years of my employment at the Survey. These observations, however, were but a few of the many attractions resulting from our repeated visits.

Field work always encourages the appetite, allowing the eyes, and the thought of having a filling meal . . . to proceed directly past common sense and the tempering of one's consumptive addiction. Hence, we usually stumbled up from the table on our way to pay at the cash register (attended always by one of the kitchen staff, never by the nonexistent host/hostess), then crawled and/or dragged one another off the premises, then pulling ourselves into the field vehicle wondering, "Will we manage to complete our day's scheduled fieldwork, before considering a dinner venue?" Reckless thought of returning to Ma Hale's for dinner—on the same day we had eaten there for lunch—was moot, as the place, thankfully, was only open for lunches during most of the years we frequented the place.

To give additional plausibility to my love for this unique venue, and why I chose Ma Hale's above all others (and there are countless eateries in my memory, most deserving of at least a quip, if not greater embellishment), I recount one conversation I had with a current Illinois State Geological Survey employee, one who shall remain unnamed, but one whom I have known for years because of our long-time physical relationship in the building (I mean, "physical" in the sense of adjacency of offices), and our collaborative musical pursuits over the years. He would drive (at the advice, and in the company of a senior geologist) for many miles across the state on IL 13, or IL 146, when working in the eastern counties of southern Illinois, just to eat at Ma Hale's; there were many others who were magnetically attracted in similar fashion (including myself, and those with me in the field—and with little coercion or humiliating pressure needed to attain a consensus on where our next meal would be). At the end of a long day in the field, Ma Hale's was viewed as perhaps the ultimate reward for a job well done. But of course, there is more supporting fodder to share with the readers . . .

In addition to the obvious draw to Ma Hale's for food , the place also had eclectic accoutrements blessing the walls, the floor, and the square (old barn-wood encased) pillars holding up the ceiling, and with many nails and screws holding pictures and other items, some of which may have had interest only to the person who hung that item up for viewing [perhaps why some of these adornments seemed to change between our visits]. The ceiling lights—mostly single, uncovered fluorescent bulbs—cast a cool, often flickering light upon the old wooden-topped church hall, eight-seat tables. Furniture in the place was not close to being new, even in the early 1970s. A couple of old electric floor lamps with long-faded shades stood silently in the entry hallway, along with the elongate glass display case that doubled as the place where you paid your bill (usually scribbled on a cheap, light green restaurant order slip torn from a booklet of the same).

My favorite pictures were of Mississippi River fauna, caught or otherwise obtained in a true southern Illinois tradition (e.g., snagged, gigged, hogged, noodled, grabbled, graveled, dogged, tickled, stumped, even trapped)—pictures that occasionally included the proud person or persons who made the catch. One was of a nearly seven-foot-long paddlefish (a.k.a. spoonbill cat); several other black-and-white pictures were of large turtles, gar fish, and other subjects that cannot be recalled at this time. Suffice it to say that the adornments on the walls, pillars, and corners were eclectic, yet interesting, often humorous, and most certainly represented the purest of Americana/Mississippiana/Illinoisana.

A couple of days after returning to Champaign from one of the many field trips to southern Illinois and Ma Hale's with Warren Brigham and others (while collecting aquatic macroinvertebrates throughout Little Egypt and beyond), my mail carrier delivered a postcard—with a picture of Ma Hale's restaurant (a cheesy, 1960s faded color post card reproduction)— to my house. It read "Having a wonderful time; wish you were here; please send money, bye." A couple of years later, I had the opportunity to send a similar courteous greeting to Warren, and that card from me to him was still proudly displayed in his office until he passed away in August 1996—with yet another visit to Ma Hale's planned by us for that autumn under the guise of collecting at two of our most favorite places, LaRue-Pine Hills Ecological Area and Burden Falls.

Ma Hale's no longer serves as a haven for hungry riverboat captains, tour operators, buskers, truckers, fisherpeople, river rats, field biologists, or those lost (for whatever reason) on their trek along the Great River Road. After Ma Hale passed away in the early 1970s, her son, Thomas, assumed management of the restaurant (the boarding house part of this establishment had long ceased to exist). A few years later, the business was sold to wishful restauranteurs, hoping to resurrect the long past fame and draw of the place; but it never regained its early, often overwhelming popularity. One or two other owners came and went, but the place closed for good sometime in the early 1990s, and the building is now in disrepair, perhaps soon destined for demolition.

Many of us miss this haven for hungry, often weary travelers, but our waistlines won't. The legend lives on in all who were blessed by a visit to Ma Hale's. I even think that Mr. Creosote would have been happy here, although I don't think he ever signed the guest book. In closing, I can unequivocally affirm that post-meal torpor and field work in southwestern Illinois will never again be quite the same—for any of us.

Acknowledgments

I acknowledge Warren Brigham (now deceased) for introducing me to Ma Hale's in 1974 and for accompanying me on many revisits to this fine southwestern Illinois establishment. Charlie Burdick (Grand Tower historian), and Devon Clifford (Carbondale, Illinois, Convention and Tourism Bureau) provided historical background on the restaurant. Additional insight, factoid oversight, and "flavor" for this article was kindly tendered by my anonymous friend and colleague, Robert J. Krumm.

Chapter 3

Work Abroad

Woods Hole, MA August 24, 1881

... I returned from a cruise 120 miles south, to the borders of the Gulf Stream. When I arrived here Monday noon, I found Prof. Baird just leaving for Newport. Had a short but very pleasant talk with him and learned that the Fish-Hawk was to start on a dredging trip that afternoon. Prof. Baird took me down to the Laboratory and introduced me to his party, and I was soon thoroughly at home. I ought to set down at once my appreciation of the cordial, kind and friendly greeting which this little band has given me. From Prof. Baird to the steward on the boat, all have treated me most courteously; and two or three have devoted themselves to me with all the generosity of friendship at first sight. Except that I was too tired to be myself completely, the trip down Vineyard Sound was very charming. When we struck the swell of old ocean, however, I began to have my doubts. Seized with a growing melancholy, I sat silent in the cabin, until, about eight o'clock, and vanished quietly but instantly through the door of my stateroom. I got a little sleep that night, and turned out at four to see the dredging begin. At five, I suddenly remembered that I had forgotten my morning devotions; and in about ten seconds I was on my knees with my head out of the cabin window, making my neglected sacrifice to Neptune, the infernal old pagan, delighted, I suppose, at having so good a Christian in his grip, wasn't content with one performance of this little ceremony, but kept me at it all day long. Whenever the trawl was sent down or taken on board, I staggered out to watch the operation, and then hurried back to pay my penalty. In this way, without a mouthful to eat, I got through the day. A little brandy helped me a little toward evening, and I think that I should have been all right to-day, but we started in at seven, and this morning got into port.

The dredging was magnificent. I felt like a dull school-boy, with so much before my eyes that I didn't understand. A new species of fish, of a family that I never heard of before, was as abundant as "bull-heads" in a mill pond, sea anemones came up, by the bushel, and starfishes by the barrel. Jelly fishes, holothurians, ... Etc. were as common as butterflies in Illinois.

It was outrageous and abominable that I could not be in the thick of it, but I finally learned all I came for; and with some further observations to be made this afternoon and some collections from ponds near by, shall feel ready to leave.

Experience life, all of it.

An Electrifying Experience
as told to Susan Post

During the early 1990s Jon Armbruster was a graduate student of INHS ichthyologist Larry Page. Jon and I shared an office space for a year and he would regale me with some of his fish tales; great stuff to a landlubber. Part of Jon's thesis was working on a project that allowed him to collect in South America for two years. He shared his journal with me of an especially electrifying experience.

The entry is dated January 6, 1995. "I saw an *Electrophorus electricus* (electric eel) swimming along shore. We surrounded it with a seine and waited until we got it in the net. It was about 1 meter long and tried to hide in a root mass. It was able to go backwards and forwards and we saw it come up for air several times. Some of us touched it and man it was weird. I felt the pulse of electricity go up my arm and felt the muscles twitch. Had to try though."

From frass to fracas—foreign field work.

Across Europe: Bathrooms, Bedbugs, and Bedlam
Michael R. Jeffords

Although I began my career working on soybeans at the Illinois Natural History Survey, in the mid 1980s I had an opportunity to turn my attention to the dreaded gypsy moth, just making inroads into northern Illinois. Thousands of researchers over the last 100 years have attempted to eradicate, control, manage, or even coexist with this insect, all unsuccessfully. Finding a research niche that might prove fruitful and relevant to Illinois was essential. This desire led me into a partnership with Dr. Joseph Maddox, an insect pathologist at the Survey and one of the world authorities on an obscure group of insect pathogens called microsporidia. Joe and I were successful, after a time, in receiving funding to conduct exploration in Europe to search for microsporidia of gypsy moths that could be imported into the U.S. for use against this most important forest pest. We agreed to search areas of Europe that had low levels of gypsy moths, likely under natural controls (predators, parasites, and pathogens), and bring them back to Illinois for study and possible release. Our destinations were to be the cork oak forests of Portugal and the forests of Yugoslavia. I will spare you the tedium of the search effort as I dissected around 2,000 gypsy moth caterpillars in Portugal and an equal number in Yugoslavia and Joe diligently screened each one for microsporidia. We ultimately found six infected individuals and isolated the pathogens for return to the U.S. That, however, is not the whole story. Over the six weeks we were in Europe, a series of adventures and misadventures occurred. To understand some of what occurred, a brief description of Joe is in order. Joe is a kind, calm, quiet southern gentleman with an encyclopedic knowledge of his field. But, things happen to Joe, funny things, for no apparent reason. They just happen. Before the trip, as we both spoke only English, Joe agreed to learn enough Portuguese to get us by and I agreed to do the same with Serbo-Croatian.

Toilets

As most of you undoubtedly do not know, one of the best ways to detect disease in insect populations is to look at their frass (fecal matter or poop). One of our first field days was spent in the vicinity of Lisbon, searching the cork oak forests for caterpillars. Not finding any, Joe asked our hosts from the Forestry Institute of Lisbon to help him search for frass under the trees. They spoke only halting English and Joe's Portuguese had progressed only to the level of ordering beer in restaurants. Yet he valiantly tried to convey his message and they finally caught on, we thought. After a short walk, we found ourselves in front of a line of ancient, outdoor privies, with our host looking expectantly at us. When we looked puzzled, we were asked by our most English-savvy host, "Joe, why for do you wish to hunt for gypsy moths in toilets?" Little frass was collected that day.

Trains

After nearly three weeks in Lisbon, we were to fly to Belgrade, Yugoslavia, to continue our search for pathogens. However, Joe, in his inimitable style, decided it would be more adventurous to take a train from Lisbon to Belgrade. While not the Orient Express, it did possess some romantic appeal, so I agreed. We trundled off to the train station to purchase our tickets. Again, in halting Portuguese, Joe purchased two first class tickets to Belgrade, and the train was to depart in a couple of hours. As we waited in the station, we noticed that several people in our area showed up with their luggage, but also had rather large bags and baskets of foodstuffs. How charming that the locals were to accompany us and that they actually used the train for the weekly market runs, or so we thought. We boarded the train and were soon on our way in a compartment for six, that included a nun and priest and a couple who smoked incessantly during the trip. Joe, polite as always, said little, while I glared at the occupants for a time, but soon gave up and ventured into the long hallway of the car. Here, too, the air was thick with cigarette smoke so I opened the window and stuck my head out for fresh air. This was a mistake as I did not realize that in Europe, the rail lines run very close together, somewhere around a foot apart, and I was nearly decapitated by the first express freight train we passed! So back into the crowded, smoky car I went for the trip across Portugal, Spain, and into France. Later that day Joe and I noticed that our fellow travelers were all delving into their food parcels and dining on wine, cheese, bread, and whatever else they had brought. Perhaps a late lunch was in order so Joe and I headed off to find the dining car. After traversing the rather short train, it had only eight cars, all identical to ours, we wondered how people on the train were fed. A question for one of only two train conductors led to the following explanation. His rather amused answer was that this was a second tier train and it had no amenities (such as food), and we could grab something at our stop in Marseilles. As that was almost two days away (it was also a very slow train), we were in for a long, hungry, smoky haul. Joe, in short, had purchased us first-class tickets, but on a second-class train.

Sleeping Arrangements

In Marseilles, we were finally able to grab a bite to eat, but had to change trains and we ended up in a sleeper car with six bunks, stacked three to a side. As the train was pulling out late that night, we were congratulating ourselves on our good fortune, when a French family showed up—mother and father, teenage daughter, a new born baby, and a yellow bird in a cage—eyed our compartment, and promptly began to settle in. No one spoke each other's language so we tried to make the best of it by partitioning space. One bunk was deemed luggage central, which left five bunks for six people and the bird. Joe ended up sharing a bunk with the bird, and I think the baby, while I was matched with the truculent teenager who eyed me like I was from the seventh level of Hell. Needless to say, we all slept in our clothing and had a rather restless night. I awoke several times to the cadence of the slow train and wondered to myself, "what the hell am I doing here." Unknown to all of us, there were other occupants in the compartment. The next morning as the train stopped briefly in Venice to exchange passengers, Joe and I looked at each other and promptly decided that enough was enough and left the train to spend the weekend there. As the train emptied of people, two guys entered to clean it, and they used a hose and high pressure nozzle to spray out each compartment. Later that day we both noticed that a ring of red welts with little red dots had formed around our waists. Bedbugs also had been our companions on the night's trip across France. When they say second- class, they really mean *second-class*.

Bedlam

I won't say much about our "quiet weekend" in Venice, as it was actually quite nice and the city was infinitely charming. We entered the city, however, in what was, to put it mildly, utter chaos. The train station in Venice dead ended in the city and opened onto the Grand Canal, complete with gondoliers, operatic strains of *Ole Sole Mio*, and quite unexpectedly, massive numbers of orange-clad, bald *Hare Krishna* followers, chanting and drumming their way along the canal. What a sight for weary, hungry travelers to be surrounded by the total bedlam of a *Hare Krishna* convention on a Friday night in Venice. Fortunately, we were able to find a local hotel and finally begin to enjoy our weekend.

Monday morning we were back on a train that would take us through Trieste to Belgrade, Yugoslavia. Again, this was not the Orient Express, but it did have a dining car, and when we crossed the border at Trieste, military police sporting submachine guns boarded the train and examined us, our luggage, our passports, gave us the once-over, but let us pass. Upon arrival in Belgrade we attempted to contact the Forestry Institute with which we were supposed to partner. Once we found someone who spoke some English, we were informed that they had no idea who we were and could not help us. While we had spent months arranging this trip, we had never really gotten confirmation for our visit, but had decided to chance it anyway. This was a mistake and "not the way things are done in eastern Europe," we were politely informed by the secretary at the Forestry Institute. After settling into a hotel, Joe and I decided to visit the institute in the hope of straightening things out. We did manage to finally talk to a very nice gentleman who sort of took us under his wing and introduced us to the director of the institute. Finally, they agreed to help us for two days, as that was all they could spare. It was 9 a.m. and we had to seal the deal with a traditional toast of Turkish coffee (a tiny cup, mostly with grounds and very little water that resembled mud) and a shot of slivovitz, the fiery plum liquor of the region. I'm not a coffee drinker and that was my first and last taste of coffee, but the slivovitz, although not bad, was definitely an acquired taste. I'll not bore you with the details of our fieldwork (more larvae, more dissections), but proceed on to our subsequent adventures. After leaving our "friends" at the institute, we decided to explore the country for a few days. When we asked our contact what he would recommend, his only comment was, "well, that would not be a very good idea." We questioned him as to why, but that was all he would say, except an admonishment to "be careful."

So off we went. Joe and I rented a Yugo to explore the Yugoslav countryside, having no idea of the ethnic tensions that were about to explode within a few years.

Our first stop was a national park in the southern part of the country where we rented a room overlooking a hydroelectric dam. The next morning we headed off down a trail, cameras in hand, to explore the park. It wasn't long until we were in trouble. I had found an interesting group of mating snails and was on my hands and knees photographing them when I was poked in the back. I looked around, irritated that Joe would interrupt me, but it wasn't Joe. It was a military policeman prodding me to my feet with his automatic weapon. Of course language again became a barrier and we were taken into custody. This was a Sunday afternoon and our unhappy little group returned to the hotel and we were stationed in a room while the policemen tried to find someone who spoke English. A fellow traveler did eventually show up and she explained that it is illegal to have a camera within a kilometer of a "nationally sensitive area," in this case, the hydroelectric dam. She stated that the policemen wanted to take us into custody, confiscate our camera equipment, and, well, I'm not sure what else. After much discussion, the nice lady was able to convey our story to the officer that we were scientists, not terrorists or spies bent on the destruction of this ancient-looking dam, and that we were merely photographing his beautiful country. Some three hours later we were back in our room, camera equipment intact, blood-pressure back down, sitting on our balcony with a glass of slivovitz, yes, overlooking that same, critically sensitive hydroelectric dam.

Yugos

A few days later Joe flew to Prague and I was left to myself. Just north of Belgrade was another national park that I wanted to explore, so against my own better judgment based on our previous experiences, off I went. The area was one of deep ravines and heavy forests, and I was hiking down a trail at the bottom of the ravines when I heard gunfire in the distance. Having never served in the military, my experience with firearms was severely limited, but when bullets began whizzing across the top of the ravines and splintering trees on the other side, I surmised that my presence here was no longer a good idea. I ran back to the car, only to find that my Yugo had a flat tire. Now I can change a tire with the best of them, but when I jacked up the vehicle, removed the lug nuts, nothing happened. The tire seemed welded to the axle. Now what? I could still hear the gunfire, although it was in the forest and none of it seemed directed at me. Shortly, a shepherd with his small flock of sheep happened along and I tried to plead my case as to what to do. I didn't really know if Yugos were constructed differently from American cars. Perhaps they do weld the tires to the axle. With signs and the few words of Serbo-Croatian I knew, I asked the shepherd what I should do. He seemed to understand, looked over the tire, and went to his pack and removed a short, heavy sledge hammer. Smiling, he walked over to the tire and gave it a tremendous whack, which broke it loose from the axle. It had been on so long that it had rusted to the frame. He smiled and said while waving his finger back and forth, "Yugos, no good."

Chicago? Cleveland? Customs?

One final event occurred on our flight home from Belgrade to Chicago. Joe had arranged with U.S. Customs and the U.S. Department of Agriculture that we would be returning from our trip with samples of insect pathogens in our possession. We were to declare that we had insect pathogens and the customs agents would have the necessary paperwork needed to process our entry with them back into the U.S. We flew on JAT Airlines (Yugoslavia Air Transport) and we were to arrive in Chicago early the next morning. The flight was somewhat uneventful, with the exception of the whole boiled chicken for dinner, until we landed and deplaned with our luggage and vials of insect pathogens to go through customs. At 4 a.m., however, one's senses can be a little addled, but Joe and I soon noticed that we were not in Chicago, but Cleveland. What's up? The customs agents said that the Serbian pilot had gotten confused and landed in the wrong city. The agent said it would be no problem, until Joe had the honesty, albeit misplaced, to declare that we were carrying insect PATHOGENS. It seems the only word the agent actually heard was PATHOGEN, and we were ushered off to another room while the regional agent in charge was rousted from bed at 4 a.m. and asked to come down and deal with us. This took some time, but after we had stated our case, including the misplaced landing, he took severe pity on us and took our five vials of insect pathogens, put them in a paper bag, stapled it shut, wrote QUARANTINED on it, and said in his sternest voice, "don't open these until you get to Chicago!"

Joe collecting "frass" in the Portuguese countryside.

Sometimes a net is unnecessary for collecting moths.

Brain Borer
Rob Wiedenmann

In 1997, the Midwest Institute for Biological Control was held on the campus of the Pan American School of Agriculture (Zamorano) in Honduras. Joe Maddox (Survey insect pathologist) and I were the organizers of the course, along with Bob O'Neil (Purdue University), Ernest Delfosse (U.S. Department of Agriculture-Agricultural Research Service), and Ron Cave (Zamorano). The course was about field techniques needed for foreign exploration for biological control agents, quarantine, and conducting in-country experiments on potential biological control agents. Heady stuff, and approximately a dozen students, including three from our biological control lab at the Illinois Natural History Survey—Charlie Helm, and grad students Claire Rutledge and Marianne Alleyne—had signed up.

The course was intense, running from early morning until late at night, each day for about 10 days. Basing the course at Zamorano was ideal, as they had many of the facilities, classrooms, field plots, and proximity to areas to which we could travel. Joe, given his Alabama upbringing, accent, and language wizardry could never pronounce the name of the school, mispronouncing "Zamorano" (Zah-more-ah-no) as "Zamorena" (Zam-or-ai-nuh), no matter how many times he was corrected.

We experienced many of the typical difficulties associated with searching for and collecting natural enemies. One day's activities included driving the group about four hours into the mountains west of Zamorano, where Bob had scouted out a patch of *Solanum* (wild potato) that held a large number of leaf beetles, closely related to the Colorado potato beetle. The intent was to collect the beetle larvae and rear them to see if any contained parasitoids (parasitic flies and wasps) or diseases that might be useful against Colorado potato beetle in the U.S. A flat tire, en route, added hours to the trip, and when we finally arrived at the site in the mountains, we found that a local landowner had just cut down the entire patch of *Solanum* plants. It is mighty hard to collect insects from no-longer-existent plants, and the lesson learned about the necessity of having secure sites for collecting was little consolation during the four-hour drive back to Zamorano.

We had planned to collect insects that night using a black light (UV light attracts insects), but due to the flat tire and our late return, we got a very late start to our collecting. We had two black lights spread on white sheets about 25–30 m apart at the far edge of the campus fields. The students and instructors (minus O'Neil, who stayed behind with a high fever—this comes into play again later) divided themselves between the two lights to see what could be collected. Ron Cave was leading the exercise and was at one of the lights with Joe. Joe was on his hands and knees next to the black light sorting through some of the insects that landed on the white cloth. All of a sudden Joe dropped to the ground, alternately grimacing in pain and laughing; all the while holding his ear. Between the pain and tickling, Joe told the alarmed group of bystanders that there was an insect in his ear. He got up and bent his head to the side and was hitting the other side of his head, while hopping on one foot to try to dislodge the insect—to no avail. One of the group suggested pouring liquid into his ear to try to get the insect out. Joe remembers the student pouring water into his ear, but I was the one who packed the vehicles for the collecting trip and I know we didn't have any water, but we did have a lot of bottles of the local beer, *Salva Vida*. So, to this day, I maintain that it was *beer* that was poured into his ear, not water. Anyway, whatever it was, beer or water, it didn't work. Ron loaded Joe (with beer coming out of his ear, not an unusual phenomenon for Joe) into one of the trucks and raced down the dirt road to the campus infirmary. For some students who were unaware of the happenings, the first inkling of anything amiss was when they saw tail lights disappear in a cloud of dust. At the infirmary Ron found a doctor who extracted a very large moth that had flown straight into Joe's ear canal. The alternate tickling and pain was from the moth trying to move its wings in the ear canal (tickling) and pressing against his eardrum (pain). The doctor removed the moth, treating it as if it were an everyday occurrence (perhaps he had met Joe before). More on the moth later.

Ron and Joe returned to the group as we were packing up the gear to call it a night. We returned to campus and everyone headed back to their respective rooms.

Joe was rooming with Bob O'Neil, who, by then, was running a very high fever and was nearly delirious. Joe turned on the light, got undressed to his white undershirt and boxers, and was telling and demonstrating to delirious Bob about the experience with the moth. Bob was mostly unresponsive, so Joe turned out the light and went to sleep. During the night, Bob's fever broke and he awakened in the morning, drenched in sweat, but feeling much better. However, he related to Joe his strange, delirium-induced hallucination of a bright light and some white-haired guy, dressed all in white, hopping on one foot and talking about a moth in his ear. Bob said he knew he was sick, but he had never had that kind of hallucination from a fever. Joe said, "That was me! I DID have a moth in my ear!" And he showed Bob the moth. Remember that Joe's an entomologist, so a specimen is a specimen. At that point, I am positive that Bob was no longer sure what was reality, what was hallucination, and whether the story was going to get even more bizarre. Joe brought the moth (probably illegally) back to the U.S., where Joe's long-suffering wife, Janice, had it pinned, framed, and mounted on the wall of their Ogden, Illinois, home, figuring this was just another in the series of Joe's adventures. The last time I checked, it was still there.

Epilogue #1: Joe made a number of trips to Honduras to search for pathogens in insects, but the trips to the cigar factory at Santa Rosa de Copan, the women's room incident, the men's room incident, dancing around to avoid having a semi-automatic weapon pointed at him while a guard looked though Joe's binoculars, causing an international incident by "renting" a string of fish from a fisherman at a volcanic lake (don't ask), or catching an eye disease from a nun (REALLY, don't ask), were all on different, equally adventurous journeys as the "moth trip" above.

Epilogue #2: The last night of the course, the students developed a song that poked fun at all the instructors and performed it for all of us. At the time, the horrendous song, "Macarena," was popular. The students developed their song using the same structure, only substituting, "Hey, Zamorena" (pronouncing it as Joe did) for "Hey macarena." When they got to the part of the song poking fun at Joe, the entire group of students hopped on one foot, hitting their heads, as if they were trying to dislodge a moth. Good, clean fun, although maybe not so much for Joe.

Epilogue #3: Joe's version of the story is that the doctor extracted the moth tail-end outward from his right ear. Joe identified it as an armyworm, *Spodoptera frugiperda*. However, Joe has steadfastly refused to submit the moth to top moth taxonomists for verification. Further, everyone that watched him and tried to help him distinctly recalled that it was his left ear into which we poured the beer. And the doctor later stated that the moth was removed head-first (not tail-first) from his right ear. So, if the students poured beer into Joe's left ear, but the doctor removed the moth from the right ear, that meant it must have been the much-feared tropical moth, the "Lesser Brain Borer" (*Spodoptera braegena*), and the doctor collected the moth as it was exiting the opposite ear it entered, after it had tunneled all the way through. That might explain a lot about Joe.

International boundaries: Insects don't seem to care, but border guards, that's a different matter!

Stuck on the Border with Bugs
Lee Solter

I stared forlornly at the back of the public bus, and then, as it disappeared from sight in a puff of diesel fuel and road dust, turned back to stare at the offending white Styrofoam ice chest on the folding table in front of me. A youthful border guard, draped in an assault rifle half his size with a dour, what-the-devil-am-I- going-to-do-with-her expression on his face, stood silently in front of me. Neither of us knew exactly what to do next, and we were not helped by my inability to speak Slovak and his to speak English. The box was filled with little plastic food containers, each lined with a mixture of wheat germ and nutrients concocted to feed gypsy moth caterpillars. The caterpillars were in there, too, about 1,000 of them, munching away in complete indifference to our current predicament.

I had arrived in Vienna, Austria, the previous day and, after 24 hours of sleepless travel I suffered through my first night of jet lag. My colleague, Gernot Hoch, appeared early the next morning with the box of caterpillars from his lab at the University of Applied Sciences-BOKU. He drove me to the bus station for the long ride to Banska Stiavnica, a mountain town in central Slovakia, where he would meet me and Milan Zubrik, our Slovak colleague, to set up a field experiment in an oak plantation forest.

Gypsy moths are native to Europe and Asia and are an outbreak species that, when populations are high, can completely defoliate an oak forest. For years, the populations can remain low or moderate and are scarcely noticed, but then will begin to build and eventually reach very high levels. During the building stage one also finds increases in their natural enemies, such as parasitic wasps and flies, and a complex of disease-causing pathogens, that will eventually cause the gypsy moth population to "crash" back to low levels. During outbreaks, the forest feels very strange. The canopy begins to open as the larvae grow and feed on the leaves, and the falling frass (insect fecal pellets) sounds like a persistent rain. The forest even smells like my lab when I am rearing thousands of caterpillars, a musty, earthy odor. At the end of the larval stages, the caterpillars are up to three inches long and may have completely stripped most of the trees and shrubs in the forest, creating the appearance of winter in the middle of summer.

What the border guard didn't know, and I didn't bother trying to communicate to him (no point in making a bad situation worse), was that a second organism was hitching a ride—the gypsy moth caterpillars were all infected with a microsporidian pathogen, a tiny, jellybean-shaped organism, a thousand of which would fit end-to-end across the head of a pin. Microsporidia are chronic pathogens that slowly weaken their hosts. If the caterpillar doesn't die as a larva or pupa, then often the ability of infected adults to mate and lay eggs is severely compromised. Several species of microsporidia infect the gypsy moth in Europe, but unlike other pathogens of gypsy moth, the microsporidia never made it to North America during or after the accidental introduction of the moth around 1869.

We hoped to release these pathogens in U.S. gypsy moth populations and I had been working for 10 years to make sure that the gypsy moth microsporidia will infect only the gypsy moth and are not harmful to other native North American moths and butterflies. Now, after doing many laboratory experiments, our international team of scientists wanted to study how infected caterpillars pass the disease to uninfected caterpillars in a natural field situation.

Gernot had infected the caterpillars in his laboratory at BOKU to have them ready for the fieldwork. All I had to do was transport them to Banska Stiavnica and we could set up the experiment on small, caged trees in an oak tree plantation. We hadn't anticipated any problems crossing the border, because both the gypsy moth and the pathogen are native across western and central Europe.

The bus stopped for a passport check at the border of Austria and Slovakia. The guards came inside the bus, saying something in Slovak, and the mostly German- and Slovak-speaking passengers turned around as if looking for someone. I think I knew before I even heard the words "white box" spoken in English by the bus driver that the commotion had something to do with my ice chest. I reluctantly rose from my seat and was escorted outside. The box was placed on the table and I was motioned to take off the lid. A chuckle (which I quickly suppressed) rose in my throat at the look on the guards' faces when they saw the transparent boxes full of dark, inch-long caterpillars.

The bus driver was growing restless. An Austrian, he spoke a bit of English and he told me that he had to leave, that he absolutely must be in Bratislava in 10 minutes so his passengers wouldn't miss their connections. I also had the connection to make to Banska Stiavnica. It would have been so easy to leave the box and climb back on the bus, especially because this was only a side project for me—I had another field project going on that was my main focus at the time. But I simply could not leave the efforts of my colleagues and their expectations for the spring's work sitting on a table at an international border to die.

I pulled out a U.S. government permit to rear gypsy moths and hopefully showed it to the guard. Although he couldn't have known that it had nothing at all to do with this particular situation, I figured it was worth a try. But it wasn't' a Slovak document and it got me nowhere. Feeling a little desperate, I asked the bus driver if anyone on the bus spoke Slovak and English. He climbed aboard the bus and asked the passengers in English and German if anyone could help. A young woman stepped down and came to my side. She was able to tell the guards, in simple terms, what the caterpillars were to be used for, but that didn't budge them. I finally asked her to tell them that I would remain with the insects, but would need someone to order a taxi for me to the bus station in Bratislava. The bus drove away.

Digging around in my luggage, I found a printed email message with the phone number of Dr. Julius Novotny, the Forestry Station Director in Banska Stiavnica. I hopefully handed it to the guard, pointing to the phone number. He disappeared with my precious paper, but returned shortly, chatting on a cell phone that he handed to me. I fully expected to hear Julius' cheery voice and his annual (sweetly inappropriate) greeting "welcome home, honey!" Instead, the voice was crisply professional and female. I was told that the bugs must stay at the border. Hmm . . . thinking a little more quickly at this point, I asked her to tell the guards that the insects were very sensitive (I didn't mention 'sick') and would need to be placed in a dark, cool spot until we could retrieve them. And, please, to order me a taxi!

I was motioned to pick up my box and follow the guard through the desolate-looking concrete block guard station and out the back door. He led me to a smaller concrete building with a little door in back, motioned me inside, and pointed to a dark corner. I placed my box of caterpillars on the floor, gave him the OK sign with my fingers and, for the first time, he smiled.

Epilogue: Three days later, armed with all the political clout my well-known colleague could muster, he was able to have the box of caterpillars released. It didn't matter that, had it been mailed, it would have easily (and legally) cleared customs; the border is controlled by the Veterinary Service and, thus, doesn't answer to the Forestry Ministry. Live and learn! The field project was a success.

Good friends, great colleagues, and a cranky truck . . .

Cultural (and Biological) Learnings of Kyrgyzstan
Chris Dietrich

During the summers of 1998–2000, with funding from the National Science Foundation, INHS entomologists and botanists teamed up with scientists from the former Soviet Union to conduct a biological inventory of the grasslands of Kyrgyzstan, a former Soviet Central Asian republic. Most of the territory of this small, landlocked country just south of Kazakstan and northwest of China consists of the Tien Shan, a mountain range of high, east-west trending ridges and valleys that has given rise to a remarkable level of biological diversity and endemism (plants and animals that live nowhere else) within a relatively small area. The goals of the project were to collect specimens of insects (primarily leafhoppers) and plants from a part of the world poorly represented in western collections (and until recently, largely inaccessible to western scientists) and to obtain quantitative data on insect and plant diversity in various grassland habitats at different elevations. In addition to the author, participants in the expeditions included the following persons:

- Georgi Alexandrovich Anufriev: entomology professor from Nizhny Novgorod (Gorky) State University, Russia;
- John Bouseman: entomologist, INHS;
- Alik Karabaev: Kyrgyzstani driver of expedition vehicle;
- Anara: Kyrgyzstani expedition cook;
- Georgi (Zhora) Lazkov: botanist, Kyrgyz Academy of Sciences, Bishkek, co-organizer of expeditions;
- Dmitry Milko: entomologist, Kyrgyz Academy of Sciences, Bishkek, chief organizer of expeditions;
- Dmitry (Dima) Novikov: graduate student from Ukraine working on M.S. in entomology with Dietrich, co-organizer of expeditions;
- Mikhail (Mischa) Mokrousov: student of Prof. Anufriev studying wasps;
- Natasha Novikova: field assistant and entomology technician, INHS;
- Sergei Ovchinnikov: entomologist, Kyrgyz Academy of Sciences, Bishkek, owner of flat where foreign participants stayed in Bishkek;
- Rick Phillippe: botanist, INHS;
- Ken Robertson: botanist, INHS;
- John Taft: botanist, INHS; and
- Chen Young: entomologist, Carnegie Museum, Pittsburgh.

First Expedition—August 13 1998
Our first 24 hours in Kyrgyzstan were very educational. We arrived at Manas airport in Bishkek on time at 3 a.m. Everything was dark. We got off the plane, entered a darkened bus, and rode to the terminal where we were

among the first in line at immigration. After an hour the checked luggage was finally brought in; we claimed the three of our seven bags that had made the journey with us, and ended up last in line to go through customs. I was relieved to see Dima Novikov (my newly recruited Ukrainian graduate student, who had traveled there from Moscow to join the expedition) peering through the door at the other end of the room. Our bags were x-rayed, I handed the inspector our letter of invitation, and he waved us through. In the lobby awaited a welcoming committee of the entire Russian/Kyrgyz scientific contingent of the expedition (two Russians and two Kyrgyzstanis) who grabbed our bags, carried them out into the parking lot, lit only by a Coca-Cola sign on the terminal building, and loaded them into the expedition vehicle—a military-style, high clearance truck with passenger/baggage compartment on the back. After filing a claim for the lost luggage in the Turkish Airlines office and being told to call on Thursday (two days later), we left the airport as the sun was rising and drove to our accommodations in Bishkek. Our quarters were a private flat owned by Sergei Ovchinnikov, another entomologist from the Academy of Sciences, who agreed to rent it to us while he stayed with his mother across the hall. Our expedition cook, Anara, a Kyrgyzstani woman from a large family (and, thus, used to preparing meals for lots of people) prepared a breakfast of noodle soup with beef, bread, and yogurt. Only four of us could fit into the kitchen at once, so we ate in shifts. After breakfast, Milko staged an impromptu welcome ceremony in which we were each presented with traditional Kyrgyzstani felt hats.

Afterward we drove to the Academy of Sciences, a stark concrete building with a few colorful panels representing a traditional motif above the crumbling main entranceway. The building seemed nearly deserted and was mostly dark inside. We climbed the stairs to the third floor and proceeded down the hall, avoiding the numerous loose floorboards, to a small office containing a very old desktop computer. Milko showed us how to use the computer to send e-mail and we each sent short "arrived safe" messages. We then briefly toured the large herbarium and the disappointingly small insect collection. Our final errand was to change money. Milko exchanged $2000 and was handed a one-cubic-foot stack of large bills wrapped in a newspaper.

We reboarded the truck and headed south, into the mountains; the location of each collecting stop was now dictated by our truck's engine, which overheated three times along the steep, dirt track.

August 18

We arrived at our campsite on the southern shore of Toktogul Reservoir, a large lake formed by the construction, in the mid-60s, of a hydroelectric dam on the Naryn River. We reached the site after driving most of the night over a section of highway that is under construction and closed during the day. Milko chose what seemed to be the only level spot in an otherwise steep-sided ravine. Unfortunately, the spot was covered with *Cannabis* and we worried about the smell sticking to our luggage and causing problems in the airport on the way home.

August 22

This morning we packed our stuff and prepared to take a short cut south through Uzbekistan, which Milko assured us would be no problem, despite our not having visas. Just as a precaution, he suggested that we hide all of our currency in a "crafty place," i.e., in a sack of flour, and tell the Uzbek customs officials that we didn't have any—that we had paid all our money to our sponsors in advance. As we were preparing to leave, Ken informed us of a news report he had heard on the radio the previous night saying that the U.S., in an attempt to take out Osama bin-Laden, had fired a missile that hit Pakistan by mistake. This caused great concern among my U.S. colleagues regarding our ability to obtain safe passage through Uzbekistan. After some discussion they managed to convince Milko to make a detour of several hours, remaining in Kyrgyz territory and avoiding Uzbekistan altogether. This afforded the opportunity to pass through the large border city of Dzhalalabad, where we made phone calls at the central telephone office, an earthquake-damaged building with inclined concrete floors. We tried a traditional drink made of malted grain, sold by street vendors from large wooden churns, and ate a lunch of fried eggs, sausage, cucumbers, tomatoes, pasta, mashed potatoes, gravy, and bread at an opulently decorated restaurant. Afterwards we headed south across the Fergana Valley past abandoned agricultural collectives and farms of cotton, corn, peppers, tobacco, and potatoes, finally reaching our next collecting site in Urumbash Ravine among the most spectacular scenery yet. We camped along a meltwater stream that had cut a 20-m-deep channel in the alluvial soil and glacial drift (debris) of the ravine. Snow-capped peaks towered around us. We spent the next day collecting, not finding many new things, but enjoying the beautiful surroundings.

August 31

It's Kyrgyzstan's Independence Day. This morning when I woke, I suggested to my tent mates (Milko, Lazkov, and Novikov) that we do something to celebrate. Milko said he didn't feel like celebrating, because, for him (and most people he knew), things were a lot worse since independence. He went on to say that the only celebrating people do is to get really drunk, to which I replied that it was the same in the U.S. Milko also said that it's best to avoid towns during holidays because the police are also drunk and their behavior can be unpredictable. Fortunately, we're safely ensconced in our campsite, literally in the middle of nowhere.

September 1

As I walked down the ridge last night after collecting in the alpine meadows, I saw a Kyrgyzstani man standing next to a corral in the ravine below. Because it would have been impolite to pass without extending greetings, I approached him. He shook my hand, walked over to a five-gallon plastic container, and poured me a large cup of koumis (fermented mare's milk), which I drank. His two friends came out of the nearby hay barn and each had a cup in turn. They then offered me some mystery liquid from another container that tasted like heavy cream. After I demonstrated how I collect insects by sweep net and explained that I was from America (not Russia, which they had assumed), we told each other our names and tried to communicate further by sign language for a while mostly regarding the availability of cigarettes in our camp. I shook hands with them and returned to camp. Five minutes later, the three of them arrived on horseback and gave us their entire remaining supply of koumis. Because we had no cigarettes to offer, we gave them a 1.5-liter bottle of Coke, with which they seemed pleased. One of the guys told Anara that he drinks five liters of koumis per day.

September 7

We returned to Bishkek late last night. Sergei once again gave up his flat and we ate a melon and went to sleep. This morning we went to the institute where Georgi Lazkov, Ken Robertson, and John Taft worked on getting the plants we'd collected ready for shipment and Georgi Anufriev, Dmitry Milko, and I tried to decide on the best strategy for getting the insects safely through customs. Milko's colleagues came in and spent a couple of hours pouring over Misha's two boxes of field-pinned specimens. Apparently none of them cared about all the stuff I had collected into alcohol—no one even glanced at it. Dr. Tarbinsky, head of the institute, never showed up and his secretary said he'd probably be busy for the rest of the week. This caused some concern because a call from Tarbinsky to the Ministry of Agriculture's Phytosanitary Office is usually necessary to avoid problems getting the necessary export certificates. Eventually we decided to pack up our specimens and try our luck without Tarbinsky's help. Luckily, we happened to show up at the Phytosanitary Office on a day when the two employees who had previously caused problems for Dmitry Milko and Georgi Lazkov were not at work. With no one in line in front of us, it took only 45 minutes for Dmitry Milko to fill out the forms stating the contents of our boxes, for the typist to type the forms in quadruplicate, and for another official to sign off on them.

September 11

It's 9:30 a.m. Istanbul time. We just boarded a Turkish Air plane non-stop to Chicago. Ken just blew up at one of the flight attendants because he didn't get the window seat he requested. We've had a rough couple of days and are pretty frazzled. The Ak-Keme Hotel in Bishkek (where they sent us for the night after our original flight to Istanbul was canceled due to engine trouble) was nice, but none of us wanted to be there. The bus arrived on time at 5:30 a.m. to take us to Manas airport. There we waited for 1.5 hours to get through customs and passport control. Then we waited another couple of hours in the same dingy, dark departure lounge as the previous morning. Our plane was the regularly scheduled flight to Ashkabad, Turkmenistan, which had been re-routed to Bishkek to collect us and the other stranded passengers. When the flight finally arrived, we were all so relieved to be on an airplane at last that no one seemed to mind much that we had missed our connections in Istanbul. An extra boarding pass stub turned up at the last minute and no one claimed it, so at least six different airline/airport officials came through the cabin to check and re-check all of our tickets. Finally, the issue was resolved and we took off, four hours late. A few hours later we landed in Ashkabad, where a large inscription on the terminal building proclaimed in English "WE SHOULD ALL WORK FOR THE GOOD OF OUR GLORIOUS MOTHERLAND." The cabin attendant announced that our wait would be 30 minutes. One and a half hours later we were back on our way to Istanbul; because of the unscheduled stop in Bishkek, they had difficulty fitting everyone on the plane. I had one of the few empty seats next to me and was joined by a Turkish mechanical engineer who turned out to be a graduate of the University of Illinois. We talked at length about politics and economics in Central Asia. He said that Turkish companies, including his which builds and manages manufacturing equipment, are now heavily involved in the former Soviet republics. I asked whether he did any business in Kyrgyzstan and he said no, because the country is so poor that the government can't afford to provide the necessary incentives.

Second Expedition—June 13, 1999
Upon arrival for our second expedition, conditions in Bishkek did not seem to me to be noticeably different from last year, but, in speaking to our hosts I learned that, in fact, things are considerably worse. The value of the Kyrgyzstani *som* relative to the U.S. dollar is less than half what is was last year and, consequently, prices for imported goods, such as gasoline, have skyrocketed. Conditions at the institute have also deteriorated; Milko and Lazkov have not been paid since February.

Corruption is epidemic. Milko had a great deal of difficulty getting official permission to carry out this year's expedition. Officials claimed the application he submitted was lost, so he resubmitted it and had to call the office every couple of days, inquiring about it. He and Lazkov refuse to pay bribes, which are expected in such situations; thus they rely on the officers at the ministry getting so sick of being pestered that they grant the permits, just to be rid of the nuisance.

Alik was pulled over by the militia twice on our way into Bishkek from the airport and had to pay a small fine to one officer. This is an increase over last year's police presence.

Today, fortunately, we left Bishkek. Unfortunately, we almost immediately ran into trouble with our "cargo lorry," a second truck that was needed because of the larger number of expedition participants this year. For the first hour we had to stop every 2–3 km to let the engine cool. Another problem was that few of the gas stations had any fuel, and those that did were charging inflated prices.

After many hours of stop-and-go progress, we reached snow-covered Teo-Ashuu Pass, waited for oncoming traffic to clear the long, single-lane tunnel through the ridge, and drove through, emerging just as we were about to be overcome by truck exhaust. We were greeted by a magnificent view of the Suusamyr Valley, broad, green, and surrounded by snow-capped peaks.

June 16

Our camp in Talas Valley is situated in a moderately dry area of gently rolling hills. When we arrived, it was warm and sunny, and cicadas were calling from the hillside. John Taft set up a plant transect and the rest of us collected on the hillsides. A sudden brief hailstorm interrupted sampling, but the weather cleared and John, with help from Rick, Zhora, and Natasha (together affectionately referred to as the "transectuals" by Milko) finished the transect in record time. A large herd of sheep came up the ravine past our camp and gave John a bit of a scare, but, fortunately, they turned away before they reached the transect.

June 18

The only road linking the Talas and Chaktal valleys, which crosses Kara-Bura Pass, is usually closed until July, but yesterday we learned from locals that the pass was open, so the decision was made to cross. This would save us three days of travel time. We broke camp early in the morning and headed up the winding road to the pass, stopping often to allow the truck engines to cool, and once to make some repairs to a section of road that was washed out by melting snow. The southern side of the pass was particularly spectacular, with large snow slides covering sections of the river and great views of the Chandalash Range of the western Tien Shan. We stopped for lunch in a pasture near the junction of the ravine with the main part of the valley. The place was swarming with black flies. We collected there for a while and continued into the valley, selecting a campsite, also infested with black flies, near the river.

June 21

This is our second day of camping in the lower reaches of the Chaktal Valley. We're camped on a bluff above the raging waters of the Chandalash River. This would be a whitewater rafter's paradise, if it weren't so inaccessible. The flora and insect fauna are very different from anything we've seen so far.

Yesterday, we stopped at a farmhouse to ask directions and were served some delicious, fresh-baked whole wheat bread and yoghurt. I took a Polaroid picture of the two girls who gave us the food and they seemed delighted when I gave it to them.

This is the first hot, dry area we've visited, so Rick and John finally have a chance to dry their plant specimens.

June 23

The only road directly connecting the Chaktal Valley to Kurp-Saj Ravine passes through Uzbekistan. Milko, having made the crossing before with European entomologists, said there was nothing to worry about, and to a large degree he was right. Before breaking camp, we gathered and counted all Kyrgyz currency and gave it to Milko, who placed it in a bag to be shown to Uzbek customs officials, if necessary. We then gathered our dollars and also gave them to Milko, who hid them in a sack of flour, because it is illegal to transport U.S. currency across Uzbek territory. We set off down the valley, stopping at the office of the national reserve we were about to cross to get the necessary stamps on our travel papers. We headed up the winding road across a 2,800-meter pass, down a spectacular canyon with a raging, whitewater river to the last Kyrgyz outpost, where we passed without inspection or other incident. We continued the last 30 km to the border, stopping for lunch at a point overlooking a deep river gorge inhabited by colorful, starlinglike birds in large flocks. After that, several hours of driving passed without any of us knowing for sure which country we were in. Finally, we drove through a large town that appeared to be Uzbek, due to the large number of men wearing their distinctive Uzbekistani headgear, and arrived at a clearly marked Uzbek customs station where Milko presented our papers and was told we were lacking one stamp and would need to obtain it at the main office in town. We turned around and drove back into town, stopping to ask some locals about possible bypass roads, and receiving several contradictory answers. We tried another road and reached another customs station where the guard said he understood our situation and would let us pass with a payment of 10 liters of gas from each truck. To this we reluctantly agreed. Fortunately, the guard could only find containers large enough to hold 3.5 liters, so we got off cheap. Over the next hour, we detoured onto bypass roads twice, both within sight of customs checkpoints. Finally, free and clear and back in Kyrgyzstan for good, we stopped for a "technical" (i.e., bathroom) break and were congratulated by Milko on successfully crossing the Uzbekistan border four times.

June 24

We're back in Kurp-Saj Ravine, the idyllic place that, last year in August, was full of plums, apples, and grapes. This time there are apricots and mulberries. Anara boiled a couple of kilos of both and made a delicious compote. We revisited the site, in part, so I could re-sample insects along John's 1998 plant transect, and also to look for more specimens of a strange, unidentified leafhopper species of which one female specimen had turned up in one of last year's vacuum (modified leaf blowers that suck up insects into mesh bags) samples. I re-located the patch of tall grass from which I had collected the original sample and vacuumed it, but found no leafhoppers, until I noticed many cast skins (exuviae) in the bottom of the net. I vacuumed again, this time at full throttle, and ended up with a net full of duff (plant debris); but gradually, one by one, small flattened adult leafhoppers began to appear. Georgi Alexandrovich looked at them and somewhat nonchalantly expressed the opinion that they were related to *Evinus*, a genus described based on one species from Iran.

The next morning, we ate breakfast, packed the trucks, and prepared to leave, but Georgi Alexandrovich had disappeared up the ravine in search of more of the strange *Evinus*like leafhoppers. We drove up to look for him and found him walking at a rapid pace, bug-vac slung over his shoulder, on the opposite side of the river, carrying specimens of a giant *Allium* (five-foot-tall onion).

June 25

Last night was Georgi Lazkov's birthday; he's 36. We celebrated with a very late dinner of fried bread, rice with veggies and meat, Kyrgyz wine (very sweet and not very good) and Kyrgyz cognac (tastes like furniture polish). We all signed a card and Dima presented Georgi with a commemorative mug with Cancer (the crab) on one side and a sticker printed with fancy lettering "1999 Kyrgyz-Russian-American Biological Expedition."

We're in Lajsu Ravine, the place we visited last year with bright red soil and slumping hillsides. It was raining lightly as we drove in after eating lunch at a typical Kyrgyz restaurant named "Titanic" in the town of Suzak. The menu says "steak and potatoes," but you get hot dogs, noodles, and buckwheat. The road was muddy and the trucks were sliding from side to side, making everyone nervous as we travelled up the one lane road into the ravine. At one particularly treacherous place Dima and Natasha panicked and insisted on walking. The rest of us decided to get out and walk, too, until the road widened.

June 29

We loaded up on water for drinking and for cooling the truck engines and headed up the tortuous road to Urumbash Pass under cloudy skies, again stopping several times to allow the cargo lorry's engine to cool. We were within two or three switchbacks of the top when the radiator finally blew. While we collected, Alik took the entire thing apart and located a large piece of rag inside, undoubtedly a major source of our problems. He sealed the leak with "Quick-Seal" and 45 minutes later we were at the pass. The wind was blowing 40–50 mph and it was difficult to stand, but Anufriev and I hauled out the bug vacs and collected at least three leafhopper species on the grass growing among the snow banks. The trip down the north side of the pass was more treacherous and we had to get out and walk twice while the drivers negotiated particularly bad spots. We passed a road crew on the way down, but they hadn't fixed several bad spots and we reached our next campsite only after bypassing a section of road washed out by the river, driving directly in the river bed for some distance while locals on horseback watched in amusement. As we reached camp, the wind

Nursing a cranky truck over a newly repaired road.

was blowing fiercely from thunderstorms in the nearby mountains. As we were setting up our canvas tents, the rain hit with a vengeance and we quickly dove inside to ride out the storm, but after 15 minutes, the rain stopped. We ate an "easy" dinner of ramen noodles and went to bed.

July 4

Chen and I are probably among only a handful of Americans who have ever seen this part of the inner Tien Shan, so little visited that the road leading up to this point is not on the map. The trip here yesterday was spectacular but gruelling. We left our camp at Issyk-Kul at 9:30 a.m. and drove east along the lake shore, then turned south up Barskaun Ravine past last year's campsite, which was just as heavily grazed as before and was also in the middle of a road construction zone. The presence of a large Canadian-run gold mine was apparently the impetus for the improvements to the road. We met several large trucks, presumably carrying ore, on our way to the pass. We stopped twice to enable Alik to fine tune the fuel pump of the truck so that we could make it over the pass. The pass was covered with clouds and it was snowing. The road to Suek Pass was good and we made good time until we passed the turnoff to the gold mine, whereafter the road was in very bad shape. We stopped briefly at the spot where the fuel pump broke last year so that Alik could make some final adjustments to the engine. It was cold, windy, and snowing, but there were large, black crane flies crawling over the ground. Our last leg up and over Suek Pass was uneventful. I attempted a group photo at the pass, but Natasha and Anara refused to leave the truck and the lens of my camera was quickly covered with snow.

We reached last year's sample site near Kara-Saj shortly thereafter and decided to try to sample in the cold wind before lunch because it looked like it was about to rain. The rain never came, but it remained cold and windy. As we were huddled in the truck eating lunch, a jeep drove up and five uniformed Russians got out and greeted us. One was from the Ministry of Nature Protection and the others were border guards. All were friendly and after they satisfied themselves that our precence posed no threat, they left. Best of all, they told us that as long as we stayed close to the road and didn't cross the river to the south we weren't technically in the sub-boundary zone and didn't need permission to go to Ak-Shyrrak. Milko had expected to have to bribe them with some food or alcohol. So, we loaded our stuff in the truck and headed east.

About five hours later, we arrived after dark at the border patrol check station. Milko went inside and shortly theraftter two soldiers came out, lifted the tarp on the truck, and greeted us. We were asked to produce our passports, which they checked carefully, and recorded some info in a book. After some additional friendly discussion, they let us go, and we drove about 100 meters down the road and set up our tent, in which we all huddled while Anara prepared our dinner of buckwheat stew.

The next morning the sun was shining, the wind was calm, and it was warm. It was our first opportunity to inspect our surroundings—high, dry desert with vegetation zones ranging from sedge meadow adjacent to meltwater streams to a seasonally wet *Elymus* zone with salt deposits, *Acnantehmum* patches at the bases of hillsides, dry hillsides with *Ephedra* and *Artemisia*, and barren flats almost devoid of vegetation. Our tent was at the margin of a sedge meadow which wound its way down to a rock ledge and waterfall, emptying into the Ak-Shyrrak River. The river's waters were turquoise blue and 200 meters from our camp was a beautiful gorge with sheer, rock cliffs on both sides. We spent the morning collecting and found many insects and plants we hadn't seen before.

After a hot lunch prepared by Anara, we packed our stuff and prepared to return to Issyk-Kul. There was a problem with one of the tires on the truck that Alik was unable to fix. Milko went to the river where several of the border guards were fishing and they agreed to lend a hand. By 3 p.m. we were on the road, headed west. We saw a small herd of yaks, and lots of marmots, eagles, and rabbits. We reached Kara Saj just as the sun began to set, and Suek Pass as night fell and, after a bumpy, tortuous drive down Barskaun Ravine, arrived at camp on Issyk-Kul around 11 p.m. The Russian and Kyrgyzstani comrades we had left behind greeted us enthusiastically, and I had the impression that they hadn't really expected us to make it back alive, and more or less on schedule.

Expedition 3—July 3, 2000

We all arrived safe, sound, and ahead of schedule. The flight from London to Baku (Azerbaijan) was 4.5 hours and we waited on the plane for 1.5 hours in the wee hours of the morning while the ground crew refueled the plane and cleaned the cabin. One of the cleaning women had really scary eye make-up. The flight from Baku to Bishkek was about three hours and we arrived just as the sun rose in cloudy skies. Major improvements have been made to Manas airport, including the installation of a motorized jetway and some yurt-shaped snack bars on the upper level. The passport control station was slow as ever, but they had a computer and the officer was native Kyrgyzstani, not Russian. The baggage system still has a few bugs, mainly because they have no conveyor for unloading the plane, so they just toss the bags down onto a cart.

Things in Bishkek seem subdued, and everyone involved in the expedition seemed more relaxed than in previous years. Milko and Lazkov seemed genuinely happy to see us. This year, for the first time we will visit the eastern part of the Alaj Valley in the sub-boundary zone adjacent to Tadjikistan. We will travel south along the Pamir Highway over Taldyk Pass and travel east along the road toward Kashgar (China). Unfortunately, there are reports (no doubt exaggerated) of thousands of Muslim extremist revolutionaries in the western Alaj.

July 11

Today we made an excursion to Bardoba Creek about 12 km north of the Tadjikistan border. To get there, we first had to pass the sub-boundary control station entering and exiting the small town at the junction of the E/W road through the Alaj Valley and the Pamir Highway, each of which took about 20 minutes. We then drove south across the valley, passing a radar installation that appeared to be abandoned. We then had to pass the customs station (another 20 minutes) and the veterinary control station. Finally, we arrived at Bardoba, ate lunch and started working our way up the ravine—some of us to the south, some to the north. After intensive collecting with limited success, Dima Novikov and I decided to climb a peak overlooking the valley with views of glaciers. On our way down, we were dismayed to see a group of Kyrgyz army soldiers armed with Kalashnikovs yelling and running toward us. One fired a warning shot. The soldiers had spotted us taking pictures from the top of the ridge and they apparently thought we might be Tadjik infiltrators. Dmitry Milko quickly joined us and some intense discussions with the commanding officer ensued, after which we allowed ourselves to be "captured" and returned to the last check station. Apparently, although the soldiers at the checkpoints had allowed us through, they hadn't bothered to inform their colleagues in the field of our presence. Seeking to avoid a diplomatic incident, the senior officer released us and we returned to our camp in the Alaj Valley.

Novikov, Milko, and Dietrich near Kyrgyzstan border, shortly before being "captured" by Kyrgyzstan army.

July 21, 2000

Our third and final visit to a subboundary zone was less than a complete success. After leaving Kara-Kol at the eastern end of Lake Issyk-Kul, we headed east up a ravine leading to the Terskey Alatoo Ridge. The water in the river was a beautiful blue-green color and the meadows were full of flowers. Some patches of white flowers were so dense, they looked like snow. There was snow at the pass (3,600 m in altitude) but it did not hinder our progress, although the constant drizzle made the road muddy and slippery in spots. We reached our camp late in the afternoon on the floodplain of the Sari Dzhas River, a raging torrent of glacial meltwater. It was dry, but would remain so for only a few hours. The next day was cloudy again, but dry, at least in the morning. John set up his transect on one of the few relatively level patches in the canyon, on a bluff 30 m above camp. I walked up river, waiting in vain for things to dry out enough to make insect sampling possible. At noon, we left on an excursion to the steppe and alpine zones upriver (and in the subboundary zone). After an hour's drive, during which we climbed out of the canyon and into the broad, rolling Sari-Dzhas Valley, we reached the army post at the border of the zone. Milko went inside and presented our papers but was informed that the phone was broken and that we would have to wait until it was fixed so the officer could call the colonel in Kara-Kol to clear our permits before we could proceed. We were given permission to sample the hills surrounding the post and did so, under the watchful eye of a guard in the tower on a nearby hilltop. I worked my way over to a small depression where I was shielded from the guard's view and fixed our location with my GPS unit and photographed the site. I don't know whether this precaution was necessary, but I didn't want to risk having my equipment confiscated. After another hour, we were given the OK to proceed, under the condition that we be accompanied by a soldier (unarmed) and the son of the officer, who we were to deliver to his family's homestead. We drove further up river for 30 minutes and were met by two young girls on horseback, the officer's daughters, who raced us the rest of the way to the homestead (they won easily). We dropped the boy off and continued north along the road, climbing into the alpine zone (3,400 m) where it was very moist and getting dark. We hurriedly vacuumed the soggy vegetation and collected some previously unseen leafhoppers, but gave up as it became increasingly cold, dark, and wet, and made the slow return journey to our camp and our no longer warm dinner.

July 24

A very good day! I woke up to find the weather clear (after it had rained off and on through the night), ate breakfast, loaded up my gear and headed up the ravine to the south, following a small stream along an abandoned and now nearly nonexistent road. My plan was to work my way to the meadows near the snow line, visible in the distance, and then come back down along the north-south ridge and sample John's plant transect before lunch. I passed an occupied yurt and the family's three dogs came running up barking. A boy came out and offered to sell me some koumis. But I said "no thanks, I'm working" (using the few words of Russian I had learned over the past three years), and went on. I reached the meadows at 11 a.m., after stopping several times to vacuum various patches of vegetation and finding little of interest, but I had the area all to myself. I watched rain showers pass through the valley below, but felt only a few drops. As I began to head back down, I noticed some low growing shrubs that I hadn't seen before growing over boulders on the southeast-facing slope of the ridge above me, so I went up and vacuumed them. As I sifted through the vacuum debris in the bottom of my net, I saw an unusual immature leafhopper with short hind legs and a flattened crown. It could only be one thing—*Neobufonaria*—the endemic genus that had eluded me for the past two years. Sifting through the remaining debris, I found an adult male, confirming the ID. For the next hour, I vacuumed every shrub-boulder combination in sight, but turned up only one additional specimen, so I vacuumed once more, dumped all the debris into a plastic bag and headed back toward camp. That evening, I carefully sifted the remaining debris and found three more specimens.

July 30
Last night we saw most of our Russian and Kyrgyzstani comrades for the last time. We toasted our success with a bottle of the finest Kyrgyz cognac. Milko and Lazkov, both teetotalers grimaced while downing the strong drink. I handed out commemorative T-shirts with which everyone seemed pleased. I felt happy to have accomplished all of our goals, but sad knowing we had to leave and would probably never come back. Lazkov wished me success in getting more grants, which I took to mean that he wanted to be included in any future expeditions. I suggested eastern Tien Shan (China) and he approved.

General Notes on Kyrgyzstan
Bishkek: The capital city bustles with the expected traffic of old cars and buses, including electric ones running along cables, but also has its share of Mercedes Benzes and BMWs, mostly driven by young, clean-cut looking men. The city has an unkempt look, overgrown with weeds and unpruned trees so that it's often difficult to see buildings from the street. The government buildings, mostly blocky concrete structures, have a decaying, post-apocalyptic look to them. The Institute of Biology and Pedology of the National Academy of Sciences is a good example. This once fine institution is now dark inside with stark offices and boards missing from the floors. The informational/propaganda posters in the hallways have been defaced by employees drawing mustaches and cigarettes on Lenin and other Soviet figures. Interestingly, the former KGB arm of the institute, which is situated between the biological and geological wings, is well maintained and its secretaries receive more in salary than the Ph.D.s in the scientific sections. The State University of Bishkek is also crumbling, in contrast to the business college, which seems well maintained and crowded with students.

Sergei's flat, where we stayed while in Bishkek, is in a large apartment block that appears identical to many others in the city. It has four rooms: living room, bedroom, bathroom, and kitchen. The bathroom has no sink, only a tub and toilet, and the kitchen has a table and stove, but no sink or refrigerator. Lazkov's flat, belonging to his mother, is larger and better furnished, but still extremely modest. Milko apparently has no place of his own and lives with his mother when he's not traveling. For those with money, first class accommodations are available, as we found out when our flight to Istanbul was canceled, but most people in Bishkek seem to be barely scraping by.

The Provinces: Outside the cities, life appears to continue as it has for millennia. Herders of sheep, goats, and cattle move their animals up into the mountains in the spring, camping in yurts, tents or, less frequently, in metal house trailers. They subsist on meat, milk, cheese, and koumis. These people are very hospitable, always willing to share a cup of cold koumis with visitors. In areas of higher rainfall, the people cut the tall grass and other vegetation for hay and cart it down into the valleys for winter silage. Large-scale agriculture seems largely confined to the Fergana Valley, which Kyrgyzstan shares with Uzbekistan. Here there were large agricultural collectives during Soviet times, but these have mostly been divided into smaller farms growing cotton, corn, tobacco, and various vegetables. On the southern shore of Lake Issyk-Kul (the world's largest alpine lake) are fruit orchards and wheat fields, but in the mountains, grazing is all important and ubiquitous. The steepest slopes are densely crisscrossed with paths worn by the animals, presumably over hundreds of years.

Pastimes: The most popular pastime among our Russian and Kyrgyzstani colleagues is telling jokes. Evenings after mealtime are occupied mostly by trading jokes and anecdotes, of which these guys seem to have an endless supply. Most were about "New Russians" or "New Kyrgyz" who speed around in Mercedes 600s and work for the mafia or government (or both).

Eating is another popular pastime, and these guys, all of whom are very thin, are able to eat tremendous quantities of food, including extremely vile-looking canned fish and meat paste that would probably be sold as pet food in the U.S.

Checkpoints: Last year, the government outlawed mobile checkpoints, which could be set up anywhere, anytime, at the discretion of law enforcement officials (the "militsia"). This change has made travel by road more efficient; previously the average rate of progress through the hinterlands was 20-km per hour). Remaining are the checkpoints outside most larger cities and towns and at the borders of administrative districts. These are generally passed without a great deal of hassle, but because we were travelling in an unusual looking vehicle, Alik and Dima often spent up to 15–20 minutes explaining what we were doing before being allowed to pass. That we passed through all but one checkpoint without having to pay a "fine" can be attributed to Alik and Dima's cleverness and quick wits. They were told at one point that no trucks were allowed on that particular road, but Alik convinced them that our vehicle was a bus. At another checkpoint, we were told that an entrance fee was required, but Dima got the officers to let us through by claiming that his family lived there. Alik's usual tactic was to act very friendly and claim that he used to be a militia man himself. The only fine we paid was 50 soms ($2.50) when Dima Novikov was spotted sitting on the roof of the moving truck, taking pictures of the mountains. The rule on mobile checkpoints apparently doesn't apply in Bishkek because there we were stopped numerous times for no apparent reason and our Russian colleagues had to have their passports checked.

Lost and found . . .

International Kindness
Don Webb

As part of an extensive program to prepare a monograph on the stiletto flies of the world, Survey entomologists Don Webb and Mike Irwin, along with Ev Schlinger from the University of California, Berkeley, spent several weeks on the French Island of New Caledonia in the Coral Sea. This is a large, tropical island east of Australia, which formed when Australia, New Zealand, South America, Africa, and Antarctic separated. In November of 1998, we set out Malaise traps (fine mesh nets suspended from poles that capture flying insects) throughout the island, using the Evasion Ecolodge at Sarraméa as our center of operations. This was the locality where on an earlier trip we had captured the male of a rare tanyderid fly (Diptera: Tanyderidae) that was known only from the holotype (the specimen from which a new species is described and given a name) female. Our return to this site in 1998 allowed me to search for the undescribed larva of this fly. Generally, larvae of tanyderids are found among the rotting logs and branches in alpine streams. With great expectations, I set off working my way up-stream from the lodge. But to no avail, as heavy rains had scoured the logs and brush of any accumulated debris. Having failed in the search for tanyderid larvae, collecting did improve with the discovery of a blue fanny-pack in the stream. Inside I found the French passport of Daniele Delbos of Bagnolet, France, a valid Visa credit card, a pair of sunglasses, 2,200 French Francs, and 9,500 Central Pacific Francs (in U.S. dollar, the Francs amounted to some $500).

Upon returning to the lodge we found that no inquiries had been made concerning a lost fanny-pack. Because New Caledonia is a French possession, there was no consulate on the island so the passport was turned over to the local Gendarmes in the hope that the person who lost the fanny-pack would think to inquire there. This all occurred shortly before Mike Irwin and I took off for two weeks to collect around Brisbane, Australia. The Central Pacific Francs were exchanged for U.S. dollars in Noumea, but the French Francs were badly stained by the blue coloration of the fanny-pack and they would take the bank three days to verify. Because this was unacceptable to our travel plans, the contents of the fanny-pack, including the French Francs continued on their way back to Illinois via Australia. Thus, it was over a month before I had the time to write Daniele Delbos informing her of our rich find. I often wondered what her expression would be when she received a letter from the United States on official INHS stationary informing her that her fanny-pack, Visa card, sunglasses, and some $500 U.S. (the French Francs being exchanged in Urbana for U.S. dollars) were in America. Four days later, I received a phone call from a colleague of Ms. Delbos who spoke English, and we ironed out the details for the return of the lost articles. Within two weeks, I received a letter thanking me for the safe return of her possessions, thanking the insects of New Caledonia for bringing us there to collect them, and thanking the insects in the stream for enticing me to collect along it banks. Ms. Delbos had been hiking the trail to the Plateau de Dogny and her group had stopped for lunch as they forded my collecting stream. She recalled taking off the fanny-pack and exactly where she had put it down, but did not miss the fanny-pack until she had returned to Noumea that night. Upon returning the next day the fanny-pack was gone, washed downstream by heavy, overnight rains, lost for all-time, that is, until I happened upon it.

Chapter 4

Odd Perceptions: Interacting with the Public

September 17, 1879

My head swims . . . all day tossing of my skiff. Harry and I have been living the life of herons, and now, like a heron, I take my evening sport. We are fulfilling our brightest hopes in the way of the collection of material, altho, I'm afraid we haven't made any very remarkable discovery yet.

. . . Now that we are completely engrossed with work, the discomfort of our surroundings make no impression, and we are as contented as possible with our pigs—Kentuckians. Their lack of fastidiousness has its advantage: but perhaps they are writing scalding reports of us "Yanks" to their friends and sweethearts.

What would you think of a crew of boarders from a foreign land who should convert your back porch into a slaughter house, dress great fish like catfishes thereon day after day, and tip all their scraps over the railing to the pigs under your house? Perhaps they don't like it any better. Tomorrow we shall [pitch] our tent and make a work-shop of that. I have worn one crop of blisters off my hands and have a second ready for the morrow.

Biologists will do just about anything to gather the data. Almost . . .

Naked Turtles?
Randy Nyboer

It was a raw, gray, March day in 1987 that took me to the field, looking for new sites to trap for the Illinois mud turtle, an endangered chelonian (group to which turtles belong) only found in the prairie ponds of Illinois sand regions. During the long winter in the dreary confines of my office, numerous sites where chosen from maps, soil surveys, and aerial photos. Now that spring had arrived, it was time to check the sites to see if they still existed and talk to unwary (or wary) landowners about "sampling their ponds" for turtles. The area I had chosen that day was in southwestern Whiteside County, near the tiny town of Erie. Long ago, the Illinois mud turtle had been found near Lake Erie, and no, not the Great one!

I had located a nice sand pond south of Erie and the Rock River that I had not seen before, and decided to conduct a drive-by scouting venture before going to talk to the owner. The pond was still there, so I drove into the driveway of the farmstead across the road from the pond. Being a rather friendly lout, landowners rarely turned me down when I asked to look at their land, even though I was from the *government*. With a smile similar to that found on a Jack-o-Lantern, only with more teeth, I greeted the old farmer, told him who I was, and what I was doing. We chatted about the current weather, the river, and planting time soon arriving. Finally, getting down to the nitty gritty, I asked him about "his" pond across the road and if I could trap it this spring. He just grinned at me while I spent several minutes explaining the process of capturing the turtles, assuring him they'd be released and not end up in a cook pot. He said, "Son, I no longer own that pond, I sold it years ago to that special campground next to it. You will have to ask them for permission and that may be tricky." With a sly grin, he pointed to the drive down the road. Thanking him for his time and information I started to leave when he uttered, "Have fun!"

I drove to the campground and found a locked gate with a buzzer to contact the caretaker. By this time those icy March winds had picked up and an occasional snowflake whisked by. I was wishing I had dressed warmer when a voice came over the speaker asking who I was and what I wanted. I told him the basics and he said he would come to the gate. After about five minutes, and me donning my coveralls, a small Cushman scooter came putting up to the gate with a wiry, 50-ish looking little man at the controls. He was wearing Bermuda shorts, tennies with no socks, a nylon windbreaker, and ball cap. Being darkly bronzed, I figured he was a snowbird just back from winter in the warmer climes. I do not know how he stood the freezing wind with his getup, but I figured it would be a short talk as long as we stayed here at the gate. Noting that I was not invited inside, I quickly gave him my spiel without going into much detail. He nodded, and then asked, "Do you know what this place is?" I told him the farmer down the road said it was a special campground, but did not elaborate what was special about it. He stated the Blue Lake Campground was a nudist colony and the only folks allowed in were members. Blue Lake also had only the *unclothed* option available. Immediately I figured I would not be sampling this pond! (Although doing it might prove to be enlightening, to say the least.) He said, however, my survey would be of interest to the members and he thought he could get me permission from the owner, a doctor in Freeport. He then went into his much rehearsed, thirty-freezing-minute lecture on the joys of nudism and ALL its health values. He included how it cured his daughter of allergies and asked if I would like to talk to her. Before I could answer, he inquired if I would like to join their camp! I quickly thanked him for the gracious offer, replied that I burn easily, spent a lot of time outside already with my job, and was perfectly healthy.

He nodded and seemed to accept my reasoning, probably because his tan was now starting to turn blue. I asked him if I could still trap Blue Lake, without joining or driving through the campground. He said he would try to seek permission for me, but the beach on one side of the lake was used for sunbathing. If I were to trap during tanning time, I would have to go *Au Natural* to prevent upsetting the sunbathers. Knowing this was a virgin pond (uh, never sampled for mud turtles), I agreed, knowing I would at least be wearing cutoffs. That is when he looked at me sharply and said it was a strict rule—nudes only—that would not be waived. Nodding my understanding, I quickly remembered that many of the sand ponds I had previously trapped were loaded with baby leeches at that time of year, and that I generally wear boots (didn't tell him chest waders) to protect my feet. He accepted that.

I did not get permission to trap the pond. I later found out the old farmer I had talked to was a bachelor, who after selling his land to the Blue Lake Club, built a second story porch on his house, facing the pond. This resulted in the club planting rows of pines and constructing a wood fence to prevent gawking by the spring and summer peepers (not frogs) from that porch. Later that summer I ran across the old farmer and he asked if I had gotten any mud for my turtles.

As long as the shell is present, no nudity in turtles.

Step lightly and carry lots of duct tape.

Looking Before We Leap: All in a Day's Work at INHS
Charlie Warwick

Ever since we were all babes in the woods (figuratively and literally), we have been taught to look before we leap. Our authority figures tried to instill the notion that a little planning and careful attention to where we were going next, whether on a long odyssey or a simple jaunt in the forests near our homes, were a prudent investment in the future. There was no telling what was on the other side of those logs we were ready to hop, so it made good sense to look before we leapt and trod on something hiding there.

Even governmental agencies have learned this lesson and in many cases have institutionalized the looking-before-leaping process. For instance, the Illinois Department of Transportation (IDOT), which is responsible for upgrading and maintaining the state's highway system, is required to make biological assessments of areas where it plans to make or replace roads. Before it leaps into construction activities, IDOT must look to determine how such construction will impact the plants and animals in the surrounding environment. Actually, IDOT contracts the Illinois Natural History Survey (INHS) to do the looking.

INHS field biologist Bill Handel, who specializes in endangered species and grading natural communities, has served as the eyes for IDOT and its construction of Illinois Route 20 that traverses the state from Chicago in the east to Dubuque, Iowa, in the west. As co-principal investigator in the biological assessment of Route 20, Handel and his colleagues in the Statewide Biological Assessment Program and the INHS Wetlands Group have studied some 70,000 acres (109 square miles) along this highway since 1993. These researchers have discovered a number of unrecorded threatened and endangered plants and animals as well as high-quality natural communities. Some of these rare species reside in Tapley Woods Natural Area, a holding of INHS' parent organization, the Illinois Department of Natural Resources.

The new knowledge uncovered by INHS scientists was very useful to IDOT as it proceeded with construction along Route 20. IDOT took measures to minimize the potential negative influences of construction upon the plants and animals along this highway

Occasionally Handel and the staff of the Statewide Biological Assessment Program, in their role of being the eyes for IDOT, get unsolicited help from concerned citizens throughout the state. Recently Handel received a phone call from a landowner in northwest Illinois near Route 20 who discovered a large timber rattlesnake sunbathing on his patio. The landowner knew the snake is an Illinois threatened species and that the Survey is interested in occurrences of such species around Route 20. So he phoned Bill who, fortuitously, was preparing for a trip to that area of the state the very next day.

When Handel arrived he was escorted to a Coleman food cooler (the kind you take on picnics) into which the landowner and his son somehow had been able to coax the rattler. Remembering to look before he leapt, Handel gingerly lifted the lid of the cooler only to be confronted by the stare of a none-too-happy, four-and-a-half-foot venomous reptile that was not shy about displaying its displeasure with a loud agitated buzz of its tail.

Handel decided to relocate the snake a mile or so into the woods, away from the house and its human inhabitants. For added security he applied a generous amount of duct tape in place of the broken latch on the cooler lid. Handel found a prairie opening in the forest that he reasoned would be suitable habitat for the snake because it had a number of fallen logs that would provide shelter and attract rodents (lunch for the snake). Carefully, he removed the duct tape from the cooler lid, stepped back the length of his hiking stick, and used the stick to flip open the cooler lid from a safe distance. The rattler had no problem figuring out what to do.

Handel explained that the rattlesnake episode culminated in a win-win-win situation—for the landowner who got rid of an unwanted intruder, for the snake that was saved by the alert timely action of the landowner, and for INHS, which was able to document the location of another threatened species and help ensure its continued survival by making sure government policymakers know its location. This kind of collaboration among concerned citizens, INHS, and state agencies proves to be an effective force for the preservation of nature in Illinois.

A rattler, a cooler with a broken clasp—just another day in the field.

The lost art of communication!

Field Talk
Joseph Spencer

Two Conversations About the Same Thing—I Think

30th of May (on the phone)

Spencer:	"Hello, is The Grower there?"
Hired Man:	"Oh, he's not here right now. I'm his hired man. I can take a message."
Spencer:	"Okay, my name is Joe Spencer. I'm a scientist with the Illinois Natural History Survey studying western corn rootworm beetle ecology and behavior..."
Hired Man:	"ah…hummmm…"
Spencer:	"…Each summer, I and a colleague, Dr. Eli Levine, have always put a few insect traps in Mr. Grower's corn and soybean fields to monitor western corn rootworm abundance. I'm calling to see if it is okay to install some vial traps on PVC posts in Mr. Grower's fields northeast of Urbana…"
Hired Man:	"ah…hummmm…"
Spencer:	"I won't put them in until you're done with your soybean spraying and corn cultivation. We'll be in and out of those fields every week until the end of the season. I promise to have them out long before harvest time."
Hired Man:	"ah…hummmm..."
Spencer:	"Take my phone number, in case the Grower would like to call me. But tell the grower I'll try to call later."
Hired Man:	"Humpf…(pause)… that's a lot of stuff to 'git written down...I'm not sure he'll git it."
Spencer:	"Okay, ah…um…will the grower be back anytime this afternoon? I can call later, but I don't want to call too late?"
Hired Man:	"Well, I don't just know when the Grower will be back. Ya'see, he's up there to the nursing home,…visiting his girlfriend. He didn't say when he was a coming home, but I'm fixin' to clear outa here pretty quick…ya know, 'fore he gits back. I'll leave the message here by the phone and he'll probably git back to ya… Goodbye…(click)."

2nd of June (once again, on the phone)

Spencer:	"Hello, is The Grower there?"
The Girl Friend:	"Yes, he's right here, may I ask who is a calling?"
(Girl Friend to the Grower):	"No, I don't know who it is…I am asking him for his name…"
Spencer:	"Certainly, my name is Joe Spencer. I'm the scientist with the Illinois Natural History Survey who's studying western corn rootworm beetle ecology and behavior…I left the Grower a message about getting his permission to put some traps in his field…"
(Girl Friend to the Grower):	"It's that boy from up there to the University…the one that wants to put the mouse traps in the cornfield."
The Girl Friend:	"…(pause)…the Grower says it okay to put them mouse traps up where ever you want,…"
Spencer:	"Tell him 'Thank you' for me, but, to be accurate…"
(Girl Friend to the Grower):	"He says 'Thank you'….(pause)…How would I know, I'll ask him…"
The Girl Friend:	"…the Grower wants me to ask if you know anything about the Japanese root beetle and whether ta' not he ought ta' got the spray…(pause)…"
(Girl Friend to the Grower):	"…I'm asking him that right now…"
The Girl Friend:	"Sorry about the interruption,… whether ta' not he ought ta' got the spray or not on the corn,…(pause)…"
(Girl Friend to the Grower):	"…because of the what was it?...Oh!..."
The Girl Friend:	"…because of them beetles and what not?"
Spencer:	"Well…(pause)…if you're referring to the corn rootworm beetle, applying a soil insecticide at planting would be a good idea in your area. The data from our rootworm traps in the Grower's fields last year indicate that there was large population of egg-laying females in fields from your area. I think you misunderstood me earlier about the mousetraps…."
The Girl Friend:	"…Hold on, he's hollerin' to me…"
(Girl Friend to the Grower):	"…he musta counted trapped beetles in one of your fields cause he thinks the bug spraying is okay for you, but it has be a lot earlier if you're gonna git rid of the mouses…(pause)…I'll ask him…Are you sure you don't wanta just talk yourself?..."
The Girl Friend:	"The Grower wonders if you wouldn't mind putting up a couple of them beetle traps once you're up setting out mouse traps?"
Spencer:	"…(pause)…I'd be glad to!..."

Biologists in the Field

Inhale? Well, yes, I do . . .

Close Encounters of the Constabulary Kind
Don Webb

In the late 60s and early 70s, a simple way to collect adult chironomid flies (small flies that resemble mosquitoes) was to travel the backroads of Illinois at night and aspirate (suck up) the adults at fluorescent and neon lights in the windows of laundromats, drugstores, and jewelry stores. The aspirator was a plastic tube plugged with a rubber stopper. Two copper tubes were inserted through the stopper: one six-inch tube through which the insects were inhaled; and one two-inch tube on which a filter was attached and positioned on the inside face. A gum rubber hose was attached to the outside piece of copper. The operator, me, then sucked in on the gum rubber hose creating a vacuum and small insects were thus pulled into the collecting tube. The filter prevented any insects from being inhaled by the collector. Armed with this piece of collecting apparatus, I would then move the collecting tube around the edge of the store windows, rapidly collecting chironomids. In the lab, this seemed like a very quick and simple way to collect flies, but in the field, it required additional diplomatic expertise to succeed. Most small towns shut down at dark, with only the illuminated store windows glowing. The local constabulary would often be parked at a corner gas station that provided an unimpeded view of the main street. Into this serene scene entered the field entomologist. In an attempt to collect at many sites during a night, I would quickly drive into town, find some illuminated window, jump out of the car, aspirate insects, then jump into my car and high-tail it to the next town. Obviously, this was strange behavior to the local law enforcement personnel, especially at 2 a.m. in front of a jewelry store. During these collecting sprees I would often notice a pair of headlights go on and a nondescript car slowly drive around the block and pull up alongside my car. What followed was 10 minutes of questioning as to what exactly I had been doing. After being involved in several of these encounters I quickly developed a patented answer, which involved some mad scientist at the university who ground up these insects and did weird things with them. Ultimately, this was a very simple, routine procedure that became complicated only until I realized that I should never approach a police car with an aspirator in hand, pointing its six-inch-long barrel at the police officer.

Rural night life.

Small Town Police
Joyce Hofmann

One summer I was conducting a mammal survey for a highway project in southern Illinois. One of the sites to be surveyed for bats was located on an extensive parcel of land near Pinckneyville that was owned by a mining company. The property was fenced and gated. I talked to a representative of the company and he agreed to arrange for someone to open the gate on the day we planned to be there. We promised to lock the gate when we finished our mist netting (after midnight). Arriving at the site in the afternoon, we found the gate open and set up our netting equipment deep in the interior. That evening we returned, drove back to our site, and began netting at dusk. Later that night, after completing our work, we drove back to the gate only to discover that it was locked. Apparently someone had visited the area during the evening and, not realizing we were there, locked the gate when they left.

So, it was nearly one o'clock in the morning and our vehicle was on the wrong side of a locked gate! I told my two companions that we could either sleep in the vehicle or walk the few miles back to our motel in Pinckneyville. Perhaps, not surprisingly, we decided to start walking, and had gone down a side road for quite a way. As we approached the intersection with the main highway into Pinckneyville, a car turned around and pulled over next to us. It was the Pinckneyville police. The policewoman asked what we were doing wandering around in the middle of nowhere so late at night. We explained our situation and she kindly gave us a ride back to our motel. At a more reasonable hour of the morning I called our contact from the mining company to tell him what happened and he once again arranged to have the gate unlocked. How to get back? We located the police station and walked in. As soon as we reached the desk, the officer in charge knew exactly who we were and that we needed a ride back to our vehicle. Small town citizens are really nice and this was hospitality at its best.

Setting up a mist net in preparation for a night of surveying for bats.

When you gotta go . . .

To Serve and Protect?
John B. Taft

It is not unexpected when conducting field work, especially when botanizing along roadways, to have law enforcement personnel inquire about my activities. So, while surveying a remnant of tallgrass prairie along an abandoned railroad right-of-way on the edge of Pana, Illinois, as part of a biological assessment of a proposed highway construction project, I was not particularly surprised when a police officer pulled up beside me. Eagerly, I approached the officer, prepared with my explanation about the proposed by-pass of Pana. I was certain that he would find this information much to his interest. Alas, I approached too quickly, for this officer, rather than being filled with curiosity about my business on the outskirts the town, actually was filled more with his morning beverage and in greater need of a place to empty its excess. There I stood, at the ready with my explanation, when I was sprayed with collateral discharge—he urinated right in the middle of the road where I was standing. Without word or acknowledgement, he got back into his squad car and off he drove. I was left dumbfounded, a little damp around the ankles, and uncertain for a moment of my own existence.

Move over David Letterman!

Top 10 Lists of Things We've Learned from the Illinois Natural History Survey Traveling Science Center
Heather Grotefend and Jen Mui

The first full year of operation of the Illinois Natural History Survey's Traveling Science Center (TSC) provided many opportunities for us to learn, both about people and about the operation and maintenance of a 60-foot trailer with a generator. The trailer housed exhibits and information about the habitats, plants, and animals of northern Illinois. Our unique geographic location allowed us to experience the best and worst of weather and traffic conditions, and also encounter a great cross-section of people throughout northern Illinois. We've been surprised to find that there is really very little difference in the actions and reactions of students, whether they are from inner city schools in Chicago or rural schools near Iowa. Some of the important lessons and observations we have made over the course of our first year operating a traveling science center devoted to the topic of biodiversity are:

10. Eighth graders give off more heat than kindergartners.

We deduced this from the past winter when we found out our "heaters" are only functional for three seasons, when they are not needed, and thus, there was really no heat in the trailer as they failed to function below about 35° F. The larger the child and the more of them there are, the more heat they generate and we scientists can begin to feel our toes and fingers again. The excited children, however, don't seem to notice the cold.

9. Humans have many misconceptions about animals and their various parts—e.g., snakes don't have bones, and a squirrel head + rabbit pelt + raccoon skull = an animal that makes total sense to children.

People are amazed when viewing the skeleton of a snake, mostly at the total number of bones they posses. Yet when we ask them, "What do snakes not have?" (looking, of course, for "limbs" or "legs" as an answer) the best guesses are bones, lungs, heart, anything but legs. We were astonished at how many people, including adults, think that snakes don't have bones, especially when they are staring at the snake's skeleton at the time. The children, and some adults, also seem to think that the squirrel head, rabbit pelt, and raccoon skull somehow should fit together, even though the squirrel head and rabbit pelt are two different colors, and the raccoon skull is far too big to fit into the squirrel head. But, comparative anatomy notwithstanding, for some reason, this seems to make total sense.

8. A 60-foot truck and trailer means "two car lengths" to some people.

When we ask groups to reserve a spot for the trailer at events, individuals seem to have a problem visualizing 60 feet. To most people, 60 feet means leaving, at most, two car lengths free in the area where we are supposed to parallel park the truck and trailer.

7. One computer + one "heater" + one 12-amp vacuum cleaner running off one generator = a blown circuit breaker and one confused Jen.

We quickly learned the limitations of our generator on the trailer. Having an iMac computer, a heater/air-conditioning unit, and a powerful vacuum cleaner all running at the same time proved to be a bad idea. We tripped a circuit breaker. Trying to find which switch was off, however, proved to be a harder task than we first thought. Having reset all of the breakers in the breaker box, but still with no power, the last two classes of the day had to be conducted by the light of the sun, and using a flashlight to look at things under the microscope. The students and teachers thought this was a great adventure, and perhaps part of the total TSC experience. It wasn't, and later, after a few choice words were exchanged over phone calls, we found that the breaker tripped was not in our vehicle, but obscurely placed on the generator, an easy fix, if you know where to look.

6. Children prefer to use a microscope to look at their hands, plastic toys, or just about anything else except what they are supposed to view, insects.

We have a rather large box of native Illinois insects, along with a few exotic ones placed around the trailer, not to mention pelts of several different animals and numerous fossils. All are potentially good targets for microscope viewing. Strangely, children seem to be more fascinated with what their fingertips or plastic animals look like under the microscope than the real creatures.

5. "This vehicle makes wide turns means," does not mean, "Please ignore this and pass us on both sides!"

Driving what amounts to a semi-length vehicle in Chicago traffic has proved to be challenging. We have had people try to pass us on the right side of the vehicle while we are making a right turn. We thought that perhaps they didn't know we made wide turns, so we purchased a sticker that says, loud and clear, if you bother to read it, "This vehicle makes wide turns." However, many must still read the sign as, "Please, try and pass us!" The worst situation was at the intersection of Fullerton and Damen on the north side of Chicago. With barely two lanes, and while preparing to turn right, two cars managed to squeezed by us, one on each side of the TSC. Fortunately, we did not crush either one, although the thought did cross our minds.

4. Handy Wipes can freeze, along with anything thing else in the trailer, during a Chicago winter.

The first winter was a learning experience on so many levels. Simple things stood out, and learning to deal with frozen items in the trailer was not insignificant. During cold spells everything froze, from the disinfectant handy wipes we used to keep ourselves "healthy," to our water jugs, and, of course, ourselves (when large children were not present, see item #10 above). We soon learned that the Handy Wipes and water jugs had to be stored in the cab of the truck. This allowed them time to thaw while we drove to schools each morning.

3. Children are worried about the germs on our animal specimens, but have no qualms about sticking borrowed clipboards and pencils in their mouths.

It is amazing that children are more worried about what perceived germs the animals have/had than what they have on their own hands. Note that many hands are fresh from wiping that snotty nose. They persist in putting clipboards, paper, magnets, and even the borrowed pencils in their mouths, which led us to remove the erasers from the tops of the pencils because we were tired of dealing with chewed pencil ends. Also, you now see the need for keeping the wipes thawed (see item #4).

2. The word "heat" on our trailer means it will work not below 35 degrees F. Who knew? (corollary to item #10 above)

We found this out the first really cold winter day in December. We were at a school program and soon discovered that the all-season heating/air-conditioning unit would not turn on. Needless to say, we did the program by using the children to generate heat by having them do jumping jacks to warm themselves and the trailer. Upon calling the manufacturer, we learned that the "heater" is not designed to operate below 35 degrees F. After that, two space heaters helped get us through the winter.

1. Zots™, silicone sealant, and Velcro™ will fix most anything.

Whoever invented Zots™ should be given a gold medal. Because our exhibits are hands-on and interactive, there have been many times when something has either broken in the trailer or a specimen animal has had to be put back together for the next group. Zots™ and archival adhesive dots have been the answer for us. Because Zots™ tend to lose stickiness in the winter, our backup solution became Velcro™—industrial strength Velcro™! On most days the trailer exhibit materials are pretty much held together with Zots™, silicon sealant, Velcro,™ and, of course, the ever present duct tape, now in a variety of colors.

Top 10 Repeated (and repeatable) things heard in the Traveling Science Center.

We hear a lot of things in the TSC (sometimes I think individuals believe we are deaf) and get helpful advice from well-meaning people. Here are a few of the most commonly heard suggestions that we can repeat:

10. "Backing up is easy . . . Hey, Watch Out!" or "Can't you just back it up right into there?"

There have been too many times when the trailer has needed to go in reverse. Most people think this should not be a problem, and this is true, it's usually not, especially when there is ample room to maneuver, and we do not have an audience, all simultaneously putting in their "two cents." However, there is rarely enough room for a 60-foot truck and trailer (see item #8 above), and there is almost always at least one person giving advice on how to back it up, or a small child trying to run either behind (or between) the truck and trailer. One woman even demonstrated for us how easy it is to back up by putting her car in reverse and driving backwards.

9. "Can't you just push that branch out of the way?"

Along with the joys of backing up, there are times when the trailer visits places that are not made to accommodate an 11.5-foot-tall trailer. We encounter trees with low-hanging branches, which many people think that we should just "push out of the way." They fail to realize or take into consideration that the TSC trailer is not indestructible and the air-conditioning/heating units WILL pop off after hitting something substantial, such as a 12-inch-diameter branch or a low overpass. Many a route has had to be recalculated because the school forgot about an overpass that we wouldn't fit UNDERNEATH, requiring a 35-point turn around on 15th Street in Chicago.

8. "You girls will never make that turn."

Many truck drivers see two young women driving a large truck and trailer and immediately question our competence. One such time, a truck driver didn't believe that being in the left turn lane of the exit ramp would give us enough room to make our turn (a turn we had made many times previously). It's always nice to have running conversations with truckers on the highway. After completing our turn successfully, we just gave him a little wave and smile and proceeded on our way home.

7. "Do you live here?"

Children always seem to think that we must live in the trailer. This perhaps goes along with younger children also thinking their teachers live at school. But most likely it's our mysterious black curtain in the front of the trailer that leads to this misconception. Whatever the case may be, no we do not live in the trailer, and no, there is no bathroom, nor heat (again, see item #10 above).

6. "Who drives that truck for you?" with the unspoken "little ladies" fortunately for the speaker left out, and "Do you need to have a special license to drive that thing?"

During school programs, children, as well as teachers are curious about who actually drives the truck and trailer. When people learn that we (the little ladies) drive the truck and that it doesn't require a special license, they are either greatly impressed or a slight look of terror appears on their faces; either look provides us great entertainment and a certain measure of satisfaction. The children, and many teachers, must imagine that we have a big, burly man stashed away, likely behind the big, black curtain, just waiting to chauffeur us from school to school.

5. "My daddy/I saw a deer/rabbit (or any creature) once."
Children always seem to want to share their stories, especially when it has nothing to do with the discussion or the answer to the question we just asked. This is especially true when we are short on time. Whether it is about their dog, their dad, or the stray cats at their grandmother's house, children always want to share.

4. "Will the pitcher plant eat my finger?"
Many children pose this question when I (Jen) am talking about the pitcher plant. My response is often, "If you chop it off and leave it in there (the pitcher) for a few weeks, then yes, it will eat your finger; it's sort of like, well, eating your own finger." This usually either grosses the children out or sometimes it gets a few "cools" (usually from the boys). Then I say, "But if you just stick your finger in there, no, it will not eat your finger," which always greatly disappoints the students.

3. "My friend's name is Savanna."
Almost every class that is learning about the differences between prairies, savannas, and forests has someone, usually a girl, who raises her hand and states, "My friend/sister/dog/cousin's name is Savanna, but it's spelled differently." Our typical response to this is, "Well, now you can go home and tell them that they are a grassland with some trees growing on it!"

2. "Oh, you need a break during the school day?"—this from teachers who have scheduled our visit.
We believe that most teachers, when creating the class schedule for a full day's visit at their school, think we (Jen and Heather) are robots. Quite often we are given a schedule that includes not a single break during the day. In the beginning, we tried to make the most of it and had one person cover the class for five minutes while the other ran to the restroom or inhaled their lunch outside the trailer. Finally, we decided that enough was enough and told all teachers we needed breaks during the day. Most teachers were apologetic for not having thought of that on their own, but a few have acted very inconvenienced, sniping, "Well, how long of a break do you really need?" We are not animals, er, I mean robots!

1. And our number 1 favorite saying, "You really should have a man driving that thing."
A man, of course, almost always makes this comment. Most stupidly, it was in response to the trailer being damaged during extraction from a playground. Note: the two dents currently in the trailer were caused by male drivers, so see, isn't it obvious that we shouldn't let a man drive our truck? We women have it under control.

A short, sad, but true, story . . .

Learning to Trust Our Instincts
Jen Mui and Heather Grotefend

Tuesday, 15 May 2007

We arrive at an elementary school and they ASK us to park in the fenced in play-lot for the safety and security of both the children and our Traveling Science Center. We examine the area and I believe we can safely get into the lot. Heather, on the other hand, is a little skeptical. After some maneuvering, we get into the lot, but then we find that we must move to the other side; the principal want us up against the far fence. Curious children, however, are in my way and we can't get quite close enough to the fence to satisfy the teacher. I am trying to avoid basketball hoops overhead while the playground teachers are doing a poor job of keeping the children away from the vehicle. They are running around behind me, so I just put the vehicle in park and wait. The teacher trying to direct us, like so many others we have encountered, doesn't understand that it takes time to get the trailer to respond when going backwards. Levitation is neither its nor my *forte*. I am not a witch (although some children might think so) and this is not a Harry Potter movie!

When the screaming children have been safely removed from the playground, we begin again. It soon becomes clear that we must pull out and back in again. First, though, we need to reverse far enough to clear the basketball hoop. I begin backing up and hear a horrible crashing noise. Heather takes cover because it sounds as though someone had just shot out our back windshield. The teacher comes over and asks, "Did anything break?" This seems like a ridiculous question as she could clearly see me through the back window . . . oh wait, there was no window; I had just smashed it out with the corner of the trailer!

Did I mention it was raining? It was and I tell the teacher that I'm going to have to sit for a minute and calm myself and that she should go inside and let me deal with the problem. We sit in shock for a moment, panic setting in . . . take a deep breath . . .

Heather gets out and promptly directs me to where I need to be. We quickly prepare the vehicle for class and cheerfully greet the first students moments later.

The school janitor brings out a garbage bag and some masking tape (what kind of school janitor doesn't have duct tape?) Between classes we sweep up the glass from the playground and the bed of the truck and attach the plastic to the back of the window, only cutting ourselves a few times.

We begin calling around to find a place that can repair the window quickly, because while we may be able to drive my car to the site the next day, it will prove difficult to tow the trailer back from Rockford with the gooseneck of the trailer duct-taped to the console and through the sunroof of my Saturn.

At 2:30 p.m. we pack up the truck to go home and finally locate a place (near Bartlett) that can replace the window the following day. The plastic holds for the first six highway miles, until we hit the expressway; all of a sudden, the masking tape gives way. A roar of flapping plastic gets louder and louder until it's really quite deafening. It is louder when we speed, but if we drive faster, at least this horrid trip will end sooner.

The plastic bag gets more and more tattered as the shards of glass scrape and cut the bag while it flaps. Water begins to pelt us; the rain is, of course, coming from behind us. Only 36 more miles to go...

Finally, we make it to our exit ramp, but still, the rain is coming from behind us. We go over a bump and all the lights come on in the truck; apparently the back door has popped slightly open because it got jarred in the earlier crunching. Fortunately, 24 hours later the truck is good as new, but the trailer is still In Rockford. Now it's time for trailer extraction.

Thursday Afternoon: The Extraction

The fun begins Wednesday night when I download an aerial photo of the school, make a few measurements, attempt to use the geometry my mother painstakingly forced into my brain as a child, and calculate that we cannot exit the school grounds without removing a portion of the fence. We just need those few extra inches. Remember that we had to jack-knife the trailer and blow out the back window to get in the spot!

At 2:30 p.m. the last class leaves the Traveling Science Center.

At 2:45 we commence our first attempt at exiting the lot.

At 2:50 we circle around and try from the other side.

At 3:00 I ask the principal if I can write her a check for $500 to let me take out part of the fence (she says, "No!"), or perhaps the wooden bench (she says, "No," again). We continue to try to exit the lot with a maintenance man trying to guide us. I'm ready to just donate the trailer to this school when a tattooed man (the night custodian) comes over and I inquire hopefully, "So, are you by any chance a trucker?" he replies, "Well, I used to be." Relieved, I say, "Perfect! Get this out of the lot." He begins trying to direct me . . . failure.

I turn the keys over to him and say, "Why don't you try?" Another tattooed man (a parent) comes over and begins to help direct the first tattooed man. They try backing out . . . they try pulling out . . . failure.

All of the teachers are now watching, offering great advice. A teacher yells, "Why don't you just take out part of the fence?" I respond, "I asked, they won't let me," to which she asks "who told you couldn't? Just do it!!" Smiling . . I say, "umm . . . it was the principal . . . ," at which point the teacher sheepishly ducks back inside.

The two tattooed guys switch places and keep trying. The district superintendent looks on. Heather's dad, via telephone, suggests unhitching the truck and realigning it, which we try, to no avail. It's now 4 p.m. and we are still prisoners in this play lot. I sit down, hold my head, and try not to cry or vomit.

The first tattooed man says, "we just need to remove this pole here," goes to retrieve tools from his car, and returns wielding a tire iron. He begins to dismantle the fence gate. We are now so close to being able to get out, we can taste our freedom. A man dressed in nice clothes (no tattoos that we can see) walks up and starts dismantling the gate on the other side, using our little crescent wrench.

A little more maneuvering and it becomes clear that we will escape! The teachers start cheering and startle the tattooed driver, who catches the back corner on the left side, putting a small dent in the trailer, but at least we are free!!! It's a bit after 4:30 p.m. and we are headed home. Two hours to extract the trailer from a school must be a record . . .

Heather and Jen, always happy . . .

Be careful, be very careful where you stretch your nets . . .

Potential Discovery of New Bat Species:
Lasiurus hominidus bicyclius
Jacquelyn Potter
Field Assistant, 2006 INHS Summer Bat Survey

Deep in the heart of the vast Chicago-land wilderness lives the world's largest known bat. This species managed to remain elusive to science until one fateful evening in August 2006. That night our intrepid team of bat researchers included INHS scientists Joyce Hoffman, Jean Mengelkoch, Joe Merritt, and myself. We were busy carrying out a survey looking for the endangered Indiana bat (*Myotis sodalis*). We split up to go to our designated netting areas to set up our nets (bats are captured with nearly invisible mist nets that are the same as used to capture birds for banding). Each net is stretched across an opening in the forest—a trail or stream—and are around 20 feet long. Joyce and Jean were in another area of the forest. Joe was busy in the nearby river, engaged in a valiant battle to keep his net from collapsing with the flow of the water. I was situated a bit more upland, with my net covering one of the trails. Standing there, it seemed an eternity, waiting for the sun to go down and the birds to stop chirping and flitting around so I could raise my net.

I breathed a sigh of relief when I looked at my watch. It read 9:00 p.m. It was a comfort knowing that no more wayward hikers would amble along as the park had closed to visitors. I walked about 40 meters down the trail where I set up a more permanent post. I made several trips to the net to see if there were any tiny, membranous wings flapping to get free. It appeared that this was not a very busy area for bats and it might be a slow night.

As the evening lingered on, the moon reflected pale off the trees and undergrowth. A family of raccoons waddled and chortled nearby, and I could just make out the faint reflection of two deer moving silently through the foliage, crossing the trail a few meters away from where I sat. Looking down the trail in the direction of the net, the forest loomed dark. I sat listening as the traffic along the expressway died down to an occasional passing roar, and for a while it was almost quiet and kind of peaceful there, just inside the suburban forest.

Suddenly, from deep within the forest darkness came sounds such as never pierced the human ear; bone-chilling sounds, something akin to nails down a blackboard, only louder. It was a booming cry in the woods that could only be produced by a large creature in the throes of terror. Something REALLY BIG had been caught in my mist net and was struggling frantically to get free!

I jumped up and ran toward the net, heart pounding with the thought of approaching such a large and angry animal. Through the dark tunnel of the trail, the mist net poles soon came into view, reflecting the light of my headlamp through the darkness. It was then that I caught sight of them; two of the largest creatures ever caught in a mist net! They were obviously mammals, but were mostly hairless, and it appeared they possessed only vestigial wings. They also had attached to them strange extensions with two large, circular and rotating appendages. Their eyes didn't glow with eye-shine, but obviously they were nocturnal and well-adapted to darkness as their eyes squinted painfully in the light of my head lamp. I knew they were too big for Joe and me to handle and take measurements for analysis, although the thought of keeping them as potential Type Specimens (the specimen used to describe a new species) momentarily did cross my mind. I didn't quite know what to do. These were two very large, frightened, and angry mammals; anything could happen! I kept a safe distance as the potential for defensive attack was a distinct possibility, and I had not finished my regimen of rabies vaccinations yet.

Before I could ponder another second, the two creatures freed themselves from the net and raced away along the trail toward the entrance to the expressway. Alas, they were gone! But being the diligent field biologist, I knew I had to document such a potentially important discovery for science. I quickly reset the mist net and rushed down to find Joe along the river and tell him about this amazing happenstance. His face froze in shock and disbelief as I told him what had just transpired. He told me to write everything down that I could remember so that maybe one day these creatures could be found again, somewhere within the greater Chicago-land wilderness.

Obviously, we are dealing with a fascinating new member of Chiroptera (the order to which bats belong), most likely Vespertilionidae. I hereby propose placement within the genus *Lasiurus*, due to its very large size. I also think it important that the species epithet (last part of the scientific name) reflect the fact that they are hairless and seemed to stand upright, giving them the appearance of hominids. I have tentatively classified them as a possible subspecies, due to the unique combination of vestigial wings and large circular appendages which, although obviously used for motility, in all probability are an exaggerated and regionally variable feature for mate attraction. *Lasiurus hominidus bicyclus*: a remarkable new species of bat!

Tend to the necessities, ask no unnecessary questions . . .

Chasing Frogs Across the "Great Corn Desert" of Illinois
Jen Mui

Over the course of five summers, several of us at INHS undertook the not-so-minor task of determining the distribution of the two species of gray treefrogs throughout Illinois. The two species are identical in appearance, but differ in mating call and the number of sets of chromosomes. We opted to do frog call surveys to determine their distribution, which led to trips totaling several thousand miles throughout Illinois. We visited towns of all sizes and met all sorts of people.

Who Ya' Gonna Call?—Frog Busters

We knew that gray treefrogs call mostly near wooded bodies of water, so we studied topographic maps to locate small ponds in forested areas. We planned our arrival at promising locations at dusk and waited for the frogs to begin singing. We quickly learned that male gray treefrogs will call from almost any body of water, including puddles in tire ruts under a highway overpass. With this new-found knowledge, our approach to determining survey locations changed. We began looking for corridors that went through wooded areas, drove those roads with the windows down, and strained to hear frogs. If frogs were detected, we stopped the car.

One memorable night, while stopped along the edge of the road with an undergrad at the wheel, a police car pulled up behind us with his lights flashing. The student turned to me and asked, "Should I just take off?" I quickly determined that this was a bad idea and we stayed to endure an interrogation. This was to be the first of many such encounters with skeptical law enforcement officers throughout the state.

A Shot in the Dark

Aside from trying to avoid the police, we also strived to stay away from angry, gun-wielding, homeowners. Often the frogs were calling from private property and it would be far too late at night to knock on the landowner's door and ask permission. Besides, my dad always taught me to "ask no unnecessary questions." If we were too far from Champaign, and not wanting to drive the several hours home and return the next day, we would, on occasion, stealthily creep onto the property, flashlights down, and voices low. One night, in a trailer park near Ramsey, Illinois, I was standing in a marsh, recording a frog calling from a nearby cattail. An undergrad assistant waited on the bank and fellow graduate student Mike Dreslik remained down the road with the truck running. Someone emerged from a trailer, letting the door slam. Our faithful undergrad thought it was a shotgun discharging and took off running across the marsh. Unfortunately, I was stuck in the muck and unable to extricate myself, so I stayed quietly crouched under the bank, finished recording the frog's call, took his temperature, and collected him. The undergrad came back, pulled me out, and we headed back to the truck—all in a herpetologist's nightly work.

Who Wears the Pants (or Not)?

In the summer of 2004, while hunting gray treefrogs in rural Marion County, Illinois, I stopped by a house one afternoon where I had previously heard a chorus of treefrogs. I rang the doorbell and was greeted by an older man. I explained to him that I was conducting a statewide survey of the gray treefrogs and that I was interested in sampling his property later that evening. He proceeded to ask me about the fish he ordered from the Illinois Department of Natural Resources (IDNR) to stock his pond—When will they arrive? What size they will be?, etc. I explained politely that even though the Survey is part of IDNR, it was a large agency and I knew nothing about that. I was a graduate student working on this frog project. His wife came out to the door, wearing only a T-shirt and underwear. She questioned my presence, but then warmed up to me and invited me into the house. The couple took me on a tour of the pond they had constructed, explained the use of re-bar in the construction of the deck, and added many more details that I really didn't need. They invited me to "sit for a spell," so I explained that I had people waiting for me in the car and that I really ought to go as I had taken up enough of their time. I returned to the car and said to my assistants, "That was a little weird," to which one responded, "She wasn't wearing any pants, was she! I called it! I told you, 'Granny No-Pants!!!'"

How Do you Spell Relief?

We had time to kill until dusk so we cruised a bit through Marion County. After a while I realized there was nowhere to make a needed "pit stop." The closest town was too far away; however, an abandoned pole barn at a curve in the road offered the best hope for immediate relief. I pulled over and had my assistants flip a few rocks (looking for salamanders and snakes) while I did what needed to be done. I finished, called them back to the INHS minivan, and as we started to pull out two pick-up trucks came flying up behind us and blocked us in. Two "good ole boys" rushed to my window, wanting to know what we were doing in their shed. Quite embarrassed, I explained the situation and apologized for the crudeness of my actions. The skeptical leader believed either that we had stolen things from the barn or that were we cooking up crystal meth on the sly. I offered to let him search the vehicle. He declined, but took down my name and other information.

I reported to my advisor what had happened and we chuckled a bit. The next day, INHS Chief David Thomas received a phone call about the incident. The Conservation Police had been contacted to track down the people in the state-issued minivan to verify that everything was on the up and up. Apparently, children being kidnapped, crystal meth manufacture, theft from the barn with no walls, and other potential activities all were bandied about as possible explanations for what I might have been doing there. Relieving myself while searching for herps apparently was an excuse that made little or no sense to the locals. My advisor and I agreed that pit stops would only be made, from that point forward, "on the road."

The site of the alleged "peeing and fleeing" incident in southern Illinois.

No irate hang ups on this survey.

Frog and Toad Surveys
Chris Phillips

Frogs and toads are unique among amphibians and reptiles in that the males produce audible calls during the breeding season. Herpetologists take advantage of this fact and conduct censuses for these species based on the calls. A frog and toad calling survey is usually conducted by driving around after dark, stopping at regular intervals, rolling down the car windows, and listening. When observed by someone unfamiliar with amphibian survey techniques, this activity can be viewed as rather odd—and in some cases, suspicious— behavior. In my job as herpetologist, I have conducted many calling surveys throughout Illinois and have frequently been stopped by a passerby and asked what I am doing. I've also had the sheriff called several times. After a few of these inquiries, I crafted an in-depth answer that I could give that I thought would satisfy anyone's curiosity—or fear. After one attempt to use this answer, I realized that not everyone is as interested in amphibians as me, so I went back to a simple, one-sentence answer.

On one very notable occasion in southern Illinois, while conducting a calling survey; driving and stopping and listening, driving and stopping and listening, a man in a pick-up pulled up beside me and asked, "what ya' doin?" I told him I was conducting a frog and toad survey. With a very serious face, he replied, "What ya' askin' them?"

Survey herpetologists processing a turtle before releasing it.

Mus mishap . . .

Mouse at DQ
Joyce Hofmann

In the early 1990s I participated in an INHS project called Corridors for Tomorrow, which explored the role of Illinois' many miles of roadsides as habitat for wildlife. I conducted a small mammal survey to compare Interstate right-of-ways that had typical roadside vegetation and native prairie plantings. My colleague, ornithologist Patti Reilly, and I set lines of live traps along stretches of Illinois Interstates 74 and 55. In the mornings it was cool and the vegetation was wet, so we wore our hip waders. We walked the lines and checked the traps, placed at 10-meter intervals. If a trap was occupied, I (being the mammalogist) dumped the small mammal into a plastic bag. Removing it from the bag, I examined the animal to determine its species, sex, and reproductive condition. I then weighed it by suspending it briefly by the tail from a scale. Finally, I released the animal from the clip on the scale and let it drop to the ground, no worse for the wear. I tried to watch the animals scurry off so that we wouldn't accidentally step on them as we moved on to the next trap.

One morning I released a house mouse (*Mus musculus*), but didn't see where it had landed. The vegetation was quite dense so I didn't think much about it. We just proceeded slowly. After we finished checking the traps, we exited the Interstate for a "pit stop." The gas station at that interchange included a convenience store and a Dairy Queen, with restrooms between the two. As I headed for the rest room, I realized I was still wearing my waders. I stopped and began folding them down. As I did so, a house mouse jumped out of one wader and began running around inside the building. We chased it for several minutes before I was able to corner, catch, and carry it outside to our vehicle. I placed it in a trap until we could release it, yet again. The only witness to our chase was a man talking on a pay phone near the rest rooms, but he didn't act the least bit surprised.

Really, it's not what it looks like.

Fieldwork is a Peach of a Job
Don Webb

Aquatic ecologists Mark Wetzel and I, both from INHS, and hydrologist Phil Reid of the Illinois State Geological Survey worked on a field project to examine several springs in southern Illinois. We traveled south every two months from April 1991 to April 1992. Examining six springs took three days of fieldwork, so we headed south on Sunday afternoons to Dixon Springs Agricultural Station, thus allowing us an early start on Mondays. We followed this procedure in August of 1991 and finished sampling the last two springs in Union and Jackson counties on Wednesday. Our route home took us past Alto Pass and Rendelmen's Orchard, where a fresh crop of Illinois peaches, the size of softballs, was being picked. To accommodate the three cases of purchased peaches, we set them atop our collecting gear, thus prominently displaying our investment to all passers by and hiding our true mission. This "unlawful" use of a state vehicle to transport peaches apparently caught the eye of a conscientious Illinois citizen, who wrote the Governor's office about his concerns that a state vehicle was being used for the express purpose of driving to southern Illinois to buy peaches. The subsequent inquiry led to our having to justify to the Governor's office that a state vehicle had not been inappropriately used to buy and transport Illinois peaches. We also noted that the vehicle in question had been correctly utilized for specific field research, part of which involved our own personal time (i.e., traveling on Sunday). Our final statement confirmed that the acquisition of said succulent peaches had been merely a fortuitous and fruitful by-product of our long drive to work.

Webb looking for aquatic insects under rocks.

Damsels in distress.

Nightly Knights in Shining Armor
Don Webb

As you have likely noted, nighttime is an excellent time to collect adult chironomids (small flies) that are attracted to store lights in small towns. Upon leaving one such town we were perplexed to see a pair of on-coming headlights disappear. Pressing on, we observed two women emerging from a car parked along the road. Although there appeared to be no damage to the car, entomologist John Marlin and I felt that they might be in need of assistance. Our first question was "Have you run out of gas?" "No," came the reply, as their gas gauge showed a quarter of a tank. Unconvinced by this answer, John shone a flashlight into the gas tank and found it bone dry. As luck would have it, the son-in-law of the older women lived in a nearby town. Following many "thank you's," we dropped the two travelers off safely and again headed out of town. Within two miles of passing the previously stalled car, we came across a young woman jacking up the rear of her car. It was 12:30 in the morning and not the best time for a young woman to be alone on a lonely road. After assuring her that we were state employees and of good moral character, we got her to lock herself in her car with her young child, who was asleep, while John and I changed the tire. This reassured her of our honorable intentions. With the job completed in a few minutes, we sent the woman and child on their way to pick up her husband from work. Finally, we could get back to the good things that made a field biologist's life worthwhile—collecting flies.

"A salamander in hand is worth, well, it's priceless!"

To Be a Field Biologist for a Day—IWIN
Susan Post

The revival of the Illinois Natural History Survey Field Guide series spawned the idea of offering the public an opportunity to be "in the field" with the scientists who wrote the guides. The Illinois Wilds Institute for Nature (IWIN) was born. The courses are designed to bring citizens (general public, teachers, professional individuals, and students of all ages) into contact with scientists, while exploring the biodiversity and natural history of Illinois. Classes are held at the best times to see the organisms in question. These classes are not only popular with the public; Chris Phillips, author of the *The Field Guide to Amphibians and Reptiles of Illinois* and instructor of the IWIN class of the same name says, "I thoroughly enjoy teaching IWIN classes. It's great to have students who are so eager to learn the material. I wish the students in my undergraduate course [at University of Illinois] had half that much enthusiasm."

Since the first IWIN class in October 2000, participants have had the opportunity to photograph mating Balitimore checkerspot butterflies in a northern Illinois wetland, do a timed butterfly walk where 46 threatened regal fritillaries were spotted at a sand prairie, watch the courtship ritual of the rough green snake at Garden of the Gods, and wade the Wabash River while using their feet as feelers for mussels. The participants have also had the opportunity to hold countless organisms, from walking sticks to fritillary butterflies, to marbled salamanders, and musk turtles. During the course of most classes a similar comment is overheard, "I feel like a kid again!"

Jumping Through Hoops

The second IWIN class was *Butterflies of Illinois*, taught by the authors John Bouseman and James Sternburg using the Survey field guide of the same name. The class was held during June at Richardson Wildlife Foundation in Lee County, Illinois. One of the items provided to the participants was an insect net. Netting techniques were demonstrated, with the then 81-year-old Jim Sternburg commenting, "I am not getting better with age!"

Nets in hand, the class participants were told to walk, to disperse, and to have fun, but with this tidbit of information—butterflies can only fly 5–10 miles an hour, but sometimes that will be deceiving, especially to a novice wielding a net! One final comment was made before the class members fanned out with their nets. "Remember, be elegant with the nets, not jabbers!"

The comment "Don't scare them away," is frequently heard. Netting techniques ranged from running and spinning in circles while wildly leaping about, to quietly stalking. One person commented, "I wish my net was the size of a basketball court!" Another stated, "This is the first time I've had an insect net in my hand since I was a kid, and you know what, it's just as fun."

You could tell when someone had netted a specimen as it attracted a gathering of people, inevitably asking what it was. . . Several participants lamented on the difficulty of telling things apart. "Don't worry, that's what this class is about," someone else commented. Eventually, a specimen appears that tests even the experts. One participant pulled out a red-brown, angular-winged butterfly and asked, "Is this a comma or a question mark?" Jim's reply was, "It's too big and angular for a comma. Does anyone have a book?" The response "Maybe you should write one!" Jim said, "The pattern looks like a question mark, although this is the first time I've seen one without the silver dot. That was a good teaching case, bring on another."

With the class's final outing, the nets were no longer pristine white; most had streaks of dirt and several had holes. The last classroom topic to be discussed was distribution. John Bouseman asked everyone to open their field guides and look at the distribution maps for the various butterfly species. Even with the resources of one of the country's largest insect collections and over 130 years collecting experience by the authors, plenty of counties had no marks. To remedy this Bousman said, " Take a look at the book, especially the distribution maps of the species. If something hasn't been found in your county, get out and document the species. Pick up your nets and run with them!" But please remember to do it with elegance and style.

Perhaps the most popular IWIN class is the Reptiles and Amphibians of Illinois, the spring 2008 class will be the fifth offering.

To Hold a Marbled Salamander

What do the words blizzard, unseasonably cold, and cold-blooded have in common? The first two obviously pertain to winter, while the latter refers to a group of animals incapable of regulating their own body temperature—insects, reptiles, and amphibians. Combine all these terms, however, and you have the flavor of the weather anomalies endured by a group of hardy individuals who sought the chance to hold a marbled salamander and other herpetological wonders during the Spring 2003 Illinois Wilds Institute for Nature (IWIN) Reptile and Amphibian Workshop. The class was scheduled during early April in southern Illinois and was to take advantage of warm, wet weather, replete with sunning snakes, basking turtles, and calling frogs and toads. Instead, there were three days of record cold, flooded swamps, and fat, wind-driven snowflakes; certainly not the type of weather conducive to bringing cold-blooded snakes, lizards, toads, frogs, and salamanders out of hibernation.

Of the state's 100 species of reptiles and amphibians, over two-thirds can be found in southern Illinois, and 40 to 45 could conceivably be found during the workshop. Class headquarters was the new Henry N. Barkhausen Wetland Center, located south of Whitehill, Illinois. The major instructor for the class was Dr. Chris Phillips, herpetologist with the Illinois Natural History Survey. Herpetology collections manager John Petzing and several

A handful of chubby mole salamanders.

students assisted Chris. At each field site Chris and his team would fan out, exploring ephemeral wetland pools and leaving no rock or log uninvestigated. Their knowledge of what should be where, and how they could find it to show the eager but cold class, led to a remarkable list of animals, considering the weather!

What follows is a brief tour of the 2003 IWIN herpetology workshop field stops. Our companions along the trails are not only our instructor, but also a small green book with a gold embossed salamander on the cover–*The Field Guide to Amphibians and Reptiles and of Illinois* written by Christopher Phillips, Ronald Brandon, and Edward Moll.

Section 8 Woods

Section 8 Woods is located less than a mile from the wetlands center and was a logical destination for day one. The woods are an Illinois Nature Preserve and contain a cypress/tupelo swamp and floodplain forest. A boardwalk enables anyone to view the area and see the state champion water tupelo. The area was quite wet, but accessible, as instructors left the security of the boardwalk to forage far and wide. Chris had a white bag into which he put specimens to show the class, leading to the comment, "It's like Santa Claus when he pulls out treasures from his white cloth snake bag!" Here we learned the difference between a green frog and a bullfrog. "Remember, the fold on a bull frog goes only to the ear drum whereas in a green frog it goes all the way down." We would find both luna and polyphemus moth cocoons, and ponder why tupelo seeds had been stripped of their glossy, black-and-white spotted covering and stuffed into the crevices of a cottonwood.

La Rue-Pine Hills

La Rue-Pine Hills is a five-mile by two-mile strip of land running north to south in the Shawnee National Forest in Union County. For several weeks each spring and fall, La Rue Road, the main north-south road at the base of the bluffs, is closed to vehicular traffic; this allows many of the 65 species of reptiles and amphibians that hibernate among the rocks along the bluff a safe route for migration to and from the swamp. This migration is what we had come to see on day two.

On the road to La Rue-Pine Hills it began to snow—large, wet flakes hitting the windshield with a smack and a patter. It was like driving through a giant ticker tape parade. We arrived and ate a cold lunch—only to be interrupted first by a spring brood zebra swallowtail. "Look at its red dot," was soon drowned out by "LOOK at this VERY COLD COTTONMOUTH!" Due to its torpor everyone had close looks at this usually very hyper snake.

Walking the closed La Rue road in the spring is like shelling on a Florida beach—you never know what will pop up next. Is that larkspur on the right? See the shooting star on the left; and look, it's a pair of Louisiana Water Thrushes bobbing ahead of us. Stop! is that a stick or a snake? One could walk this road a 100 times and never see the same thing twice. With all the birds and flowers we see along the trail it's easy to forget why we are here. That is, until John Petzing comes down the road with a snake that resembles a large earthworm. "What is it?" we all clamor. "Key it out" is his reply. Soon the conversation is littered with, "Can you see a preocular scale? My eyes are too old, where's a hand lens." Finally, we all agree that it's a smooth earth snake—a very descriptive name for the rare catch of the day.

Heron Pond

Our final day (and the sun is finally shinning!) is spent exploring the Cache River State Natural Area and one of its jewels, Heron Pond. It features a trail through a floodplain woods, a boardwalk into the heart of a cypress swamp, and up-close views of the state champion cherry bark oak. From the boardwalk we see herons in their rookery, a Pileated Woodpecker excavating a nest cavity, and red-eared slider turtles basking on a distant log. One of the herpetological highlights of Heron Pond was a pair of marbled salamanders—cool, moist, smooth bodies with black and gray/silver markings. Everyone in the class had a chance to hold them before moving on to the next find. While not a salamander, another silvery black and gray wonder was discovered under a turned over log—an eyed elator or click beetle—an insect that is not an everyday occurrence, and certainly any entomologist's delight.

Wildcat Bluff

Wildcat Bluff is a sandstone outcrop found above Little Black Slough. We are looking for sandstone-colored, cryptic fence lizards. Chris spies a large example, but the lizard also sees Chris and tries some evasion tactics—down a log and up a tree. Chris is not deterred; he taps the tree with his snake stick and nonchalantly catches the fleeing lizard using a Willie Mays basket catch. A one-in-a-million chance and Chris made it look easy.

Just as the class is leaving, we hear "Wait! Wait! What's this?" Field guides come out and we quickly key it to Fowler's toad—species number 28 on our list and the final discovery of the class.

The Real Test

After the class was officially over a small group went looking for more, testing our knowledge without the crutch of Chris. We find a turtle shell and agreed that it was some kind of slider. By turning the shell over we noted the spots on its plastron. Easy, it's a red-eared slider! One class member commented, "I must have learned something as I wouldn't have known to look on its underside. Before the class it would've been some kind of turtle—now it's a red-eared slider. Thanks Chris!"

I win
You win
We all win with IWIN
(poem by class member Steve Lyons)

Be careful what you ask for.

Directions
Michael Jeffords

Even when you are not lost, getting around can be tough. My first job at the Survey was to conduct insect sampling of selected soybean fields across Illinois. These 33 fields were scattered hither and yon and since there are tens of thousands of pretty much identical soybean fields in Illinois, finding a particular one can be tricky. On an initial trip to Pulaski County in far southern Illinois, a colleague and I stopped in the sleepy town of Mounds to ask directions of a lady working in her yard. We knew the field was in the vicinity of Horseshoe Lake Conservation Area so we began our inquiry with that. "No problem," the lady said, "just go down the road apiece and turn right where the Dairy Queen used to be. Y'all can't miss it."

Needless to say, we did.

Chapter 5

Ah, the Weather!

Chicago, IL September 14, 1881

It has rained all day but I have been busy, this forenoon looking up the various workmen who have my apparatus in hand, and this afternoon down on the dock, canvassing the subject of boats. Came back wet through but satisfied. A Mackinaw boat that will outride any gale, and "beach" with comparative safety, can be had for $2 a day, and a man to run it for about as much more. This won't haul the trawl, however, I think, in any ordinary breeze; and for a steam jacket of proper size and sea-going quality, I am afraid that I shall have to pay $20 or $25 a day. Our S. Chicago fishermen will give us a start with the trawl gratuitously, with their fishing tug and then I can tell what more I can afford. The Mackinaw boat will be perfect for dredging, and we shall have to use the trawl as a luxury. . . the little boat is as trim as a wood duck and as clean as a dinner plate. . . .

September 19, 1881
Another disappointing delay, but the very last, I verily believe. I could take boat in half an hour now, but I couldn't at noon. It is an abominable place to get anything unusual done. There is such an Assyrian habit among the workmen of always doing the same thing over in a monotonous way, and never doing anything else, that they are lost when they take up something new.

the weather is lovely here, the winds are strong and steady, and the lake ripples away to a horizon of thick haze. The invitation to try our fortune is all we could ask, and to-morrow we go.

September 20, 1881
I have tried my hand at making things happen. As a grand result, I fed my breakfast, and everything else I could possible get up my throat to the fishes of Lake Michigan, and then got driven in by a rising wind and a dense fog. I think we really might have stayed out; but my "skipper" didn't want to risk it, and I am too green in such matters to have any judgment of my own. We shall try it again in the morning, perhaps keeping in shore if the fog continues. I am going to conquer this detestable, disgusting and disgraceful weakness of seasickness right here, and you needn't expect to see me

home until I have become a good sailor. But I don't think that you want to go to Grand Traverse. A big dose of tartar emetic, repeated at short intervals for three or four days, will do you just as well...

September 21, 1881
Before you sink to the extreme of sympathetic disgust over my note of this morning, let me narrate my more successful venture of to-day. I started out more than half sick, but most thoroughly determined to dredge my best, got under way at eight, worked out four miles in almost a dead calm, and at last began operations. Our apparatus worked to perfection, and everything went off without trouble or delay. I evidently have the art of dredging all at command. We spent about seven hours on the lake, which I think will do for a beginning, considering that I again promptly fed my breakfast to the fishes, and spent the whole time in a state of absolute disgust and misery, and went without my dinner. . . .

I don't yet know what we got, in detail. No great quantity, at any rate, but we found out what was to be had, and that is the main thing, and all I have undertaken. To-morrow, if the weather is right, we shall go out ten or twelve miles, and stay all day. I feel so much better this evening that I think I shall fare tolerable to-morrow. At any rate, I shall finish it through.

"Rain happens."

The Field Botanist's Mantra*
Steve Hill

Written in field notes of August 18, 2005 along the Fox River, northern Illinois.

[present] I Hope it Doesn't Rain.
[later—] I Hope it Doesn't Rain Too Hard.
[later—] I Hope it Doesn't Rain Too Long.
[later—] Please Let it Stop Soon!
[later—] Oh Well, Back to Work—I'm Soaked Anyway.

*Mantras are sounds—words or phrases—that are used as objects of concentration. The sounds may be chanted out loud or heard internally.

With a sky like this, no amount of chanting will change the inevitable.

Good stories can only be told if the tellers survive the experience. This was a close call.

A Trip to Illinois' Sinkhole Plain: In which Nature Hints, Warns, and then Speaks
Steven J. Taylor

Illinois has a number of caves, with many concentrated along the Mississippi River, southeast of St. Louis. The evening of Tuesday, June 6, 1995, Jean Krejca and I drove to Waterloo, Illinois, to conduct three days of biological inventory for the U.S. Fish and Wildlife Service under the leadership of our boss, Don Webb (an entomologist at the Illinois Natural History Survey). We were to sample five Illinois caves where the amphipod, *Gammarus archerondytes* (a small shrimplike animal, commonly known as a scud or sideswimmer), had been reported in the past. Our job was to spend the next three or four days making an intensive survey for this animal in each of the caves.

Prelude
The drive to Monroe County was interesting. Because of flooding on the Mississippi River, Route 3 was closed near Chester, Illinois, and we had to detour around the problem area. Back on track at Redbud, we drove on Route 3 toward Waterloo. Along this stretch of road we encountered many downed trees, destroyed barns and outbuildings, and more than a few houses with portions of their roofs destroyed, all the result of tornado-force winds that swept through the area three weeks earlier. Farmers were just now beginning to venture back into their fields.

After breakfast the following morning the three of us headed off to the first cave, Illinois Caverns. The weather forecast predicted scattered, isolated rain, but the morning was very nice—sunny with only a few clouds. After several hours in the cave we had completed our work there. Next stop was lunch in Waterloo. I had been experiencing knee problems and by now, after hours in the cramped cool, wet, rocky cave environment, my knees were a little sore. I resolved to move a little more slowly and carefully after lunch.

Later, we drove south of St. Joe to the main entrance of Fogelpole Cave (Monroe Co., IL). Because we were doing research for the US Fish and Wildlife Service, we had special permission and a key to enter the gated cave.

Listening to Mother
As we suited up to go in, we noticed that the clouds were beginning to build. The gate required a considerable amount of hammering, generous quantities of WD-40, and brute force to finally get it open.

The "main entrance" to Fogelpole is actually two adjacent entrances in the same large sinkhole. One entrance, almost never used, is at the very bottom of the sink where a rocky stream bed with a faint trickle of water drains into the cave. The other entrance, which we used, is perched about 10 feet higher on the side of the sinkhole and is typically dry (as it was on this day). Only the faintest trickle of water was present several feet into the cave.

We noted the clouds and decided that it would be prudent not to stray too far from the entrance. The passage began with a 15-foot crawlway over large cobbles and rock; the lowest point was about 2 feet high. The cave opens almost immediately into a beautiful, narrow, winding, smooth-walled bedrock passage (3 to 7 feet wide, 10 to 20 feet tall) that ends abruptly at the top of a 10 to 15-foot waterfall. Jean and I had been here several times before and knew that this could easily be bypassed via a narrow bellycrawl along a ledge on the right side of the dropoff. Don, with his rather thick, burly build, had some trouble with the crawl along the edge. From this ledge, it's a short climb down to the stream level, about five feet downstream from the waterfall. Here again, Don was a little hesitant (The first time I came to the spot, I, too, thought I couldn't do it.) but he made it just fine. The "waterfall" was only a few drips of water. As we passed this point we discussed that even if rain came, the waterfall bypass route was, fortunately, up out of the water and would be perfectly safe.

We continued down the passage, now at least 20 feet tall and about 5 feet wide, with a rubble floor and occasional pools of water, fed by the seeping "stream." Soon, 150 feet into the cave, we joined up with the passage from the lower entrance in the sinkhole. Here, the passage from the other entrance joins the one we were in, but connects up about 30-feet above us, as we had been continually working our way downward. This spot is normally very drippy and pretty. On this visit we noticed that there seemed to be a little bit more water coming down than usual. After this point the passage becomes 15 feet wide and the ceiling temporarily drops to 5 feet, before rising again at the junction with main stream of Fogelpole Cave, another 200 feet down the passage. The junction of the entrance passage with the main stream is easily one of the finest sights in any cave in Illinois. A massive borehole heads off from this location in three directions, not including the relatively small entrance passage, a respectably large passage in its own right.

We took in the view for a few minutes—this is a very special place—before beginning our collecting. Given the building clouds and the massive size of the cave, we felt it would probably rain somewhere in the Fogelpole drainage basin. We decided to stay close to the entrance passage for our collecting and keep an eye on the water levels. If the water began to rise, we would be close enough to the entrance to just stroll out and call it an early day.

The water in the mainstream (an underground river, really) was clear and at normal flow. Jean and Don began collecting and I moved upstream into a major side passage, still within sight of their lights. We all settled into our usual routine, happily collecting cave macroinvertebrates from the stream.

Feeling Very Much Alive

Soon, Jean noted to Don that she could hear thunder, and that it must really be raining if she could hear this some 300 feet into the cave. From where I was working I heard neither the thunder nor their conversation over the sound of the stream. Moments later I heard a funny noise and looked over at the Jean and Don. Almost simultaneously, Jean was shouting in my direction as we all heard the ominous thundering of floodwater!

I slapped my collecting kit shut and ran to Don and Jean, who for some strange reason seemed to be trying to finish closing up vials and such. Out of the corners of my eyes I could see muddy floodwaters roaring down the entrance passage. I shouted "GO, GO!" to the others, which really got Don, who had little caving experience, clued in to the immediacy of things. I started up the entrance passage. Alarmingly, in a matter of two or three minutes the passage had gone from a virtually dry stream bed to a 15-foot-wide raging flood! Immediately realizing the danger, we picked our way upstream, carefully, but with amazing speed. My knees underwent a temporary, miraculous cure and the others took a while to catch up. As we continued upstream, the water became deeper as the passage narrowed. I was concerned that if the water had come up this fast (which in itself was quite puzzling) it might continue to rise. Shortly we arrived at the point where the lower entrance joins the passage, now a 30-foot waterfall, a torrent of stormwater cascading down onto the floor right next to us. Fortunately, after we passed this obstacle, the flow lessened considerably. Still, we had the climb up the 15-20 foot waterfall to negotiate, followed by the crawl through the two-foot-high passage at the entrance. Our concerns were the climb (Would we be in the waterfall while climbing?), the crawlway (Would there be sufficient airspace?), and, most importantly, would the water flow continue to increase?

Luckily, the climb at the waterfall was free of water. We were unable to communicate over the roar of the falling water, and could only shout to get each other's attention. We handed gear up the climb and negotiated the crawl along the ledge above the waterfall. Don's minor problems with the climb and crawlway miraculously vanished and he was at the top of the falls faster than Santa goes up a chimney. Here, we reassembled our gear and headed toward the final obstacle—the crawl. Fortunately, the water flow had not increased and the crawlway was open, with only about six inches of floodwater flowing through it. Finally, we reached the entrance!

As we stepped from the cave, we could hear the faint sound of sirens in the distance. From the entrance we looked down to the lower entrance in the sinkhole. The stream bed leading into it, which had been virtually dry when we entered the cave, was now, no more than half an hour later, a raging torrent of floodwater. At the lower gate to the cave, the water had formed a large, foam-covered pool that poured through it.

It was, of course, raining fairly hard when we came out, but NOT hard enough to account for such a rapid and massive increase in water flow. We had expected that if it rained, the water would begin to turn cloudy and rise steadily, not suddenly change from almost zero flow to a 15-foot-wide frothing, roaring monster!

We talked excitedly for a while and admired the awesome power of the water pouring into the lower entrance. After the adrenaline subsided we kicked ourselves for not bringing a camera to photograph the flooded entrance.

Entomologist Webb processing samples deep in a cave.

The Aftermath

As it was still early, we decided this would be an excellent time to look at a couple of nearby springs to see how they responded to the flooding. It took us 15 minutes to lock the cantankerous gate before we could climb out of the deep sinkhole, all accomplished in the rain. Near the top of the sinkhole I pointed out a fallen tree, and in the adjacent field we noticed the grass had been knocked over and was lying uphill. While changing from our wet, muddy cave gear into street clothes, the rain stopped. It had only rained for a total of 30–45 minutes.

We had a celebratory beverage back at the vehicles and discussed what had happened. We noticed there were still amphipods in one of the nets (!), so we preserved these and updated our field notes. We had actually managed to sample two habitats, in spite of the excitement. In the distance we could see black clouds and lightning moving away toward the southeast as we drove off to look at other springs.

Before we reached the paved road, we began to get a clue as to what had really happened. Small branches and occasional larger limbs lay scattered across the road and fields of wheat were flattened. Around the next bend our progress was stopped by a 3-foot-diameter, 50-foot-tall tree that had fallen across the road! It was much too large to move or drive around. We consulted our topo map which showed a lesser dirt road, and we soon made it to the pavement.

By now we had pieced it all together. It seems our sinkhole had been in the path of either a tornado or a near-tornado force storm that had abruptly dumped massive quantities of water in a very small area. We weren't, however, out of the woods just yet!

Driving back the other direction we saw more damage from the storm. Trees were downed and some smaller outbuildings on farms were destroyed. Rounding a curve, we were again stopped by a fallen tree. Trapped! This tree was a little smaller, and with all three of us pushing, we were able to bend many of the limbs to break them so the lower limbs could then be driven over. One critical limb, however, just refused to break. Don, having the mass of Jean and me combined, held back the limb as far as he could, and we drove the vehicle through, scraping the undersides on the limbs and hanging two tires over the ditch. Past this obstacle, we continued on. One final turn and we'd be on pavement, but here again was a tree. Fortunately, a farmer had beat us to it with his chainsaw, making a neat path through the fallen tree. Perhaps a new chainsaw should become part of our standard caving gear!

While driving about it became obvious that the storm had cut a swath, one to two miles wide, and of varying severity, from Maystown to south of St. Joe, and directly over the Fogelpole drainage basin! Soon we met power company trucks and a police car heading in various directions to take care of all the storm-related incidents (apparently, no people were hurt). We later heard that a tornado had actually touched down in the area.

We proceeded to Maddonaville Cave (Monroe Co.) and looked at the entrance. Silt laden water flowed out at least twice the normal rate. We then drove to the highly flood-prone Stemler Cave (St. Clair Co.). Here, the water was at normal flow and not murky—the rains had totally missed this area. A stop a Sparrow Spring Cave [the resurgence of Stemler] confirmed this observation, as flow was normal here also.

Enough was enough, though, and off we went to St. Louis for a fine dinner, then back to Waterloo to find a motel and watch the Weather Channel. The reports for today and tomorrow were not favorable for continued field work (sure, NOW they tell us!), so after breakfast we headed home, the remainder of our trip aborted by rain.

Analysis

Naturally, we discussed the Fogelpole trip in some detail among ourselves. We feel that we were not in error to have entered the cave. Jean and I are fairly experienced cavers, having, at the time, each gone in over 300 caves, and Don is strong, mature, and has traveled throughout the world, living sometimes in relatively primitive conditions. We were aware of the weather forecast (scattered showers) and the potential for rainwater to drain into the cave, and we had calculated how far we should go into the cave based on these factors. We could not anticipate that a tornado or near-tornado would pass over (there were no storm watches in effect at the time) and dump such massive quantities of water in such a short time. We were prepared for, even expecting, rising water, but not such a massive flood pulse. Fortunately, we had given ourselves a considerable margin for error.

As field biologists we felt sufficiently prepared for any "normal" situation. We had approximately 40–60 hours of artificial light among the three of us, garbage bags (for hypothermia protection), carbide lamps (for heat and light), and cave food. Back in the car we had even more gear: rope, come-along, cable ladders, first aid kit, more carbide and batteries, etc.

Unlike many caves in Illinois' sinkhole plain, Fogelpole has many high areas. Had we been trapped in the cave, we could have easily reached high ground to wait out the water. If we had been uninformed flashlight cavers, though, who might have ventured much further into the cave—the story could have easily turned out quite differently, perhaps tragically.

Conclusion

Mother Nature had hinted to us (the fallen trees we saw on the way up to Waterloo from an earlier storm)—and we looked; she warned us (the building storm clouds as we went into the cave)—and we listened; and then, Mother Nature spoke (the flood pulse in the cave)—and we learned!

I, for one, will never forget the awesome power of the floodwaters raging down that passage as we bolted for the entrance!

A high stakes game of dice.

#12
Michael Jeffords and Charles Helm

One of the arts of field research is designing cages that do what you want them to do. For an insect research project on soybeans we constructed a series of six-feet-by-six-feet-by-six-feet mesh cages with aluminum frames to isolate small plots within soybean fields. Each cage was sturdy, designed to withstand the somewhat capricious weather of east-central Illinois, and open on the bottom so each could be dropped over a group of soybean plants and anchored down with tent stakes. An experimental field adjacent to our laboratory served as a convenient plot and during early June in the early 1980s we had placed a dozen cages across the field. Secure in our belief that our design was adequate and the cages well-anchored and safe, we left for a survey of field plots across the southern third of Illinois. While returning to Champaign, Illinois, three days later, we encountered a rather vigorous thunderstorm just south of town, but thought little of it as we returned, tired, dirty, and hungry after a long day in the field. Driving into the Illinois Natural History Survey's Annex parking lot in the slanting light of late afternoon, we noticed that it had recently rained, that the nearby trees were a bit windswept, and that our experimental soybean field, was, well, empty of cages. Where could they have gone? No one was about so we began a quick investigation of the site and quickly found one of our cube cages lodged against a nearby pole barn. No others, however, were in sight or on site. This certainly did not bode well.

Our laboratory was adjacent to the University of Illinois' (UI) South Farms and immediately across the road was the UI Swine Farm. While traversing back and forth across the hundreds of acres of field plots, we encountered the farm manager who had witnessed the intense thunderstorm and he inquired whether those cages that had gone cavorting across his lands, "like dice in a Vegas crap game" (his words), belonged to us. Needless to say, they were ours and we found them scattered across several hundred acres over the next couple of hours. We ultimately located 11 cages, all in relatively good shape, but number 12 proved elusive. It turned out, however, to have traveled the least distance of all the others, as it had hopped the nearby hog fence and nestled itself into the mud of the adjacent hog pen. Unfortunately, it had rolled around in the pen before coming to rest on its side, coating itself with rancid mud in the process. We noted some very peculiar activity in the pig pen. The pigs were quite agitated and milling around in what we initially took to be their shelter. Not so, as we looked closely, there was cage #12. Pigs, being the curious animals they are and likely nearly bored to death most of the time, had immediately noticed the intrusion of our cage into their world and promptly decided this must be some new distraction. In short, our cage was filled with yearling pigs, all happily treating it as children would a new playhouse! Actually, a more apt analogy would be that they thought of it as an outdoor pig privy. It took some herding to rid our cage of its occupants and retrieve it. Remarkably, it was still intact, although certainly odoriferous, after its sojourn in a pigpen for a few hours. We hosed it off and placed it back in the soybean field for the rest of the field season.

Over the ensuing years, we used those cages many times, but we always knew each spring when we got to #12. The *eau de swine* persists to this day.

"Honey, don't forget your coat!"

Winter Sampling Blues
David Thomas

As every field biologist knows, sampling during frigid, winter conditions can complicate even the most routine sampling event. This story goes back to the winter of 1966 when R. Weldon Larimore (now retired from the Illinois Natural History Survey), David L. Thomas (now retired Chief), and Paul Fishman (retired biologist in Portland, Oregon) were doing their winter drift sampling (catching organisms that float or swim in the water) in the Kaskaskia River near Sullivan, Illinois. The site for this ongoing, intensive sampling for invertebrates and fish was located near the mouth of Jonathan Creek, some five miles east of Sullivan. We left our warm hotel room around 11:30 p.m. to go to our field station for the midnight sample. These drift samples were conducted for one hour and included two nets anchored on construction rods: one near the bottom and one near the top of the water column to sample drifting invertebrates. The reason we decided on a midnight sample has now escaped me.

We drove to our site in an old blue pickup truck that we affectionately called the Blue Whale. After putting the nets in position in the river, we retired to the truck to attempt to stay warm for the next hour. The outside temperature was near zero with a very strong wind. For some reason I had on a one-piece flight suit (coveralls) and no coat. When we began to lift the nets, around 1 a.m., we discovered they had become filled with anchor ice (has anyone documented the movement of anchor ice in a stream?), meaning we found basically no invertebrates in the net. For the record, anchor ice is ice that has become attached to the bottom of a stream, and in theory, shouldn't be moving around! We packed up our equipment and prepared to head back to warmth—except that the battery of the truck was now dead as a doornail (which, I'm told, is pretty dead).

At most times, five miles is not that great a distance. However, at night with a cold wind it can seem like an extremely long way. Fortunately, I had a sleeping bag in the back of the truck and I was able to wrap that around me to serve as a coat. Nearly half-way back, along the main road into Sullivan, we decided to get out of the cold wind for a few minutes and rest. We dropped down into a ditch along the road and lay against the embankment. At that moment a truck stopped in front of us and begin backing into a dirt road next to us to turn around and head back to Sullivan. We immediately saw this as a potential ride to town and jumped out of the ditch and offered the driver help in turning around. He thanked us, but once he was lined up, the next thing we saw was dirt and gravel flying in the air, and a truck speeding away from us as fast as its lower gears would take it. I never realized that a truck could gain so much speed so fast.

Larimore electroshocking for fish.

Our disappointment at not getting a ride, and some anger, quickly turned to a good laugh. At 2:15 in the morning on a windy, sub-zero night, the sight of three men leaping out of a ditch, one wrapped in a sleeping bag, was probably enough to scare anyone. In fact, the driver may this very day be writing an article for some truck-driving magazine about the various strange happenings on the road, likely featuring us.

Storm sampler.

All in A Day's Fieldwork
Diane Szafoni

Newton Lake is a 1,750-acre cooling lake built in 1975 for Newton Lake Power Station in Jasper County, Illinois. It was formed by the construction of a 50-foot-high dam on Weather Creek. The lake filled in behind the dam, extending six and a half miles up Laws Creek and five miles up Sandy Creek. On April 27, 1985, 10,775 barrels of heavy Louisiana sweet crude oil entered Laws Creek, the result of a ruptured pipeline owned by Marathon Pipeline Company. Although floating booms were installed to contain the oil, heavy rain that spring caused the booms to fail and the oil spread to other portions of this arm of the cooling lake. Clean-up operations by Marathon were completed in August 1985. However, field observation showed that little recovery had taken place by spring of 1988, so a more intensive environmental study was called for to document the habitat and biota recovery. I was a member of the research team at the Illinois Natural History Survey (INHS) that undertook this study.

Subsequently, I found myself in a Johnboat on Newton Lake in late May 1990 with Steve Kohler and Lewis Osborne, two aquatic ecologists at INHS. We were collecting benthic macroinvertebrates from 20 sampling stations in this restricted arm of Newton Lake. Benthic macroinvertebrates are the aquatic worms, immature crayfish, clams, snails, aquatic insects, and other organisms that live in the sediment at the bottom of the lake. When they mature, some become dragonflies, damselflies, and mayflies that many people recognize. Macroinvertebrates are important because they feed on the algae, bacteria, plant leaves, and other organic matter that washes into the water. Besides recycling nutrients as they feed, they also are food for many fish. However, unlike fish, they are not able to move around very well, so they are a good indicator of water quality. Scientists are able to determine the quality of the water by the kinds and number of species of macroinvertebrates present. This was one of the biological indicators we were using to assess the lake's recovery.

To collect our benthic samples, we used a petite Ponar dredge sampler, a device that looks like a big metal jaw and was about six inches by six inches. A rope was attached to it and it was sent to the bottom of the lake. It was spring-loaded, so when the sampler hit the bottom it snapped shut, taking a big bite of the lake bottom. The sampler (with sample) was then pulled back to the boat and dumped out. In many places of Newton Lake we found the bottom was scoured clean, so we shifted over a bit, using a depth finder to assess our position accuracy, and tried again and again until we got a sample.

Steve and Lew took turns using the Ponar dredge to take the samples. My job was to fill out the chain-of-custody form, make a sample label, then start processing the sample. I would rinse the sample through a fine-meshed sieve, transfer it to a wide-mouth canning jar, add a 7% formalin solution to preserve the sample, and finally, place a label in each jar.

Our day started out bright and sunny. We sampled all morning, working our way up the restricted access arm of the lake. At noon, we pulled over to the bank for lunch. After a brief rest, we continued with the sampling. Soon, the sky began to darken, but as this was our last day of sampling, and we really needed to finish, we continued to work. Soon, we could hear thunder and see lighting in the distance. By then we were too far from the boat launch to return, so we pulled off to the side of the lake to wait out the storm. We covered our depth finder with an upside down five-gallon bucket to protect it and stowed the rest of the equipment. The banks were wooded and we exited the boat to stand on the edge of the forest, conscious of not being the highest objects on the water. We waited patiently, watching the sky for a break in the clouds that would either let us return to work or get off the water. The storm, however, continued coming and advanced up the arm of the lake as a huge wall of white! With a warning shout to each other, we ran into the woods, just as large, golf-ball-size hail rained down on us. We crouched by the base of a tree and tried to protect our heads with our arms. Steve and Lew were yelling "Ouch!, Son of a ….(bucket??)." I couldn't tell exactly what was said as the sound of the hail hitting the tree branches and the crash of the thunder above us drowned out any conversation. I soon realized that I wasn't getting hit and looked up to see Steve and Lew taking the brunt of the hailstorm, standing over me so I didn't get hit. "I'm okay," I yelled. "Don't worry about me. Protect your own heads!" I don't think they heard me over the noise of the storm and their own yelling.

In typical Illinois fashion, the storm didn't last very long and we were able to return to the boat and assess damages. The chivalrous Steve and Lew had sore heads with a number of bumps and bruises. Steve, wearing shorts that day, developed a nice case of poison ivy from running into the woods as the storm approached. I was merely soaked to the skin (even with a rain suit). The five-gallon bucket, however, didn't fare as well; the bottom was cracked in half from the force of the hail! But it had done its job, and the depth finder came through unscathed. Both I and the equipment had been protected from the storm to work another day.

The real story behind the hike!

Red Oak Backpack Trail
Susan Post

Working at the Illinois Natural History Survey provides interesting opportunities. I took advantage of one during 1996. Human Kinetics, a sports/health publisher, was looking for an Illinois author to write a book on hiking Illinois. They contacted the Survey wondering if anyone would be interested. While the project was an after hours (on your own time) project, my field work had taken me all over Illinois, and I had also made some valuable contacts around the state who could make suggestions on where to hike. I embarked on the project, and for nine months—using all my vacation time, weekends, and holidays—hiked and wrote *Hiking Illinois*.

Have you ever wondered if the hike is as accurate as the writer has portrayed it? For once such hike, the Red Oak Backpack Trail at Siloam Springs State Park, "the rest of the story" was quite different than what appeared in print. The only hints in the book are, "The trail can be very muddy and slick when wet, and some stream crossings may be difficult in wet weather," and, "If the water is low, this presents no problem. If you happen to hike during or after a heavy rainfall, you might have to retrace your steps and find a suitable log on which to cross." While these sound only like cautionary warnings and nothing more, such was not the case.

The Weather Channel in the hotel said rain, locally heavy, with possible flash floods in low-lying areas. My trail partner and I shook our heads; this translated into another day of hiking in the rain.

We easily found the park and prepared to hike—waterproof hiking boots, raincoat and hat, and umbrellas. We went ahead and donned our raincoats, as the sky was already gray, and embarked on the trail. The trail showed signs of the previous week's rains—everywhere wet and soggy, some parts with deep puddles, and the mud a light tan and slick as ice. Upward we climbed, quarter-mile markers keeping track of distance. When it began to rain, out popped the umbrellas and we continued on. This was nothing new; after all, this was hike # 63 and it had rained before (quite often!).

We marveled at the ferns and an oak opening on a ridge with a scattering of bi-colored bird's-foot violets as we descended into the floodplain of Silver Creek. A tributary had overtaken the trail as its own. We fanned out, looking for any dry spot or sticks and logs to walk on. My feet were now wet as we rejoined the trail. The next obstacle was the creek—an easy crossing at any dry time, but not today. The waist-high, light brown water was (no exaggeration!) a raging torrent. Back up the trail, we retraced our steps for almost half a mile to eventually practice our balance beam act on a slim tree (moss-covered and slick of course). We managed to cross the stream without plunging into the water swirling beneath us and blazed a trail back to the original spot. With pedometer back on, we headed upward. Ah, "dry" ground again.

We now heard distant rumblings, but they went unheeded. Suddenly, at the trail's half-way point a loud CRACK! celebrated the start of a massive thunderstorm, undoubtedly a deep red on Doppler radar. The umbrellas (now aluminum lightning rods) were quickly stowed. I wanted this hiking guide to be an electrifying experience, but not that kind. With the loud crash, the rain came down in sheets. The speed of the hike picked up, as the downpour continued. Our feet now sloshed in our boots, while our clothing clung to us.

At 3.25 miles we were nearly done; only one last descent remained. We headed downward, although sliding would be a better word for our descent as a river of water accompanied us down the trail. Near the bottom I saw a rapidly spreading sea of brown—the final "creek" crossing. I was barely able to make the leap across a small, but rapidly rising "rivulet." The trail was now gone, covered by a river of brown, muddy water. But we only had half mile to go! The trouble was, we could see no trail under the swirling water in the valley, and dozens of alternative "trails" were now actually streams cascading down from the surrounding uplands. Just which one was the trail? We made a quick decision; too bad it wasn't made at the top of the hill, and decided to backtrack and try to bushwhack the last half mile.

First, my husband stopped to wipe his glasses and I commented "that's why I have contacts—no wiping!" Two minutes later, while attempting to make a trail, a branch hit me in the face and my left contact disappeared into the wet leaf litter—a present for a damp vole or centipede. With somewhat obscured vision, and much swearing, I managed to releap the still-rising rivulet. Luckily, there were strong, albeit wet hands to catch me on the other side.

We slogged our way back up hill on wet leaves (the trail was now impassable) to a forest road and had to guess which way led out. Our map had disintegrated into a sodden mass. The lightning, fortunately, had stopped and so had the sheeting rain. It was now nothing more than a gentle downpour. Finally, a park trail board came into view, and we were back on an asphalt path and returned on park roads to our vehicle. Between us and the dry, safe vehicle, however, was a rapidly rising brown cascade—a miniature Colorado River in an equally miniature, but growing, Grand Canyon of Siloam Springs State Park.

We managed to cross in the drizzle, and we were back at the picnic shelter. Hike #63 was finished (if not technically completed), my notes somewhat soggy, but readable. We savored our first hike in a flash flood, but the day was young, so we put on dry socks and continued on, consoled by the fact that somewhere in the park was a vole with 20/20 vision, at least in one eye.

Epilogue:

I did not visit Siloam Springs State Park again until 2007, when I again was working to write an updated version of *Hiking Illinois*. I chose to hike in early September; of course, it was dry with no threat of rain. The hike proceeded without any problems, and I finally got to hike the "real" ending of the trail, marveling at the trickle of a stream that was a raging torrent not so long ago.

The hike finished, my spouse and I were on to the next site. As I was driving I felt a tingling or crawling sensation on my ankles. I said "Chiggers!" (I am chigger phobic, having had more than my share of red welts.) My spouse said "no, it's too late in the season." I said, "something is crawling on me, you must be wrong." He insisted that he knew what he was talking about.

Soon my spouse was scratching as well. I could not stand the itching and tingling, so I headed the car into a pull off, got out and lifted my pant leg, revealing socks covered with tiny (size of a pin-head) ticks; hundreds, even thousands crawling on my socks and ankles. (I was busy looking at migrating warblers prior to starting out on the hike, so I forgot to spray with repellent.) Of course my first reaction was to scream, but then I went into action. Using insect repellent (DEET) cloths, I wiped both ankles and legs (luckily I was wearing pants in which the legs zipped off.) As soon as the repellent touched the ticks they shriveled and died. (This was a good, satisfying feeling.) My husband noticed he too was infested. Luckily, it was a Sunday afternoon on a back road and no one came by, wondering what these two people were doing jumping up and down, ripping off half their pants, and repeatedly wiping their legs.

We put the used wipes, our socks, and the bottom leg portion of our pants in a plastic bag, hoping this would kill any remaining arachnid vermin. The next day, when I looked at my legs, the scars of my hike were evident. I had red welts that outlined the ribbing of my socks. This "reminder" lingered, and itched, for over a month. Needless to say, my next visit to Siloam Springs will probably not be for another 10 years. I just can't handle the stress of a park so noted and touted for its calming and soothing qualities.

Not a night on Bald Mountain, but close, very close . . .

Job of My Dreams: A Night on Bath Chute
Kevin S. Irons

Coming to the Illinois Natural History Survey (INHS) as a technical research scientist fulfilled two of my life-long dreams: working with natural resources and being able to catch fish on a daily basis. The INHS is a vital player in a Long Term Resource Monitoring Program (LTRM) that monitors fish communities (as well as invertebrates, water quality, and records information on land use and water levels) on the La Grange Reach of the Illinois River. This program, with the help of other agencies, also monitors five Mississippi River reaches to gather long-term data. What a great opportunity! I pinch myself on a daily basis while launching boats on this wide, murky river to collect fish, using everything from a common seine to the typical river sampling gear of hoop nets, and ultimately an 18-foot-long pulsed direct current (DC) electroshocking boat. How cool is that! Perhaps it is my short attention span or need for instant gratification, but shocking has always been the most enjoyable way to "fish."

During my first sampling season we were going out daily on the Illinois River to collect fish. We shocked fixed sites, both during day-time and night-time hours. A typical night included launching the boat after dark and shocking up to six sites, usually until the wee hours of the morning. In 1991, the river had just experienced a couple of years of drought with low flows, which had left logs and trees strewn throughout the river and its side channels. One night in particular, we were "puttin-in" at Bath, Illinois, on Bath Chute, home of the floating boat bar (locally notorious for all sorts of wild tales). Over the years many people have exited the boat bar (even after it was dry-docked some years later) to comment to us on current river ecology events. We've heard, "What's up with those zebra clams (mussels)?" "What are we gonna do about all those (Asian) flying carp?" "How is the river doing right now?" "Those bass boats need to slow down a bit when runnin' by here!" or simple questions such as "Whatcha you guys doin? Shockin?"

I've always enjoyed talking to the locals here. The people around the Illinois are genuinely concerned about their river and amazingly up to date on the issues. Yet, I digress. We were launching our boat at the ramp on this balmy fall evening, making sure to put on bright orange rain suits to protect our clothes from the thousands of fish we were sure to encounter during our six, 15-minute shocking runs. Generally, 400–500 fish would surface during these runs; everything from ancient-looking gar, minnows, and bass, to large flathead catfish. On this particular night, however, something else grabbed our attention. After our second shocking run, estimated at around 11:00 pm, a storm blew in. Although we had seen it flashing a warning over nearby Fulton County, we thought (hoped?) it might skip us to the north. It did not. For the next three hours we were stranded on the shores of Grand Island, discussing our faith in God, hoping that the boat wouldn't be swamped and sink, and wondering, "Is it really safe to be standing under these tall cottonwood trees when lightning is bouncing off similar ones just across the chute?" We huddled around each other with three of us taking turns, every 10 minutes, to run down the muddy bank to turn on the boat's bilge pump. The water in that short time period would fill the bilge (the area under the floor boards), and begin flooding the floor. We also were using the five gallons of extra fuel to help start a fire (and keep it going), but to no avail. Even with the able assistance of gasoline, the torrential rain was quickly putting any fire out.

Escape was neither an option nor possible. The dangerous, log-strewn, watery, path back to the boat ramp (10–15 minutes in good conditions) was beyond boating. The strong winds had ripped the fading leaves from trees and they covered the chute like a blanket, hiding any safe passageway between the logs. Additionally, the lightning was going off like flashbulbs, and each of us mentally asked ourselves, "Would it be wise to travel in a boat, moreover, one that was wired for electricity, in such a storm?"

The storm lasted for nearly three hours, when, as suddenly as someone turning off a light switch, the winds calmed to barely a breeze, the trees stopped dancing, and the few remaining, straggling leaves fell like helicopters to join their fellows already covering the water. It was amazing. The chute, some seven miles long, was totally leaf-covered. Everything in view of our floodlight, river channel and banks included, looked just like the floodplain forest floor. Where one stopped and another began was impossible to distinguish.

We did manage to finish our shocking runs that night, returning to town with the rising sun. In retrospect, what I learned that evening was that it was important to spend the night on the river and get to know the innermost (although strained) thoughts of a couple of biologists who are now my close friends, to survive the ordeal, to arrive safely back at the field station with data in hand, and perhaps most importantly, to learn to keep a better eye on the radar. By the way, this continues to be the job of my dreams!

Chapter 6

Field Mishaps

Freeport, IL May 5, 1880

I haven't been out of the house for some time. Indeed (don't be very much alarmed) I have been confined to my bed for several hours. It happened this way. The boat we had yesterday was about large enough for one, and we, foolishly perhaps, made it carry three and all our belongings. By sitting flat on the bottom and balancing skillfully we got on without accident until the middle of the afternoon, when we tried to get the boat around the dam. As we started across I told the oarsman to pull up the stream a little way before striking for the other side, so as to avoid the rush of water as it poured over the brink. He obeyed, carelessly, struck a snag . . . .there was a smooth gliding and a deafening rush of water down the straight front of the dam, and, notwithstanding Pearsol's most violent exertions, we found ourselves on the jagged rocks at the foot of the fall. We were some of us seriously hurt, but, after trying to work a while longer I came home and went to bed (at ten o,clock) and slept like a log until a few minutes since, when the songs of the birds and streaming of the sunlight through the blinds aroused me to fond remembrances of the little flock in the fold at home. (About our boat, of course you understand that we landed quietly on the other side and carried the skiff around the end of the dam.)

A bored INHS editor gets to experience the thrill, the exhilaration, the shock, of field work.

The Electric Canoe
Charlie Warwick

One spring morning in 1995 I was at my desk dealing with the minutia of desktop editing—*em* dashes, smart quotes, or reduced leading in the lines of a title, et cetera. At that time, my office was in the Natural Resources Building, a classic brick Georgian structure on the University of Illinois campus. The building was designed to blend in with others with similar features to give them a unified, "planned" appearance. Unlike the low-bid architecture now in vogue, hermetically sealed from the elements outside, the Natural Resources Building had windows that could be opened to invite a bit of the outdoors inside.

That morning, my window funneled a pleasing, multi-sensory background to the more focused attention I was giving to the computer screen. Almost subconsciously, my ears gathered in the call of an American Robin in the red oak only a few feet away; my peripheral vision absorbed the lavender and ivory wavelengths of blooming magnolias across the street; my face reveled in a breeze laden with the scent of lilacs—all made available by a simple piece of glass that could be raised or lowered at will.

These sights and sounds of spring began to overshadow my focus on editing. I felt envy for my colleagues who perform the crucial fieldwork for the Illinois Natural History Survey. They had the good fortune to be out and about, luxuriating in this vernal abundance, while I was imprisoned in an office. Little did I know at that moment how naïve and idealistic I was about scientific fieldwork.

Gradually the sound of footsteps in the corridor superimposed themselves upon my awareness. Each of us has a unique way of walking, as individual as fingerprints. We announce ourselves to others even before they see us by the sound of our footfall.

The steps now approaching were those of INHS researcher Michael Jeffords. Although he treaded lightly, he was betrayed by the tell-tale jingle of keys on his belt. Like any custodian worth his broom, Michael resorted to wearing his keys because they were too numerous to fit into his pockets. There, they would only wear holes in a day or two and all his loose change and personal detritus would slide down his inseam and tumble out his cuffs along with the keys. No, Michael kept his keys easy to access and ready for action—a kind of authority symbol like a doctor's stethoscope or a judge's gavel. The poet in me saw those keys as fitting metaphoric tools for his status as a scientist and educator. His keys might open many closed doors to real rooms; yet, they also proclaimed Michael's calling to unlock knowledge and inspiration of the natural world in the minds and hearts of his fellow citizens.

The rhythmic jangle of keys ceased as his lean silhouette stood quietly, framed by my doorway. He said he had a proposition, a kind of key to get me released into the great outdoors. The Illinois Nature Conservancy had asked him to document the natural history as well as land-owner impact upon the Mackinaw River in McLean County, between Colfax and Lexington. He would do a photo reconnaissance of the river near its source to create a multimedia program to present to a group of landowners called the Mackinaw River Consortium.

Ironically, Michael wasn't interested in whatever editorial skills I might bring to bear to this project. He said he only required "my body and my canoe"—not necessarily in that priority. He had to have some way of getting down the river with his tripod, cameras, and lenses, not to mention lunch. However, someone else would have to do the "driving" so he could concentrate on taking photos. He hypothesized, perhaps not completely accurately, that as a canoe owner I could handle whatever navigatory challenges the river could throw at us—that I would provide him both a chauffeur and aquatic limo in one stroke.

Michael is a quick study on everything. He thinks, decides, and acts before most mortals can blink. I was still trying to process his proposition internally as he stood silently tapping his foot, waiting for some kind of intelligible acknowledgement from me.

As my thoughts became less whirlpool and more flow, I notice that Michael's face had an incredulous glare. His thoughts, though silent, were both palpable and unmistakable— "Dude, this is a no-brainer, what is there to ponder here?"

Consequently, that night I found myself in our garage, contemplating the canoe and which paddles to use. The beaver-tail paddles were a joy to hold. With their glossy varnish they looked and felt good in your hands. There was something that felt natural and inevitable to their touch, as if they had evolved and formed precisely to be grasped by hominids with opposable thumbs. The blades of these wooden masterpieces could simultaneously slice through and push against water as fluidly as the proverbial hot knife negotiating a stick of butter.

The collapsible, aluminum kayak paddles, on the other hand, were all lightness and utility. What they lacked in poetry and ambiance they made up for in efficiency. A single person wielding kayak paddles could propel and maneuver a boat faster and easier than a canoe with two paddlers. Because I was going to be the sole paddler on this expedition, I went with the aluminum kayak option—a fateful decision if there ever was one.

It felt good to be in the canoe going with the current as Michael perched in the bow with his camera poised and ready. I was anticipating our arrival at a stand of old-growth sycamores a mile or two downstream. These pale giants along the river's banks were said to house a nesting colony of Great Blue Herons. This bird was special to me because it was our older daughter Aliyah's favorite, and intimately associated with canoeing in our family.

The first time we used the boat was on the Salt Fork of the Vermilion River system near Homer Lake. As we drifted around a bend, a heron arose and soared in Jurassic dignity over the bow. Aliyah, then a three-year-old, seemed to be in a rapture as the seven-foot wingspan of this heron disappeared beyond the next bend. I told her she had seen her first Great Blue Heron. And she wondered aloud if it had "another name," like the House Wren in the Mister Roger's song she knew that celebrated this bird using its scientific binomial *Troglodytes aedon*.

She was thrilled to learn that the Great Blue Heron was also known as *Ardea herodias*. This was how she would refer to the Great Blue from then on, and she would judge the success of subsequent canoe outings according to the number of *Ardea herodias* we encountered.

As Michael and I floated along the Mackinaw, which at this point was little more than a brook, I was hoping to report to Aliyah that evening that we had visited an entire village of Great Blue Herons. I imagined that by her definition of success, today we would be having the best canoe adventure ever. Little did I know that we would be giving a new meaning to the definition of "best."

The flow of my thoughts was soon interrupted by a sudden, almost imperceptible, flash of sun ahead of the canoe. An incongruous and out-of-kilter horizontal band of light persisted in my field of vision, although my mind could neither grasp nor give name to this phenomenon.

Like the "instant replay" technology that is the stock and trade of sports castors these days, I must back up the tape in my memory banks and replay slowly what happened next to attempt to describe the blur of events that now occurred. In reality the ensuing action was not a sequence neatly ordered in the space/time continuum, but an instinctive blast from the limbic system—a pure and primal fight/flight reaction that overrode the rational mind.

The horizontal band of light that my "rational" cerebral cortex was unable to process, but which my primitive "reptilian" brain perceived clearly and immediately, was the wire of an electrified cow fence stretching across the river in front of us. It was about to catch Michael chest high.

I found myself thrusting the paddle deep into the current and pushing back against it with a fury I didn't know that I possessed. The canoe swung instantly 90 degrees to the right, where Michael was now facing the river bank instead of the cow fence spanning the stream. However, the full 17-foot aluminum superstructure of the canoe, now parallel to the cow fence, was swept sideways by the current toward an imminent encounter with hundreds of volts of electricity.

Perhaps there was some residual rational function in my cortex, a blurry, smudged remnant like the cloud of radiation at the edge of the universe that belies the original big bang. This distorted rationality that condensed in my consciousness thought it saw a way to avoid the big bang that was now approaching. It became convinced that the canoe was going to slide under the cow fence without contact. All I had to do was leap over the fence's live wire as the canoe floated, untouched, under it and I would land in the boat downstream of the fence.

Obediently my body arose to standing position in the canoe with knees bent and ready to spring. I pushed off at the last moment, but somehow never became air-borne. The very act of exerting downward pressure on the canoe with feet and legs caused it to slide out from under me. Instead of deftly hopping the fence and coming down in the canoe, I was flailing backward out of the boat, simultaneously pushing it closer to the cow fence. A second consequence of my inspired great leap was that without my weight in the back of the canoe to hold it low in the water, it rose several inches higher with disastrous results for Michael, who had elected the opposite approach to me.

With an assemblage of camera equipment and film attached or stashed about his person, he opted to protect the tools of his trade by folding himself forward in the position recommended by airlines before a plane crashes. His very sensible and yes, rational, act had the potential to save both himself and his equipment if he could just clear the electrified wire as it passed over him and the canoe. Unfortunately, as he was ducking, I was falling and pushing the canoe toward the fence.

When I bobbed to the surface and stood chest-deep in midstream, I heard a nauseating "zap," "zap," "zap," "zap" . . . . I immediately understood why my dairy farmer friends in Minnesota referred to their cow fences as "weed zappers." The term not only described the sound of contacting such a fence, it also described the result.

The canoe, with a hunkered Michael Jeffords, was caught on the fence. Rather, the whole length of Michael's back was snagged on the wire. His spine was receiving continuous pulses of electricity that announced their contact with him in an insistent rhythm of zaps. And he could only sit there and take them.

Inexplicably, the kayak paddle was still in my hands after the plunge. Desperately, I lunged its full length at the boat, attempting to push the canoe and Michael out from under the cow fence. The paddle's aluminum shaft, however, touched a now very electric aluminum canoe, and I became the recipient of an electric jolt that surged from hands to feet. The accompanying zap, while the paddle bolted from my grip, was a kind of backbeat to the zaps that Michael was continuing to produce.

I was the lucky one, though. My ordeal was over after a single zap.

Somehow, by blind luck, divine intervention, or Michael's inner instinct for survival, he extricated himself from the cow fence. He finally broke the circuit of which he had become an unintended on/off switch.

Dazed, but apparently still residing in his body, Michael and the canoe drifted soundlessly to the shore. Our field trip down the Mackinaw was not yet 10 minutes old.

We took a quick inventory of equipment, supplies, and body parts. Nothing was missing or even damaged, so we decided to continue. The lure of the unknown was greater than the fear of the unexpected.

We floated on to find the nesting colony of *Ardea herodias* and were rewarded by a deer that loped beside us for many yards as we drifted nearby. Rare mayflies and dragonflies in the air and mussels in the water indicated that this reach of the Mackinaw had a fairly high degree of biological integrity. In spite of human-induced changes, such as the six electric cow fences we encountered that day or cattle grazing in the riverbed, the Mackinaw stood a good chance of surviving, if people living along its waters could be persuaded to make relatively small changes in their land-use habits.

There was something noble and uplifting in the memory of Michael Jeffords' refusal to abandon his cameras to save his skin. He persisted in the face of danger and bodily harm and went on to take the photos by which he educated the very folks who had, perhaps unmindfully, strung live electric wires for private use across a waterway that belongs to all of us. His images, acquired with some rather intense physical discomfort, would be the means by which he attempted to change the thinking and behavior of landowners along the Mackinaw.

For me, Michael became the personification of all the field researchers at INHS. Each of them willingly sacrifices personal comfort year in and year out in the pursuit of knowledge to benefit both their environment and their society.

Our little adventure in an electric canoe became a metaphor for private interests constantly colliding and interacting with the natural functioning of the state's plant and animal communities. In part, those electric cow fences are a wake up call for the custodians of the environment to stay alert and constantly active in pursuing natural science to influence environmental policies that will benefit our biological heritage.

In part, the cow fences tell us that the tug of war between private and collective interests will be with us as long as humans walk this planet. We are at once selfish and selfless, provincial and universal—solitary and social creatures who must continue to act locally but think globally. This is our nature, our destiny, our function in the scheme of things.

"My boots, my boots, my kingdom for my boots."

Up to My Ass !
Anne Bartlett

While working on a graduate student's wetland bird study at Chautauqua National Wildlife Refuge (NWR) near Havana, Illinois, I went to the water's edge to collect benthic invertebrate samples (bottom-dwelling insects, crayfish, worms, etc.). I was admiring the student's collecting invention, and didn't worry that my feet were sinking into the pure, wet silt. Samples in hand, I tried to turn and leave. I was stuck. With great effort, I pulled first one, (THWUCK!) then the other (MWICK!) foot from the silt. Pant! Gasp! Every time I pulled a leg out, it had to go back in. Ugh! I could have crawled, but it was spring, chilly, and there was a long field day ahead of me. Each stride sank deeper than the last.

My hip waders were too big, so I could only pull them out of the muck with my toes pointed up. With my toes pointed down to decrease resistance, my feet simply came out of the boots. The mud wanted those boots, but I wanted them more. Finding waders that almost fit had been a coup. I'd been handicapped by huge men's boots at a previous National Park Service job. Knowing the extreme difficulty of finding waders for women, I'd purchased a pile of them for the park and a pair for myself. Giving these up was not an option. After all, I was only about 10 paces from the grassy area and maybe 20 from the truck.

By the fourth step, my legs were mired too deeply to pull out with their waning strength. I pushed my arm into the cool, silky, muck, past the elbow, grabbed my heel, and wrenched it out. Oh well, staying clean and dry wasn't really that important. I hesitated to step down, causing the other leg to sink to an alarming depth. Dowsed in cold, wet sludge, gasping, fatigued, and aching, my composure had fled with my strength. Every effort was accompanied by grunts, curses, pleas for help, and the occasional useless, but satisfying scream of rage.

It took nearly 20 minutes to extricate my leg from each step. It drained me. Unable to bear stepping back into the muck, I laid my left knee across the mud and rested briefly. I had moved six steps in about an hour. The right leg was buried almost to the top of my thigh. I tugged with my legs and from every reachable angle with both hands. The leg wouldn't budge. The mud was starting to constrict my ankle and I was out of strength.

Physical power never was my trump card. It was time to think my way out of this. What could I do? A rope! I had a good strong rope in the truck, but the truck was still 30 feet away. I could empathize with Tantalus, but not pull myself out with a rope. What about getting help? My cell phone! Also, in the truck. At least it wouldn't suffer the same fate my binoculars were in for. Aargh! If someone drove by, would they see me? Probably not. The truck blocked my view of the road. No matter; no one came by.

Although teetering on the brink of insane frustration, I wasn't afraid. Then my seething brain started to mess with me. A heart-breaking episode of "National Geographic Explorer" began playing in my mental venue. A herd of mighty elephants labored to rescue their adorable baby mired in mud. He wailed, and his mama and aunties worked and trumpeted for days. He died there. The herd stayed with him until hunger drove them away. Hang the stupid boot! It was to blame for this predicament. I yanked my leg up out of the boot, sprawled across the mud, and wallowed to the grass. Three inches of boot stuck out of the mud, like the tongue of an impudent brat. Aside from a few damp depressions that remained of my "footprints," the soil once again appeared smooth and firm as a baby elephant's butt.

After nearly a half an hour of wheezing and venting on the grass, I hobbled to the truck, drove to a spot where rocks went down to the water, and washed off as much filth as possible. At the end of the day I limped into the NWR office. The staff's curiosity at my disheveled state was obvious, so I shared the story. Their uproarious laughter helped to wash away what remained of my mud-hued irritation, but I could only muster a feeble grin in gratitude. I won't soon forget how that boot leered at me throughout the season. For all I know, it may be there still.

Where did that come from?

Collecting Alfalfa Weevils and Other Critters
Ed Armbrust

My most memorable alfalfa weevil collecting trip took place at Dixon Springs in southern Illinois with several of my graduate students. While crawling around in waist-high alfalfa looking for adult weevils on the ground, I felt an intense itch in my groin. Upon investigating, I was horrified to find a critter clinging to the hair. I yelled for Judy, a student who was making a required insect collection, to bring a vial.

I suspect she was one of the few students, likely the only one that year, who had a *Phthirus pubis* (crab louse) in their insect collection. I suggested that she not list my name on the label as the host.

Beware of witches on All Hallow's Eve!

A Halloween Adventure
Matt O'Neal as told to Susan Post

I had just returned from the Peace Corps in 1995 and was not sure what I wanted to do. Luckily, I was able to get a job at the Illinois Natural History Survey as a summer hourly with Dr. Eli Levine. Eli was a corn entomologist, specializing in corn rootworms and diapause (how the beetles overwinter and where—either in corn or soybeans). During that summer I worked extensively with corn rootworms and bean leaf beetles.

All things considered, it was a pretty good summer. The corn rootworms had been laying eggs in soybeans and we needed to sample those fields. We tried digging the samples by hand with a cup sampler (a.k.a., golf ball cup digger), but it was a hot, tedious process and took forever. In the mind of this overheated, sweaty, even feverish field hand, there had to be a better way. Why not use a Ditch Witch?

We rented said implement locally and went to pick it up. Along with Eli and me came Jimmy Finger, one of the Survey's farm assistants. The machine proved to be a monster. It was great—self-propelled with a 10-horse power engine. Already, I envisioned zipping across the field at near breakneck speed while generating mounds of the necessary samples.

Jimmy managed to maneuver the Ditch Witch onto the trailer where we started it up. The grand, hulking machine, although a little too noisy to say it purred like a kitten, ran just fine. Jimmy hooked up the trailer lights for us and we were ready to go. After assuring Jimmy that we could handle this by ourselves, off we went. It was a fall day, but felt more like summer—hot and miserable. Boy, was it going to be great to be automated! No more sweaty digging for me!

At our first field site we stopped near a culvert to unload the Ditch Witch from the trailer and pulled the truck and trailer out of the field. I started up the digger and everything was going great, for about 100 yards into the field, when Eli decided we'd better check the oil. The Ditch Witch stopped, and for the next three hours refused to start. We even used an entire can of Spray N' Go to speed the process—nothing.

Our "easy" day was done. Even though we couldn't use the machine, we still had to complete the sampling, so we returned to the back-breaking hand digging. Finally it was completed and we loaded the now dead machine back on the trailer, hooked the trailer up to the truck, and hit the highway. After an hour or so, we needed a break; the digging had been brutally hard work and we were hungry. A stop at McDonalds was in order; it was a large one with a truck stop attached—good for us and our large load. We parked and went in.

After lunch, we headed to the next field site. I was half asleep and we were halfway to the next site when it dawned on me that we had a big truck with a loaded trailer, and I didn't see its shadow on the road. I looked out at the mirror, yet still didn't see a shadow. I was thinking, maybe it was in our blind spot, so we pulled over—no trailer! Hmm! We were a half hour from our lunch stop so we decided to go on to our next field site and pick the trailer up on the way home. The trailer must have become unhitched at McDonalds, and we just left it.

As we sampled this site the old fashioned way, we were laughing to ourselves, wondering how we could have failed to notice the absence of the large trailer and orange Ditch Witch.

When we returned to McDonalds no trailer was in sight. We rationalized this away by saying, "Oh, it was probably moved for safety reasons." It didn't occur to us how the McDonalds staff could have moved the heavy trailer, just that they probably had. We drove around the parking lot, but the trailer, with the Ditch Witch, was simply not there.

In a mild panic we retraced our route back to the first field site as fast as possible, and there, stuck in the field at an odd angle, was the Ditch Witch, but, alas, with no trailer. At that moment Eli and I looked at each other and said, "Holy #!*%." The trailer had become disconnected from the truck, ejected the Ditch Witch, and gone off to do who knew what. This was not a good day.

In fact, we were frantic; we had to find the trailer. One would think that such a quest would be easy in mile after mile of mind-numbing, Illinois flatness, but the offending trailer was nowhere to be seen. We retraced our steps again, this time going slowly, searching down each back road we passed. We nervously approached the occasional house, hoping not to see the trailer protruding from someone's living room, or worse, having a local news crew on the site of a hot breaking story of a runaway, mystery trailer that impaled grandma so-and-so as she sat in her kitchen shelling peas.

The nightmare had to end and we finally spied, not the trailer, but its path of destruction. There, at a bend in the road, we found a newly created path that led through a pulverized fence, into a cemetery, leaving a trail of broken tombstones. Now we spotted our trailer, askew and embedded in a large gravestone.

Now what? "Let's just leave," I thought to myself, "after all today is Halloween and no one will know. They'll just think it was Halloween pranksters." But then I turned around, and standing at the side of the road was a young kid with a wide-eyed, blank look on his face. All of a sudden it dawned on me, "Holy #!*%, we have a witness."

We managed to retrieve our trailer from the cemetery, this time taking care to connect it properly. Next, we drove back to the first field to collect our useless Ditch Witch, made sure it was secure, and limped back to Champaign at 45 mph. It was late on a Friday night by the time we got back to town, and Eli (of greater moral character than I), wanted to know what we should do. I said, "I'm not sure," and went home to prepare for some (more) Halloween fun.

Eli, bless his soul, did not have as carefree a weekend as I did. I later found out that he had worried and stewed the entire weekend. He kept thinking, "We need to do something."

On Monday morning, Eli called the cemetery caretaker, told him what had happened, and asked how to pay for the damages to the cemetery. The caretaker's response was simple. "Thank you for calling," he cheerfully said, "but don't worry about it, it happens all the time!"

All your senses . . .

A Rattlesnake Tale
Kenneth R. Robertson

On, May 12, 1987 I attended a meeting of the Illinois Nature Preserves Commission in Galena, which is at the extreme northwestern corner of Illinois. During the meeting, a new area was proposed for listing as an officially dedicated nature preserve—Hanover Bluff. This sounded like an intriguing area, with hill prairies and other unusual habitats, plus several rare species of plants. One rare animal species was also mentioned, the state-endangered timber rattlesnake.

The mention of the rattlesnake did register with me. You see, I am hard of hearing, a genetic condition shared with both my parents as well as my brother. Why do rattlesnakes rattle? Obviously to warn larger creatures that they are in the vicinity and to stay away. Alas, that warning adaptation does not work well for me. Now, I don't mind snakes when I see them, but I would prefer that my defective genes not be eliminated from the human gene pool because of a rattlesnake that I could not hear!

But, back to the story. Hanover Bluff. In looking at a map, Hanover Bluff was not much out of the way on the route back to Champaign from Galena. It was a beautiful day in May, I was by myself and had no set schedule, and there was still plenty of daylight, so why not stop for a visit? Even though I had detailed topographic maps showing the precise location of the hill prairies at Hanover Bluff, it was rather difficult to find them. They are up on the top of bluffs and cannot be seen from the road that runs along the base of the bluff as forest covers the lower slopes. I parked the car, grabbed my camera bag, and hiked up through a wooded ravine that promised to lead to the hill prairies.

Soon, I saw an opening in the woods that led out onto a large hill prairie with a fabulous view over the broad floodplain of the Mississippi River that contained the Savanna Army Depot. At that time, the Army depot had been closed to the public, as well as botanists in search of rare plants, since 1917. The hill prairie was ablaze with some early spring plants (remember that May is indeed early spring up near the Wisconsin line), such as *Oxalis violacea* (purple wood sorrel), *Lithospermum incisum* (fringed puccoon), *Nothocalais cuspidata* (prairie dandelion), and *Besseya bullii* (kitten tails). So, I started taking photographs.

Hill prairies usually occur on steep, southwest facing slopes, and that is the case at Hanover Bluff. After taking some photos, I sat the camera down on the ground in order to collect a few herbarium specimens. What I did not anticipate was that the slope of the hill was so steep that the camera bag tipped over and the camera and contents rolled out and tumbled down the hill and off the cliff!

I worked my way down a rocky slope to the base of the hill prairie near the top of the bluff and then down the bluff a few ledges, going as far as I could. I found a lens cap and my Swiss Army knife, but the camera was long gone. It was a new camera too, so I was rather upset. Slowly, I worked my way back up the ledges, none too carefully, still angry at losing the camera. And just as my eyes became level with a ledge, what before my wondrous eyes should appear? Yee gads, a timber rattlesnake!! All coiled up! Looking me right in the face! The tail vibrating. Not that I, with my bad ears, could hear any rattling, of course. It's amazing how quickly the adrenaline kicked in, and my heart was racing. I know what you're thinking now—but the answer is no, I did not soil myself, or even scream, er, at least not very loud.

Reflexes kicked in and I jerked backwards, grabbing hold of a sturdy red cedar branch with my left hand to keep my body from joining my camera at the base of the cliff. Unfortunately, I knocked my glasses off in the process, and I'm pretty well blind without my glasses. (It's bad to have a semi-deaf, blind guy on a cliff near a rattlesnake.) The glasses went to my left, while the rattling rattlesnake was to my right. Hoping that there was only one snake around, I felt around on the ledge to my left and found my glasses.

By now, I was far enough from the snake that I could get a good look at him. Nice rattlesnake, too. Gee, I sure wished that I had my camera—could have gotten some great photos—would have called them "Eye Level with a Rattlesnake." It turns out the rattlesnake was on a ledge right beside the trail I had come down, so I must have walked right by it before. Fortunately, timber rattlesnakes are not very aggressive, unlike some of their western cousins. But now that I saw the snake, no way was I was going to walk right past him again!

So, the snake and I looked at each other for quite a while. Finally, the snake decided that he should get out of my way, uncoiled, and started working its way along the face of the bluff. Another great photo opportunity gone to waste! After he had moved on, I scrambled back up to the hill prairie, retrieved my camera bag, and, looking ever so carefully where I walked, headed back to the car. It took quite a while before my heartbeat returned to normal.

This could be the end of the story. But it's not.

When I got back to my office the next day, I called Randy Nÿboer, then with the Illinois Department of Natural Resources, to let him know that if they ever found a camera at the base of Hanover Bluff, it would be mine. They were actually much more interested in my sighting of the rattlesnake than my lost camera! Since it is an endangered species in Illinois, they conduct yearly surveys to see how they're doing.

The last photo from the camera before the "incident."

A couple of years went by.

At a conference at Eastern Illinois University, following the lunch break, I was summoned onto the stage. Randy Nÿboer told the audience that sometimes I had been known to leave behind more than footprints. Randy grabbed a large, burlap bag from behind the lectern, put on a long thick leather glove, opened up the bag (my eyes were pretty wide open by that time), and pulled out a large, plastic snake, which he tossed through the air to me! That, of course, got a big laugh from the audience. Randy reached into the burlap again, and this time he brought out my camera that had been found at the bottom of the bluff. It was one, very smashed-up camera to be sure. They actually found the camera the year after I lost it while surveying for rattlesnakes.

That camera now sits in my office on a shelf as a kind of trophy. And when persons visiting my office ask about it, well, you know, out pours my rattlesnake tale.

Robertson and his "famous" camera.

Dirty jobs.

Entering the Retch Zone
John B. Taft

You might not consider livestock rendering and the 1993 flood (an event that had devastating consequences to Illinois citizens along the Mississippi River) to have any plausible connection to a botanist or a herpetologist. I, too, would not have assumed so, until I entered the retch zone. This story involves the events on a stifling, hot, mid-September day in 1997, but has its origins in the 1993 flood that caused a rare Illinois endemic plant species, the decurrent false aster, to expand its range.

The decurrent false aster (*Boltonia decurrens*) is one of the very few plant species that has a range that is geographically limited, almost entirely, to Illinois. It occurs in scattered populations in wetlands along the Illinois River from LaSalle County to the mouth of the river, as well as a few locations in neighboring Missouri counties (which makes it not a true Illinois endemic, but this is about as close as we get in a state with few natural barriers to dispersal). In recognition of its rarity, the U.S. Fish and Wildlife Service listed it as a threatened species in 1988. Following the 1993 Mississippi River floods, several colonies were discovered near wetlands in the East St. Louis area of Madison and St. Clair counties, well below the mouth of the Illinois River. The establishment of these colonies is possibly a result of seeds transported in floodwaters. This asterlike species is a short-lived perennial that grows to about six feet tall. It has leaf tissue that extends down the petiole and onto the stem. The botanical term "decurrent" is descriptive of this characteristic

The decurrent false aster.

(it means the leaves run down along the stem) and appropriate for both the scientific and common names of this species. The decurrent false aster behaves like an opportunist colonizer of open ground and probably was historically a member of the sparsely vegetated shore community of the back-water lakes, wet prairies, and marshes along the Illinois River. Now, with these habitats largely altered, the species has found other niches, including roadside ditches, recently fallow ground, and cropland. The largest populations I have seen, comprising thousands of plants, have been in soybean fields—quite unusual for a species classified as a federally threatened species. However, to emphasize the often ephemeral nature of colonies, many of these bean field populations have become extirpated in recent years. Through the Conservation Reserve Program, fields left fallow in the Illinois River floodplain have converted to young, floodplain forests. For its population to persist in a site, *Boltonia decurrens* needs a lot of available light and open spaces for seedling establishment.

The colonies of decurrent false aster in Madison and St. Clair counties were discovered during botanical surveys for a proposed highway development project. They were found in wetlands and abandoned crop fields in an area between Horseshoe Lake and a small industrial community called National City (once the home to one of the largest stockyards in the world, and where some "byproduct" industries remained). Given the sometimes short persistence of populations, an up-to-date survey in this area was needed in 1997, and the prime time to search for this species is during its blooming period in mid-September. Surveying populations of this species requires long hours of counting plants and estimating colony sizes, and despite the heat on this particular September day, work progressed routinely, without incident except for the annoyance of the malodorous drift from an upwind livestock rendering facility. On this occasion, my field partner, Chris Phillips, was surveying the same areas, examining habitats for fossorial (soil-inhabiting) species of reptiles and amphibians.

Somehow we managed to save for last the survey of a *Boltonia* population found very near the rendering operation. By 4 p.m., the heat only seemed to grow in intensity, and as we approached this facility, so did the strength of the smell. To describe the smell is not easy, as I have nothing in my experience with which to compare it. Simply put, the odor severely limited the desire to breathe. As you might guess, hiking across fields and holding your breath can only provide limited rewards. Eventually, a breath has to be taken to avoid the risk of suffocation. Through the waves of heat we could see a hapless employee tossing carcasses into a furnace, and we wondered aloud just how he was able to cope, thankful our duties were not exchanged with his.

We walked along a long line of rail cars (probably waiting to receive "product" from this rendering operation) that provided a sort of temporary, though porous, olfactory shield. I somehow was able to plod along, breathing solely through my mouth as infrequently as possible, and surprised that I was able to tolerate the conditions. Perhaps knowing that soon I could find escape in an air-conditioned vehicle with a cold can of soda kept me going.

However, as a clear sign of impending danger, Chris, who had forged ahead just beyond the rail cars, quickly reversed course, pulling his shirt over his mouth and muttering something about "I don't know how you can stand it." I have been a vegetarian my entire adult life, so I was indeed proud of my endurance of this volatized meat odor and wore this minor accomplishment as a badge of honor. However, as I rounded the end of the train cars, the wave that had forced Chris' retreat hit me like a linebacker. Here the odor was not merely an annoyance, as I could sense the essence of this fetidness penetrating every cell in my body. I instantly fell to my knees and retched. I could see Chris had stopped, and for an instant I thought he might be coming back to assist me, but he was only fumbling for his camera. Later, I had to choose my words carefully in a technical report to explain why this last population had not been confirmed for 1997. I could not easily explain that I had entered "the retch zone."

Epilogue: Safe from the smelling fields, Chris and I stopped at his hotel room to clean up. I had lost my lunch and wanted to replace it with dinner, prior to heading home. An hour later the stench was still hanging in the hallway where we had momentarily paused to open the door. For anyone who has ever had a bad day on the job, remember the poor soul working in the rendering plant, and take some relief in knowing that you might not have it so bad after all.

Strange, but, unfortunately, very, very true.

Fragrant Fields
Michael R. Jeffords

In my position of Education/Outreach Coordinator at the Illinois Natural History Survey I'm asked to give lots of presentations to a variety of groups. Other than an occasional equipment mishap, this would seem to be a rather tame type of field work. Such was not the case several years ago when I was asked to be the banquet speaker for a group in far southern Illinois. The event was held at a local restaurant in Dongola called Fragrant Fields. The restaurant was really quite charming. It was a converted mule barn, and the dining room was adjacent to an area that was raised and contained a bed of pea gravel; unusual, but remember that this was a converted barn. My host suggested that I set up my screen in this gravel area. I set the screen up, as usual, and was ready to have dinner when I noticed that my shoes had a layer of gravel stuck to them. Not really thinking, I wiped the gravel off just as something diverted my attention away from my hand. I inadvertently swiped my hand across my nose, and wow, what an olfactory shock! The material binding the gravel to my shoes turned out to be cat feces, and I had just filled both nostrils with this odoriferous mass! It seems the local cat community had been using the gravel pad as a litter box, and for some time. So there I stood, dressed in white shirt and nice pants, in front of a room full of diners with both nostrils full of the aroma of cat crap. Fortunately, no one was paying much attention so I quickly exited stage left to the men's room. It took some time before I was able to remove the last vestiges of "feline essence" from my nostrils, shoes, and hands. Miraculously, my shirt had remained feces-free and the evening proceeded fairly normally from then on. And, by the way, the talk went well.

Chapter 7

To Be a Biologist

Cairo, IL September 13, 1879.

I saw my fishermen yesterday morning and found the promise good for active work, made the preliminary engagements with them, and took the ferry for Bird's Pt. I gathered up much pleasant gossip from an old Cairo doctor whom I picked up on the way over, and we trampled through a cornfield together, he after a patient and I in search of a carrying place. . . . . A dinner rescued from the flies at a boarding house for railroad hands . . . left me with an hour to wait for the ferry boat, and I walked a way of the Cairo and Fulton R.R. I remembered so well. It plunged at once into an almost primeval forest so alive with birds that one might have supposed the place had been named by an ornithologist instead of an arch rebel in honor of himself.

I got back, I went over to Kentucky in a skiff, and arranged to board at a long low country house on the opposite bank, putting up our tents in the vicinity for work-shops and sleeping rooms. I could see through the doors that the beds were at least five feet deep, and that mosquito bars hadn't yet been thought of, and came over to the St. Charles again for an evening's work on my birds and fixtures. A stirring episode was offered by the breaking out of fire in the hold of a large steamer at the levee. She lies now on the opposite bank, where they ran her into shallow water and scuttled her to flood the hold.

Encounter with a turtle.

Journal of Susan Post

July 3, 2004

"Did you see that?" asks Michael, "It looks like a leather purse trying to cross the road." We are heading down the busy Wilmington/Peotone Road near Jordon Creek in early July, scoping out sites for a field trip. We stop the car, turn around and head back; there, slowly crossing the road is a large, dinner plate-sized turtle. We stop, I jump out and whisk the turtle to the safety of the roadside.

I am holding a large, spiny softshell turtle. It is so big that its leather shell has turned to bone. It feels like wet leather and it looks at me with its leech-encrusted head. It is olive green with a pointy nose and flippers with claws. Instead of letting it resume its slow amble among the flooded cornfields, we decide to drive a few miles to the Des Plaines Conservation Area to release it. I put it by my feet in the car and it sits there looking at me.

At the Conservation area we measure its carapace (15 inches long) and then it takes off like a flat, discus-shaped torpedo. Splash—out of site! It is only after the rescue that Michael bothers to tell me that spiny softshell turtles have a nasty bite, just like a snapping turtle.

Sue and her "leather purse."

Outsmarted by a gosling.

Goose Killer
David A. Enstrom

Mom and dad goose and the goslings.

In 1999 I was doing an avian (bird) survey at a typical state-of-the-art wetland mitigation site (a created wetland to replace one destroyed by development) in Cook County, Illinois. This restoration consisted of a series of steep, flooded ponds, each several hectares in size, distributed along Interstate 355. These wetlands are a paradise for Canada Geese; with unlimited food and few predators they are perfect goose nurseries.

At the time I already had a great deal of experience working with wild birds. I had handled everything from Atlantic Puffins to hummingbirds. But I had never held a baby goose. And I wanted to.

One of these wetlands was very isolated. Interstate 355 roared 80 feet overhead along with a maze of on and off ramps, and the only way into the site was a dirt service road and a quarter-mile hike. When my survey was over I was alone with a few Redwinged Blackbirds, a muskrat, and 10 grazing adult Canada Geese with 53 goslings of several sizes. I knew the precise number because I had counted them. I looked around and decided to pick up a gosling, one of the downy ones. There was no harm and the action was sure to be covered by my banding or collecting permits. Why not!

I put down my field gear and quickly had a lovely yellow-grey downy gosling in my hands. The adults sounded the alarm and streaked to the middle of the pond with the rest of the young. After a minute or two of satisfying examination, I went to the edge of the pond and let the gosling drop into the water from a height of three to four inches.

The gosling went straight down and disappeared under the water. The adult geese trumpeted their fury. The gosling stayed down. I stared at the spot where the chick had disappeared. I could see nothing in the murky water but a few tiny, rising bubbles. The bubbles stopped. Time passed. The adult geese stopped trumpeting. The gosling stayed down. I watched the now placid water where the young goose had disappeared. The flotilla of geese moved to the opposite side of the pond. Still the gosling didn't come up.

I can't be sure how long I waited, but after what seemed like a sufficient amount of time to be sure of the gosling's fate, I left. I had most certainly killed it, but how? Shock? Not likely, the corpse should have surfaced if it had simply died. Perhaps it had been eaten by a turtle. There were some big turtles in the pond. I half convinced myself that a turtle had taken my chick.

I pondered the fate of the yellow ball of down for several days until I finally got up the nerve to ask Pat Brown, a waterfowl expert at the Illinois Natural History Survey, about the incident. Pat listened to my account and to my turtle theory attentively, and then with a gleam in his eye and a smirk on his face, described, in prolonged detail, a defensive maneuver often used by young waterfowl. Apparently young geese can hold their breath a very long time; longer than guilt had allowed me to wait for a lifeless corpse to pop to the surface of that pond. When threatened, a gosling will sometimes dive and hold on to the bottom substrate (material) until the threat has passed. It appears to be an effective strategy, especially when the harassment is coming from a naive source (that would be me).

For a while whenever I saw Pat in the hall he would shake his head, chuckle, and mumble, "Goose killer."

Attracting a crowd . . .

A Close Encounter
Susan Post

During the late 1990s Michael Jeffords and I were members of the Society of Invertebrates in Captivity, a most unusual organization. Members of this society come from butterfly houses, insect zoos, nature centers, and universities—anyone who uses live insects as an educational outreach tool. The annual meeting was held in southern Arizona during early August and was timed for the seasonal monsoon rains and abundant insect emergence. While our days were filled with talks and workshops on insect rearing, how to build an exhibit on a shoestring budget, and how to conduct insect field days, the evenings were for collecting! Many of us still had that collecting passion that sparked our interest in entomology as children. Southern Arizona, however, is not central Illinois!

The meeting always opened with a few words (read rules!) about collecting—what we could and could not collect with the group's blanket permits, and more importantly, where we could collect. A final warning was "remember, you are near the Mexican border and there have been incidents with 'illegals'." This is one of those announcements at a meeting where you only half listen and hope they get on with the business of the day. After all, Zack was soon giving a talk on "If you can't be a bug, pretend." Intriguing, to say the least.

As soon as the afternoon's talks were over, we headed to our rental car and hit the desert with cameras, high powered flashlights, a jar or two for collecting, and eager friends and colleagues from the meeting. We headed south, toward the border, but we weren't worried as we had photographed and collected near here before with no problems. Once the sun had set we set up our makeshift blacklight—a sheet with a couple of Coleman™ florescent lanterns. At first a few moths and some tiny beetles came in, but soon there was the prize we were looking for—large (two inches) dark beetles with "horns;" we commonly call these rhinocerous beetles. I wanted to bring back several pairs to rear, so we could use them in Illinois for our own "show and tell."

When blacklighting you are so focused on the white sheet and the bright light that you are "blinded," literally and figuratively, to everything else. Your surroundings are in total darkness and insect collecting is your only focus. Another advantage to blacklighting in the desert is there are no lights to compete for the attention of those prized arthropod catches.

One of us heard something and we stared into the inky darkness—nothing. We were excited as maybe it was a coatimundi, a unusual mammal that none of us midwesterners had seen. We continued to hear a rustling, and it kept coming closer and closer. We shined our flashlights—nothing. Suddenly, I flashed back to the morning's warning about collecting too near the border. I was now very nervous. What were we supposed to do if we encountered "illegals?" Why hadn't I paid attention! The rustling came very close and our flashlight picked up an eye glint of the largest brown eyes I had ever seen. The possessors of these large eyes appeared equally afraid of us. One of us yells "Who are you?' To which the brown eyes reply, "Moo!"

Call me Ishmael—my great, white carp!

Sixty-Minute Cruise
Susan Post

Asian carp are one of several introduced species of fish. They were brought into the United States to clear algae and parasites from ponds in Arkansas and Mississippi that grow catfish. Floods washed the carp into the Mississippi River, where they worked their way upriver and are now thriving in the Illinois River. Asian carp consume up to 40% of their body weight in plankton each day and they push out weaker native fish species.

The 2007 summer Illinois Wilds Institute for Nature (IWIN) class, Sun, Sand and Skippers was held in the Havana area. While the class focused on the sand prairies and most things Lepidopteran (butterflies, skippers, and moths), I wanted to take advantage of the Survey's field station in Havana—The Forbes Lab. I contacted Director Greg Sass to arrange boat tours on the Illinois River so the class could experience Asian carp. What our cruise focused on is the fish's ability to leap out of the water when startled by a noise. I had seen videos of fish leaping all around boats as they traveled on the river. And for some reason, I thought participants in a field class focusing on butterflies should be exposed to all things flying, and that included fish.

After dinner Greg announced we were ready to depart. The response was greater than expected, even overwhelming; all class participants wanted to go, so more than one cruise had to take place. I thought to myself, "If I play my cards right, I might not have to go." While I wanted the class to see this phenomenon, I wasn't that keen on it. I am not a "water person," so I usually avoid anything aquatic.

Those that stayed behind cheerily waved to the first group as they embarked on their cruise. Ninety minutes later they returned with glowing eyes and nervous tales of fish slamming against the boat and flying out of the water. The second group was eager to board the boat for their fish experience. Again, the boat filled quickly. I "missed the boat" again and stayed on shore to have another dessert. After about an hour they too returned with more barely believable fish tales.

Greg asked if anyone else wanted to go. I noted it was getting dark, but no, there was still time for another cruise. I reluctantly climbed aboard and was seated in the rear on the left. I am thinking, great, I'm too near the water! My friend Karen was sitting next to me. As we boarded, the group I was with started to sing the Gilligan's Island song. They were very happy and a little too excited.

We shoved off with the sun starting to set and the waters calm. A pair of Mallards swam along the river's edge and a startled Great Blue Heron noisily squawked off. Periodically, I heard a thumping, which were fish hitting the bottom of the boat, but otherwise the water was serene, the scene idyllic, and I was glad I came on this soon-to-be moonlit cruise. Greg was telling the group about the fish and his recent experience with a CNN news crew, where, as soon as the fish started to jump, a female reporter started to scream. Karen then smirked to Greg, "I bet she had on high heels and lipstick!" Greg just smiled and shook his head.

We rendezvoused with a second boat somewhere in the middle of the river. The second boat was outfitted with electro shocking equipment—a generator and underwater electrodes. At Greg's signal his colleagues started the generator and put the electrodes in the water. As soon as they hit the water 50 fish leapt out of the water at once, as if in some odd, synchronized swimming routine. What a sight! Then smack, they hit the water; the fish kept jumping as our boat moved along. Greg carefully piloted between the jumping fish.

All of a sudden I was hit from behind. A fish scraped across my face, knocking my glasses off, hit my right thigh, and landed, wriggling and bleeding, in the bottom of the boat. Like the fish, I was stunned. Karen started to scream, flailing her arms and her feet. (I am not sure why, as I was the one hit! And I was hoping that she wouldn't tip the boat with this performance.) I, on the other hand, stared at the white slime left on my pant leg, still trying to comprehend that I had been just whacked in the head by a rather large fish. I then remembered that I had glasses on. They had landed underneath Karen's flailing feet. Although a little bent, I could still use them. After reassuring Greg that I was fine, we headed back to shore. Karen eventually ran out of energy and calmed down.

I still remember the look Greg gave Karen when she made fun of the reporter screaming. It was a look that said, you don't know half of what to expect. I'm glad my reaction was one of calm dumbfoundedness. And now I get to add "getting pummeled by a 10-pound carp" to my life's accomplishments! Thanks, Greg for a great cruise!

Real life Loonie Toons.

A Fox Goes to Work
Joseph Spencer

For years, my summer workday didn't end at 5:00 p.m.; it only paused. That was because the western corn rootworm beetles' (WCR) ascent and aerial dispersal from cornfields occurred between ca. 6:30 p.m. and sunset. My aerobiologist collaborator, Scott Isard (of tower fame), and I had a project where we characterized seasonal patterns of WCR ascent and dispersal from Illinois cornfields by catching the high-flying beetles as they flew around above our corn and soybean fields.

After a full day of ground-based bug-collecting, I had about an hour to re-group and run through my check list of supplies (aerial insect nets, stopwatches, safety harnesses, vials, pens, tape, notebook, and small coolers of ice to chill the samples) before rendezvousing with Scott at the "Lost 40" field site, two miles north of Trelease Woods, near Urbana.

As long as it wasn't too cool or too windy or raining, Scott and I would meet in the field, split up the collecting equipment and scale a pair of 40-foot-tall scaffolding platforms (a.k.a. the "patented, life-threatening towers") to wait for the evening rootworm commute. Spending the last two hours of the day perched 40 feet above Champaign County meant that I often had a prime balcony seat for spectacular sunsets.

Around 8:00 p.m., after one particularly long day and evening of insect collecting, I had returned to the Survey I-Building to drop off my collecting gear and retrieve my things before heading home. I came down the backstairs on the north side of the I-Building with my briefcase in one hand and laptop in the other. Without a free hand, I tripped the latch with my hip and used my arm and shoulder to ease the door open. In all likelihood, tonight, like the day and evening, was probably still blistering hot. My suspicions were confirmed by the ominous warmth of the window glass against my forearm as I went to shove open the door. I held my breath, closed my eyes and stepped out.

"Not so bad." I thought. It took only a second or two for the clinging layer of dry, conditioned air to fall away and dissolve, exposing me to the reality of a hot July night in Champaign. I took a few steps down the sidewalk when, just ahead, at 20 feet and closing, I saw a fox walking toward me from the west. I didn't know what to do, so I kept walking, wondering how close I might get before this mirage would run away, or melt. The fox seemed to be wholly unconcerned by my presence and just kept coming; perhaps because my hands were full, it knew that it had the drop on me. We passed each other, not more than five feet away. I took another step or two and stopped to look back over my shoulder. Just then the fox stopped, and turned to look back at me. It regarded me for a moment before making what seemed like a fox's shrug of the shoulders and continuing on its way east, into the long grass toward the deepening dusk and the sheep barns beyond.

I felt compelled to follow it. I continued to advance and I stood in the grass where the fox had been, looking in the direction that it had disappeared. I wondered about where that fox was heading and what a fox does at night. Those thoughts occupied my mind as I turned and resumed walking toward the parking lot.

Sheep barns and lambs to the east. "Was the fox going to work or going home?" I wondered.

I turned this question around in my head as I opened the car door and tossed my things into the passenger seat.

Just then, a familiar cartoon moment came to mind and I laughed out loud. I recalled how Wiley E. Coyote and Sam Sheepdog would cordially greet each other before punching in and out of work in the Warner Brothers cartoons. The ridiculous circumstances of a predator and a protector meeting at the close of business, with their differences set aside 'til scheduled to resume the next business day always amused me. I never imagined I'd ever walk out of the I-Building and onto that cartoon stage to actually play one of those roles.

"How rare and unusual," I thought.

I think I was playing the Sheepdog.

Saga of a swamp . . .

Capturing Mystery
Michael R. Jeffords

The dirt road ended abruptly in an old cemetery. Sloping off to the south, a field of corn stubble stretched toward the wide floodplain of the Ohio River. The sight was a common one in this part of Illinois; after all, the annual cycle of flood and silt deposition made this land some of the most fertile in the state. The great river, however, was not visible from this relatively high vantage point; a line of hazy grayness, uniform in height, spread across the horizon. Trekking across the relatively muddy cornfield was only a prelude to the wetness that was to come. As we moved closer, the gray haze changed into a mass of uniformly spaced boles, each angled slightly, and topped with a tangle of branches waiting for early spring foliage.

While I had grown up in southern Illinois, accustomed to swampy landscapes such as this, relatively few times had I had occasions to "discover" and explore new terrain, untrammeled except for the occasional proximity of a laboring tractor. A colleague, Charles Helm, and I were on a soybean insect sampling mission when we had the opportunity to visit this stretch of bottomland known on topographic maps as "Black Bottoms." As we approached the edge of the swampy woods, a distant yet distinctive squawking could be heard. A colony of pterodactyls or pteranodons immediately came to mind, but only fleetingly, for were we not in the twentieth century—modern scientists on a quest no more mysterious than the cataloging of insect pests of the ubiquitous soybean?

As we entered the buttressed, ancient trees—water tupelo and bald cypress—the time period ceased to be important. Only the senses played a role here and they, it appeared, had become timeless, subject to the mood of this ancient place. The ill-defined squawking soon became a serious of focused, raucous calls from messy bundles of twigs, woven into massive nests high above. We had discovered a Great Blue Heron rookery of nearly 200 nests, all evenly spaced and ancient in their own timescale. Upon approaching the edge of the activity, the ground became a speckled mass of white, gray, and tan—remains of the fishy meals enjoyed above. As if to reiterate their culinary preferences and demonstrate their displeasure at our proximity, a slight whistling sound from above caused us to look up, just in time to see a partially digested, hand-sized bluegill come hurtling down and plop wetly at our feet. We gladly retreated, nodding with wonder and awe at the spectacle. As we left the swamp, the eerie call of a Barred Owl somewhere in the distance was answered by one not so far away—both to serenade and likely applaud our departure.

I will always remember this visit in the early 1980s. I was just beginning to attain a small measure of competency in photography and had carried my camera along on that day—no tripod, just a wide-angle and a short telephoto.

After all, we were seeking soybean pests, and were likely to see little else. I took only a few shots that day, because the season was early, the light not particularly pleasing, and when leaving the car, I had not imagined seeing much worthy to capture on film.

A few years later I returned to that same site with another colleague during high water and canoed through the trees. The herons had not yet returned, but the nests were still high overhead. Another visit only a few years ago proved to be much less satisfying. The view from the cemetery parking lot now showed only a uniform expanse of farmland, stretching to the brown ribbon of the Ohio. The land of the herons and Barred Owls was no more.

While looking through my photo files one day, I happened upon a couple of the images from that first visit. I was struck that perhaps the only records that this place had ever existed could now reside in my polyethylene slide files and in the now somewhat-less-than-descriptive "Black Bottoms" from a topo map. I've often pondered ideas and sought reasons why I have such a passion for biology and for photography, and I think this episode may best epitomize why. Photographing landscapes that are ancient and undisturbed is like recording history, or in the case of this special place, "capturing the mystery" of a place too perfect for its own survival.

This spring I visited Heron Pond, a similar habitat along the Cache River in southern Illinois, but one that is protected, hopefully, forever. In the distance I heard the call of a Barred Owl, answered by another nearby. The cypresses were an ephemeral green, the calling owl a brown blur through the trees. My mind went immediately back to that day so long ago and that perhaps I had a chance to recapture a piece of that long-lost mystery.

Chapter 8

Personal Introspection

East Cairo, Kentucky, September 13, 1879

I am working alone on an indescribably dirty table covered with my traps and with dead birds in the genuine Kentucky farm house—built up on stilts apparently to afford shelter for the pigs under it—furnished with a porch the whole length which serves as a sort of garret on wh. everything is stored for wh. the rest of the house affords no place. Two wooden [porches] at one of which we work . . . over the river water where I was instructed to toss my dead birds into the front yard, while on the other we will sit after meals and smoke and gossip.

In the third room . . . . the family live, in the fourth is a long table, at which a little while ago I ate my supper of biscuit and southern butter and clabber and fried fish meat and brown beans and molasses and coffee innocent of sugar or cream. There is no plaster in the house, the wooden walls are all covered with white-wash except where this has been worn off by children's heads and hands or cracked away with age. The boards of the floors are all loose and slip and rattle under our feet, and whatever is dropped falls through to the pigs.

A dog . . . is gnawing with some canine visitation apparently resembling nightmare, the pigs grunt and squeal, my room-mate a graceless scalawag snores, the steamboats in the river pant and roar, the lights of Cairo show brightly opposite, the night wind wanders in cool and sweet, crickets chirp, the leaves of the great forest behind mingle their nocturnal rustling with the rippling of the water along the shore and I am happy.

I have had a glorious day in the woods. I am on comfortable footing with these southern Gentlemen. I come in so ravenous with hunger that the fare is as good as if I paid $3 a day for it instead of $3.50 a week.

The novelty of the day has been a half hour . . . watching at short range with my field glass a large party of white and blue herons with five wood ibises (a bird I never saw alive before) at their evening sport on the sands.

I stalked through the smothering woods sometimes on my hands and knees and sometimes in the attitude to which the serpent was doomed when it tempted Eve, to within ten feet of a capital shot, and was pushing aside the weeds to get sight when a gun up the river startled my game.

Being "in the field" is what matters most to INHS biologists.

The mind of a botanist, the words of a poet . . .

Images from the Field—Field Work
Connie Cunningham

Maddening mosquitoes,
Stinging nettle,
Chiggers, ticks, and poison ivy,
Multiflora rose,
Awl-sharp honey locusts thorns,
Weltering, sultry, stifling heat,
Ah, field work!

Worrisome storm clouds in the distance, running to the car, thunderclaps, and crashing branches, downpour! — soaked to the bone.
Long days in the never-faltering heat and sun, still grateful to be outside rather than indoors looking out.
Pauses by the roadside to watch a brilliant sunset, spectacular storm, thousands of fireflies emerging from rolling farm fields edged with woodlands!
Kneeling in waist-deep stinging nettle to watch a luna moth emerge from its cocoon.
Tree tops swaying to and fro, timeless voices telling tales to those that carefully listen.
Ah, field work!

Cool early mornings, wet with dew,
Refreshing breezes,
Shaded woodland coolness,
Whispering grasses,
Chirping tree frogs, singing toads, fluting Wood Thrush, scolding woodpeckers,
Ah, field work!

Solitude,
Gratitude,
Wonder,
Belonging,
Peace.

Field work.

It's all a labor of love.

Why Do This?
Michael R. Jeffords

A variety of topics, a variety of audiences . . .

As I drive south from Champaign for over three hours to give a talk at Southern Illinois University for an unknown audience, assuming one shows up, my thoughts inevitably go to my wife's comment as I left the house. "Why are you doing this, I thought you were going to learn to say no!" This leads to a little soul searching (very little actually) as to what propels me to give the seemingly endless array of presentations that I do (some 1,100 over the last 20 years). The answer is quite simple, really, I like it! Also, it is my way of trying to change the world, at least a little corner of it. Over the years, whatever skill I may have acquired as a photographer, as well as the thousands of images I have accumulated, must be put to some use. Now I could attempt to make a living selling images for the marketplace, but I would likely starve pursuing that avenue. Thus, I choose to use photography as a tool for education. Fortunately, I have a day job as a biologist that allows me to do this on a regular basis—thus my jaunt to southern Illinois. Most of the presentations I make revolve around the central theme of "biodiversity," the great array of life the covers our planet. I have found that my niche in all of this just may be the re-creation of that intimate contact with nature that is missing from most individuals today. There is, there must be, more to life than malls, minivans, and motor homes if we are to preserve at least a significant proportion of the life that exists around us.

It is thought that humans have an innate affinity for life; this theory, termed "biophilia" is eloquently described by prominent Harvard biologist E.O. Wilson. The hypothesis also states that biophilia is only partially genetic and must be nurtured from a relatively early age if it is to manifest itself in an individual. Thus, I view my role as a "biophilia facilitator" via the medium of photography. I have long since given up on the concept that humans will preserve Earth's biodiversity based solely on its potential economic value to us. Exploitation wins out over conservation in virtually every instance. Thus, we are left with reasons for preserving biodiversity, not for any direct benefit it may provide to us, but because we choose to, and because we like being surrounded by an endless multitude of fascinating organisms. Ideally, we could take all those skeptical individuals into the world's great natural habitats and let them experience its biodiversity first-hand. While this is sometimes possible, it is far more feasible to present images of the natural world to them in a context that says "these organisms are wonderful and are worth preserving for their own sake." This, at least, provides a first line for nurturing biophilia. It is my experience that the visual elegance of the natural world is its own best friend and can sell itself if given the chance. As I look back over the last 20 years, I know why I seldom say "no" to groups which want talks on biodiversity. If they seek the knowledge and awareness of the natural world, it's the least I can do to attempt to provide it. I also believe that the organisms of Earth deserve to be portrayed in as favorable a light as possible. This ultimately falls on the presenter, in this case me, to be (sorry Army) "all that I can be" with regard to photography and to biology. Each program might add that special grain of sand to a person's psyche and tip their balance in favor of preservation, and that can only be good. Person by person, sand grain by sand grain, we just might make a difference.

Parallel universe.

The Fawn
Ben O'Neal

One of the greatest joys of being in the field each spring is the opportunity to witness all the young animals as they learn to live in the new world around them. During my two years of Master's degree research, I came to love the thrill of being startled by bounding young fawns bedded in the thick Conservation Reserve Program fields (CRP) I frequented. There's something humbling and humorous about a 20-pound fawn stopping the heart of a grown man. On one occasion, I jumped a doe and her fawn in a grassy ditch along a desolate gravel road in rural Fulton County. The mother promptly leapt over the roadside fence, expecting her little one to find its own way across. The clumsy little fawn decided that diving through the hog wire was its best bet for keeping up with mom. That would have been true were it not for her larger than expected rump, which couldn't quite squeeze through the holes in the fence. She quickly found herself halfway in and halfway out, with no chance of escape. I had to laugh as I freed her, sympathizing with the folly of youth, because it wasn't more than a mile away that I had recently gotten myself equally stuck in a mud hole; one that I was sure I could cross.

Getting very, very close to a fox.

Stalking the Fox
Joe Spencer

My student, Tim Mabry, and I had ascended our respective 40-foot-tall scaffolding towers in preparation for an evening of collecting insects. We planned to use our insect nets to catch flying western corn rootworm beetles as they zipped past and over our perches. Tim's tower was near the west side of a soybean field, 80 yards from the tower I occupied on the east side.

Western corn rootworm beetles (WCR) express a strong, daily periodicity in their activities. We were in place, anticipating the onset of an evening peak of WCR flight. This evening, there was a northwest breeze strong enough that few WCR could take flight, even as prime flight time approached. Tonight was looking like a bust.

I had waited around 30 minutes, net in hand and eyes focused on the horizon, for the burst of flight that would never come, when Tim called my name from across the field: "Joe!" Roused from my attention to day-dreaming, I began to call back, when Tim waved off my shout and pantomimed an exaggerated "Shhhh!" In his best field-approximation of a stage whisper he communicated one word, "Fox," and pointed to the north. There, at the edge of the soybean field was a red fox wandering down the alley that marked the boundary between the 40 acres of commercial soybeans to the west and my set of experimental corn and soybean fields.

This fox was known to us as we'd seen it many times ducking into one or another plot as we came and went throughout the field season. From our roosts, high above the field, we could clearly see the fox 100 yards away, and watch it unnoticed.

Tim made a downward motion and descended from his tower in no time. I did the same, careful to establish a secure, if only brief, grip on each rung as I clambered down and sprinted across the soybean field on a path connecting the towers. We anticipated that the fox would continue down the alley and eventually enter the large cornfield at the southwest edge of the field site. With little time to spare, if we hoped to see the fox close-up, we ran down the grassy alleyway that paralleled the fox's course and turned west at the end of a cornfield plot. We sprinted 50 yards along the south side of the field and ducked into the corner of the cornfield in advance of the creature's approach. We crouched just inside the rows of corn and waited.

The fox did not disappoint us.

The northwest wind favored our scheme and meant the fox would not detect our scent as it neared. Moments after we took up position, I could see the canine making steady, but slow, progress toward our hiding place. I was struck by its small size and amused by how lightly it bounced along, its bushy tail "bobbing" up and down like a helium balloon, trailing behind a running child. This little fox was too distracted with his explorations to notice Tim and me. Its steady progress was broken by brief pauses to sniff deeply from holes along the field margin. In a token concession to caution, the fox occasionally stopped and looked back over its shoulder to the north before continuing. When Tim first spotted him, this fox had just emerged from a soybean field. Now, despite a fast falling layer of dew on the grass, the fox's paws still wore muddy booties that belied an afternoon of stalking prey amidst farm fields. As the fox neared the end of the field and made its closest approach, my heart was pounding. Never was I so close to a fox that was so unaware of me. Peering at this wild thing from behind a row of cornstalk bars, I felt protected from it, yet I also felt excitement at how vulnerable this creature had become, thanks to our wary exercise of stealth.

There was a moment, just as the fox passed not more than two feet from where we crouched, when I realized that if my intention had been to take this animal, I would have done so just then. Instead, at that instant, in that second when the fox crossed the alley between our hideout and the safety of the cornfield, I stuck my head through the cornstalks and into the fox's world. The animal turned toward us and stopped stock still, staring for what seemed like an eternal moment of startled recognition. In that split second of connection when the fox and I were nearly face-to-face, the fox's instinct took over. Fueled by a gusher of the same adrenaline that would later leave me shaking, the fox shuddered and sprung forward with all four feet leaving the ground; in an instant it was gone through the curtain of corn. I turned to Tim, and laughed as if to ask whether this had been real. The fox was here and then gone, disappearing so quickly that it could have been argued that it had never been there at all. Who, other than a red fox with muddy paws, would ever believe this field tale.

"When in the course of human events . . ."

Finding My Calling
Gail Kampmeier

Being interested in science requires an insatiable curiosity about the world around you: wondering what things are; making hypotheses about how the world works; using evidence to shape new hypotheses to test; and weaving together a credible story. Although I'd always had that curiosity, my high school only spent 37 cents per student per year on science. Looking back years later, it was little wonder that I was the only person in my class who became a scientist, and that after first attaining a bachelor's degree in French. When my husband and I arrived at the University of Illinois at Urbana-Champaign (UIUC) in August 1977, I decided to return to school for a second bachelor's, choosing something with actual employment potential—ornamental horticulture. I began to pick up science courses, like chemistry, which I had managed to avoid while pursuing French. But among my courses that first semester were two that would leave an indelible mark on my future career: agricultural entomology and introductory plant pathology. The entomology class was team-taught by Drs. Stan Friedman (department head and insect physiologist at UIUC), Marcos Kogan (biological control and agroecology expert working in soybeans), and Bill Ruesink (a mathematical modeler working with pest management decision making, and lover of beetles, especially leaf beetles). Each of them was an amazing scientist; the latter two were both members of the Illinois Natural History Survey (INHS). Michael Jeffords, who was finishing his Ph.D. studying mimicry and predation in butterflies and moths at Allerton Park, while not my teaching assistant (TA) for the lab portion, was also involved in the course. While the general public may not appreciate the great impact these men have had on scientific research and outreach conducted at the Survey, as I look back on this, I am amazed at my luck to be associated with them and the impact they had on me!

When the semester was over, I asked Stan Friedman about a student job that might make use of my newly developed skills in discerning one insect order from another. He pointed me toward the INHS. Shortly thereafter, I was hired by John Bouseman, also a beetle guy. However, he was mainly a pre-eminent naturalist, more reminiscent of the old- fashioned Victorian breed whose love for the land would only be revealed to me in the annual field trips he organized. These introduced me to areas of the state I would never have otherwise seen. John hired me to pin soybean insects from Brazil, which were part of IRCSA (International Research Collection of Soybean Arthropods). I was to get rather proficient at daubing a small paper triangle into a spot of Elmer's glue and then affixing it to the side of a tiny insect (just under the wing on one side of the bug), all the while trying not to entangle wings or legs in the glue.

The INHS insect collection at that time was a social nexus of numerous characters, such as George Godfrey, a lepidopterist with a million stories, and John Marlin, who was torn between finishing his Ph.D. and a burgeoning interest in the political side of science policy. It was there, too, that I met Mike Irwin, who wandered in one day looking for John, but found only me. He mentioned that he was looking to hire students for the summer and his research involved insects as vectors of plant pathogens—bet you thought I'd forgotten about that other course I told you had made an impression—and I couldn't believe my luck! So, that summer I got to join a crew of students doing field work in soybeans.

I bicycled to work from Orchard Downs, UIUC's married student housing. I took the sidewalks as far as possible, past the giant mushroom of the Assembly Hall, and turned off St. Mary's Rd. onto Griffiths Dr., and followed the line of Osage orange trees that separated the INHS Biological Control Lab from St. Mary's Cemetery. One morning, I happened on the biggest moth I'd ever seen alive, just sitting on the drive, apparently exhausted from a night's carousing, and waiting to be run over by the next car. I picked up my prize and took it into the lab, where technician Suan Chu kindly gave me one of her moth rearing cartons, a plain, round ice cream carton lined on the inside with brown paper and topped with gauze for breathability. Much to my surprise, the moth proceeded to lay eggs all over the brown paper, just like the corn earworm moths that Mrs. Chu normally raised. I learned that my moth was a *Cecropia*, and that her babies would become very colorful caterpillars with exceedingly voracious appetites! The local chokecherry trees that also lined the drive gave up their photosynthetic bounty that summer as my babies grew larger, changing from yellow and black to green, with brightly colored spiked knobs of blue, yellow, and red.

This was only one of the many insects I brought to my fellow workers that summer, Charlie Helm, among them. Charlie worked with Marcos Kogan, and would patiently answer my questions when I asked what this or that bug was, expecting to hear such nonspecific terms as "beetle," or the like, but he'd tell me "*Ceratoma trifurcata, Leptinotarsa decemlineata*," and a host of additional scientific names. This was a new language to learn—different from the French I'd been studying since the third grade. Not one to shirk from a challenge, I decided to enroll in the insect taxonomy course the following fall, taught by Ellis McLeod. I truly fell in love with the marvelous diversity of the insect world and the way McLeod wove its stories together. Who knew you could stand in a stream, parting the water with your legs, and reach down and find a caddisfly larva enclosed in a case built out of debris, clinging to the underside of a rock? Or find immature dragonflies (nymphs) with their hydraulic powered, steam shovel-like jaws just waiting to scoop up unsuspecting prey? When these ancient, speedy predators finally emerged from the water and took to the air, they provided additional entertainment to any who happed to watch our class try to sweep one out of the air with a net for our collections! The ones that we managed to catch were inevitably the copulating pairs that were distracted enough to be occasionally caught by our lumbering lunges.

This class finally tipped the balance for me. Although I'd had more training in botany than zoology, entomology won out as a career path and course of graduate study for me. Yet even today, plant pathology still weaves through the stories I tell of aphids and how their movement and behavior can affect the course of plant virus epidemics. While many scientists knew and tell of their calling at a very early age, mine took somewhat longer and a more circuitous path before I discovered who and what I am—an entomologist.

Explorations.

Dissection Haiku
Joseph Spencer

Vials of dead bugs
Hard tools tear soft parts away
Look inside and see!

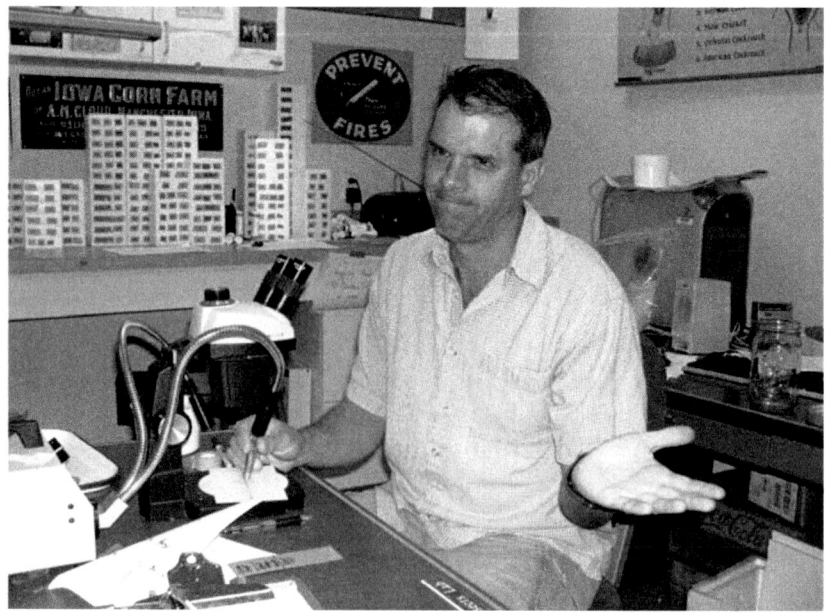

One down, 499 to go.

Delve into the mind of a botanist doing transect work.

Reflections on a Quadrat
Jamie Ellis

I stare down at the jumble of green leaves at my feet. Plants on the forest floor are neatly framed in the dark wood of my half-meter by half-meter quadrat (an area outlined by a square made of PVC pipe). I begin to write names in the blank spaces of my data sheet. *Laportea canadensis* (wood nettle), *Elymus virginicus* (Virginia wild rye), *Impatiens capensis* (spotted touch-me-not), *Pilea pumila* (clearweed). I stare into the quadrat again. How much of this quarter square meter of earth is occupied by *Laportea*? I lick the itchy red spot on the back of my hand where I errantly brushed against a stem of *Laportea*. Woodnettle, as it's otherwise known, frequents moist woods and floodplain forests across Illinois. This plant grows to about three feet tall and its large, darkgreen, oppositely arranged, egg-shaped leaves with regularly toothed edges are easily recognizable. Wood-nettle is armed with sharp, stiff hairs along the stem and underside of the leaves. These stiff hairs easily poke into the unsuspecting (or even suspecting), soft skin (like the back of my hand) and inject a little formic acid; hence the itchy, burning sensation I feel. Luckily, a little splash of water or well-placed spit dilutes the acid and soothes my skin. It's hard to believe that this painfully offensive plant, as well as its close relative, the stinging nettle, is edible. When they first emerge in the spring, the young shoots can be gathered, washed, and wilted in a hot skillet with a little butter and salt. The stinging hairs are rendered harmless as the plant wilts. I can only describe the taste as *green*. After a winter of root vegetables and meat, nettles were a nutritious and welcome food source for early settlers of Illinois. I think a better use for wood nettle (other than pushing unsuspecting friends into a patch) is for cordage. The fibers in the outer wall of the stem can be processed and then twined into string or rope. This was the bowstring material of choice for many native peoples throughout the Midwest.

Glancing quickly back to the mostly blank grid of squares on my data sheet, I write the letter C next to *Laportea canadensis* for quadrat #1. The C corresponds to 5–25% coverage. It looks to me that more than 5% but less than 25% of this square is occupied by wood-nettle—not particularly precise, but close. If a fellow botanist looked into this little square, he might say that *Laportea* occupies 15% while I think it is 20%. Fortunately, we both agree that *Laportea* occupies somewhere between 5 and 25%. That's C! A smart man by the name of Daubenmire came up with this ingenious system of categories to quantify how much we see when we look into a quadrat. How much indeed!

What's next? *Elymus* gets a D, *Impatiens* a B, and *Pilea* a B. I wrap up my quadrat estimation with some summary information—how much space do the herbaceous plants occupy? The woody plants? Everything together? How much leaf litter is on the forest floor? How much bare dirt do I see? How much moss? I perform this methodical routine for each quadrat.

I pick up the quadrat, move five meters up the transect, step over to the right side, measure out one meter from the tape, and carefully frame the next set of plants. The transect I'm working is 50 meters long. A tape measure marks the line. To record ground-cover vegetation I place the quadrat every five meters along the tape, starting at zero and ending at 45. Ten quadrats along this transect, 10 along the next transect, and 10 along a final transect. That makes 30 quadrats in all for each forest site. I'll end up staring down 30 times into my little wooden frame, writing down the names of the plants I see and estimating cover from A to G. This is what I do—identify, quantify, and record. This is the work of a field botanist.

"Hey, Jamie. What's this?" I look over at the young man standing 20 feet away. I'm not alone out here. "Just a minute. I'll take a look," Actually, I'm rarely alone in the field. We botanists are fairly gregarious folks who need a lot of encouragement and second opinions. Sometimes you'll spot a whole pack of us wandering through the woods, marshes, or prairies, examining leaves and pointing excitedly at flowers. Of course, I don't hire assistants just to keep me company—we all work together. We take turns driving, carrying equipment, and making sure data are recorded.

I stand up and stretch my cramped legs, leaving the quadrat behind to dutifully remind me of where I left off. The person who called my name is standing next to a tree, clipboard and pencil in one hand, a diameter tape in the other. As I reach the tree in question, I examine the dark, deeply furrowed bark and strain my neck to look up at the pinnately compound leaves high above our heads. "*Juglans nigra*, black walnut," I proclaim, as if I had just figured out some secret of the universe. Happy with my determination, he writes down the name, hooks the end of the tape into the bark, and wraps it around the tree to measure the diameter. Satisfied, I walk away.

Besides the chore of recording plants found inside a quadrat, I (really we) identify, measure, and count trees. What would the forest be without trees? Of course we don't count all of them—just the ones in a 10-meter by 50-meter rectangle positioned along each transect. As a reminder, that's three transects per forest site, which means three tree plots.

Luckily there are relatively few tree species in Illinois, and they're much easier to learn than the hundreds of possible herbaceous species. That's why our summer assistants, with their limited botanical skills, can work on recording trees while I stare at my quadrat. It's quite a nice division of labor. Of course if I take someone out who doesn't know any of the trees, then I have to identify all the plants as they record on the data sheet. They're stuck listening to me call out scientific names and letters. They're also stuck listening to my botanical anecdotes or nuggets of plant knowledge. We botanists can be dreadfully boring.

I work my way back to the quadrat I abandoned only minutes before. There it sits, faithfully waiting. Thankfully, the plants haven't run away. I stare into the wooden frame again. Most of the same plants as before. Oh, here's a new one—*Viola eriocarpa* [Smooth yellow violet], How much for that? I write down C. And another one—*Parthenocissus quinquefolia* [Virginia creeper]. That gets a D.

Parthenocissus quinquefolia. What a mouthful. This one usually goes on the data sheet as PQ instead of the complete name. A very common and harmless plant of Illinois forests, it is too often maligned because of its similarity or proximity to *Toxicodendron radicans* [poison ivy]. Yes, these two plants are ubiquitous across Illinois. Yes, they often form vines on trees and can grow side by side, but they're easy to distinguish. *Quinquefolia* means "five leaves" for the five leaflets on each palmately compound leaf. As for poison ivy, you probably learned this as a child—leaves of three, let it be! This is where knowing plants to avoid a rash comes in handy.

My mind drifts. I lose track of the plants below me. Did I just brush my hand against some poison ivy? As a botanist, you'd think I'd be able to stay away from the damn stuff. Oh well, I'll make sure we stop by that Casey's gas station in the little town nearby. It's routine to stop in the rest room of a Casey's to wash the dirt and grime from our hands and enjoy a cold drink.

What does it all mean? What do I really do? My colleagues and I spend hours in the office pouring over maps, looking up addresses, and making phone calls to get permission to access private land. We spend dozens of hours each summer sitting in a vehicle, traveling from site to site across this big state of Illinois. Long days are spent walking, wading streams, climbing fences, and avoiding cows. We take pictures and record GPS coordinates. We write down our observations and data. At the end of the day we're sweaty, sunburned, bruised, cut, bug-bitten, sore, tired, and just plain worn out. And what do we have to show for it? A fist-full of papers scribbled with words and names and numbers. That's all. Information. Data that are later turned into graphs, charts, and most importantly, trends. No fields plowed, no roads built, no buildings constructed. Our lasting legacy is in what we know, not what we did. After all, knowledge—knowing what is happening across the Illinois landscape to our natural resources—is important. It is power. It is how we know how to manage our natural resources in the ever-changing world of the twenty-first century.

Yup, there it is, the 77th sample of the day.

To think like a snake . . .

Comparative Cognition or A World Divided
Jim Sechrest

In 1997, the Illinois Natural History Survey launched a study on the habitat use by predators of nesting migratory birds at the Middle Fork Conservation Area, near Danville, Illinois. We put radio transmitter collars on 12 raccoons and 4 opossums, and surgically implanted similar transmitters into 4 fox snakes and 4 black rat snakes. We followed these animals during the spring and summer and created maps of their various locations that were then overlaid on a habitat map of the area. We were particularly interested in how these predators utilized the forest edges where bird nests were common.

In an earlier part of the study, mammologist Ed Heske and his graduate student Julianne Newton had found that 100% of the first batch of eggs laid by migratory birds in their study were preyed upon (eaten). As berries and other food became available in late spring and early summer and birds relocated their nests further from the ground, approximately 50% of these second batch eggs were destroyed.

Black rat snakes are approximately four feet long and easily capable of climbing up tree trunks, using the scales on their flattened undersides. While they can be found in bird nest holes 40 feet above the ground, they also occur on the ground or in rodent burrows underground. Mainly, these very versatile predators are found in wooded areas. Fox snakes, on the other hand, are found mainly in grassy areas. All this information we gleaned by tracking our transmitter-implanted subjects.

I had located one black rat snake near a campsite in a large, hollow tree stump. However, the broken roots of the tree still supported the horizontal trunk high off the ground. When I actually found the snake I was ducking underneath the trunk, listening intently to the pings on my headphones. Suddenly, I realized the snake had to be somewhere directly above me, and although harmless to me, its presence produced an involuntary shiver through my body.

Subsequently, I often found that same snake inside the hollow tree trunk or curled in the upper branches of a cluster of small cherry trees beside it. Once, while probing around with my radio antenna, searching for this snake, I encountered a married couple camping nearby. When they heard there was a snake in the vicinity, they quickly decided to move to another campsite. On that particular day, I found the snake curled up in a grassy field close by. I cheerfully pointed to the snake as the couple drove away.

Compared to driving around the countryside in trucks with large antennas to track raccoons, locating black rat snakes was somewhat of a problem, mostly because we were forced to use hand-held receivers in the middle of often dense woods. It was difficult to get a bearing on one particular black rat snake, because every tree trunk reflected the radio signal. Thus, I decided to leave the woods where I assumed it was and go down the hill into a nearby field to get a better angle on the snake. That's when I discovered that the snake wasn't actually in the woods. The signal originated from the opposite direction from where I was standing in the field, and from its last location, I wound up tracking the snake a few kilometers, through a woods, down a wooded hillside, across a cornfield, through a hedge row, across another field, across a small dirt road, and into a hollow tree whose roots dangled above the Middle Fork River. The tree was obviously well used by other animals, as it had a number of entrances at different levels, including burrows at the base. This site seemed more like a chosen destination than a random discovery by the snake. After tracking it this far in the last 24 hours, I began thinking, "This snake knows where it is and where it wants to go."

Sure enough, a colleague found that a black rat snake would stay in one hollow tree for a couple of weeks, move to another for a couple of weeks, and then return directly to the first tree. Each snake might have 6 to 10 of these locations which it used over and over. As it turns out, snakes don't just wander around, they have a home range and a pattern for utilizing the habitat. We found these snakes had home ranges of about two kilometers wide. They would utilize one area for hunting and then move to another area. After a meal, snakes hole up for weeks while digesting their food. One snake in particular was creative about its den as we found it in an old refrigerator in a large pile of junk. It had used a small hole to enter the space behind the plastic shelves in the refrigerator's open door.

An important question then arose: How does a snake find its way around its home range? Surely, we speculated, it must use smell, as snakes are known to rely on smell in a way very similar to how humans rely on sight. But do snakes really just follow their own scent trails, or do they have a plan? Is there some sort of learned map of their habitat in their heads?

Dr. Patrick Weatherhead, University of Illinois, relates that one black rat snake spent the winter in a hibernaculum (overwintering den) with other snakes, and then headed back to its home range in the spring, in a straight line, for four kilometers! Colleague Larry Keller also tracked a snake across a railroad bridge, from its hibernaculum to its home range on the other side of the Middle Fork River. This does seem to indicate that a snake has some capacity for learning and memory, far beyond its simple use of smell. It is doubtful that the snake laid a scent trail that lasted for six months and over the winter, or that the overall scent of its home range led it back to that area.

Thus, we've concluded that these snakes are not wandering around randomly. Even honey bees can communicate the direction and distance of nectar sources to other honey bees in the hive. The study of how animals use their brains to utilize their habitat is a quickly growing field of study called cognitive ecology. One hypothesis is that an animal experiences increased fitness (the ability to leave viable offspring) by being able to utilize its habitat efficiently (random wandering just doesn't cut it). One story passed along to me is that black rat snakes don't wander up and down trees in search of bird nests, as this would take a lot of effort. Instead, they watch birds entering and leaving a nest hole from the ground, and then climb up the tree to the nest.

Very efficient indeed!

Raccoons, as you might expect from their reputations, are even more versatile in their behavior than snakes, and use different areas of their home range on different nights. Two male raccoons that we tracked seemed to share the same home range and often used the same areas of their overlapping home ranges on the same nights. They might even have been sharing the same den during the day, or their dens might just have been very close together. We couldn't tell from our tracking.

These raccoons would travel down paths, also frequented by deer, in the middle of hedgerows at night. Our raccoons followed a path to the nearby park ranger's house where they always found fresh water and cat food to eat. One hedgerow, on the west side of their home range, marked the edge of their territory during early spring. Another large, male raccoon held the territory on the other side of this hedgerow, and also shared the hedgerow path that defined the border of their territories. But, when the corn grew high and began to put on green ears in the early summer, all three of the raccoons moved into the cornfields, even further to the west of their home ranges, without any apparent regard to previous territorial agreements. We often parked our trucks at the entrance to the park at sunset and prepared for our night of raccoon and opossum tracking. Right on schedule our two raccoon would walk past us on their way west to the cornfields. We could easily track them as they went by with the pings of their specific radio frequencies. Later in the night, we would get accurate fixes on their locations in the cornfields.

On other nights the raccoons would head in the opposite direction to old fields filled with raspberries when spring turned to summer. We had speculated that the 20-foot-high walls on either side of the river would present an obstacle to the raccoons, but they crossed easily each night. When we put their location fixes on a map we were able to see where they were crossing the river. I went to visit that location and found an easy access to the river on the near shore, and a tree that had fallen into the river on the far shore that provided a convenient way to scale the steep bank. Consequently, on a given night, the two raccoons might travel one kilometer east together across a fallen tree to get to the other side of the river, or head two kilometers west, down a path or corridor to get to the fresh corn. Or, they might go south one-third a kilometer to the ranger's house for cat food. Sometimes they would head off together, and other times they went separately. Whatever the pattern was for that evening, it was clear from early in the study, and confirmed later with maps, that they were not simply wandering around aimlessly. They were using the same places again and again.

It is difficult to understand and document what mammals and reptiles can learn and remember, because they can't tell us what they are thinking. We might say that it is better to just limit our speculating of learning and memory in mammals and reptiles to identifiable, fixed-action responses, because there is simply no way to know what they actually know. We can only rely on second-hand, empirical evidence.

Humans have taught sign language to chimpanzees and human language to parakeets in at attempt to get a better understanding of their intellectual capacities, but interpreting the results is difficult. But when it comes to researching raccoons and black rat snakes, it is up to us to discover ways to study them in an attempt to determine what they know and perhaps how they know it. Spatial ecology studies, such as those above, are one useful method to get detailed information on what reptiles and mammals learn and remember in nature. That, in turn, gives us a better understanding of the natural history of these species, including a more accurate understanding of their evolution and ecology.

For a long time, I was not inclined to debate whether animal cognition rises to the level of conscious thinking, because we don't yet have a scientific understanding of human consciousness, let alone that of animals. Then, Donald Griffin, who discovered echolocation in bats, published a book in 2001 entitled *Animal Minds: Beyond Cognition to Consciousness*. In the book, Griffin outlines many anecdotes on animal thinking processes and intentionality in behavior. These observations led him to conclude that animals are capable of conscious thought. In one example, Griffin explained how a hummingbird learned the location of a mist net. It perched right on the net. Instead of chasing off other hummingbirds that intruded into its home range (the usual behavior), the hummingbird flew low to the ground, behind the intruder, and then chased it into the mist net. Very intriguing behavior, to say the least!

After studying where and how mammals and reptiles travel, I now have a greater appreciation of what they know and how they use what they know to interact with their environment. I continue to wonder, though, what cues they use and how much is learning and memory and how much is reaction to various stimuli. Eventually, though, these types of studies may shed more light on how we humans evolved and developed our individual self-awareness, and that can only be a good thing.

If you can't laugh at yourself, well . . .

The Black Sheep
Greg G. Sass

Regardless of status or position, every biological field station has at least one person, euphemistically called the "black sheep." Such individuals continually provide hurdles to accomplishing research objectives and inevitably cost the program additional money. All field scientists who have successfully avoided this affliction (and moniker) are intimately aware of these black sheep, as they continually seem to have a dark cloud hanging over their heads. More often than not, black sheep are the butt of many jokes, both in isolated, whispered confidence among nonblack sheep colleagues, or even in situations where the black sheep may be subject to public humiliation by gangs of "normal thugs." Most commonly, the black sheep are simply regarded as, "having no business in the field," and are often assaulted with quotes such as, "Don't quit your day job." Black sheep that persist going in the field are also the most consistent winners of many annual derogatory awards, often created by principal investigators to further humiliate them. For example, the Survey's Illinois River Biological Station has the "Gold Prop," awarded annually to the recipient(s) who has found the most creative way to destroy state property. In my field experiences, past winners have accomplished such feats as submerging a laptop computer in a lake because "the computer said water proof;"continually running straight gasoline in a two-stroke outboard until it seized because "engines do not need oil;"nearly burning down a battery shack next to a fuel shack because "they were not aware that red denotes positive and black denotes negative" when charging a battery; running over a brick flower planter in a cul-de-sac with a jack-knifed boat and truck because "there was no where else to go;" jamming a syringe through a co-worker's hand when asked to please hand it to him to collect a lake benthic core sample; and, my personal favorite, flipping a combination limnological/meteorological raft priced at several thousands dollars because "they were unaware that the raft was only anchored at one point and thought that the six-foot-by-six-foot raft could easily support their nearly 300 pound, unevenly distributed weight." Black sheep not only cost additional money to field programs, they often cost time. Time-shearing black sheep can often be detected standing around a boat while all others are prepping the boat for launch or landing, asking the same questions, even though the protocol has been the same every day for the last six months, or by frequently having to run into the woods from a lake or river shoreline "to use the facilities," only to return with pieces of T-shirts or socks missing, and deprive the crew of yet ANOTHER white bucket.

    Black sheep can also be very entertaining in field research, particularly if you're not one of them. The worst case scenario for "the phenomenon of black sheepness" occurs when the field station director is the ebony culprit. One would expect that the simple title of "Director" of said field station would imply some measure of demonstrated competence. Matters can only be made worse for the designated black sheep director of an Illinois field station when they hail from Wisconsin and are of Polish descent. These factors, however politically incorrect, are recognized and exploited quickly by nonblack sheep field workers. Jeers of, "Why don't you go have another brat, beer, and some cheese, eh;" "The Packers suck;" and the trite, but inevitable, "How many @#*^ people does it take to screw in a light bulb?"

It should be noted, however, that nonblack sheep must be cautious when prodding black sheep, because the infliction is unpredictable and may be exacerbated by the continued harassment of the designated black sheep.

In the recent past, I would like to believe that I was a very competent field ecologist, having conducted two, whole-lake habitat manipulations among my daily, routine field activities. In fact, I was only awarded the "Broken Prop" award from the University of Wisconsin-Madison's Center for Limnology once in eight years of summer field study, and that was guilt by association (my summer technician was the one who nearly burnt down the aforementioned battery shack). In the very recent past, I also recall being on the other dishing-it-out side of the fence with regard to black sheep. How can it be that only one year later, the "black sheep" label has been figuratively, yet firmly affixed to my shoulders. In fact, that very personal label now literally adorns the door of my office.

Why? Maybe it was my treatment of black sheep in the past. Perhaps I became overconfident in my field capabilities. I like to think that perhaps my increased responsibilities as a new field station director, a yellow lab puppy owner, or the bliss of a new marriage, may have contributed to my loss of field savvy. Likely it was choice number 4, "all of the above." The reality is that the answers to my questions may be as unpredictable as asking, "How many licks does it take to get to the center of a tootsie-roll pop?" In all seriousness, it really is difficult to lose a $350 telescopic dip net in the Spoon River, immediately after it was working so nicely for a technician, or to have a cobble-sized stone magically go through the wind shield of a brand new Ford F-150, or to not catch silver carp routinely in the La Grange Reach of the Illinois River when they are literally jumping into everyone else's boat, and, finally, to cause one of the coldest winters and two of the worst blizzards in Illinois' history. Well perhaps, not the last, even though I was blamed for it. And yes, to satisfy your curiosity, I have been seen running into the woods in search of a white bucket a time or two.

In case you, too, are a black sheep, and have not yet figured out that I am the one this story is about, let it be known that all these things above I have managed to "accomplish" in my short tenure at the Illinois River Biological Station. These examples provide only a snapshot of the many field misfortunes that I can recall from the past year. For unknown reasons, a stationary front has stalled above me recently, and the forecast is consistently cloudy with a 99% chance of unpredictable, strong and severe weather; including gale force winds, softball-sized hail, blinding snow, frigid temperatures, tornadoes, freezing rain, sleet, extreme humidity, hurricanes, tidal waves, and meteor col-

View of current black sheep director Greg Sass' office door at the Illinois River Biological Station. The picture plaque was awarded to Greg by the staff of the Illinois River Biological Station after a cobble-sized stone of unknown origin smashed through the windshield of a brand new Ford F-150 state vehicle that he was driving.

lisions. Unfortunately, for this black sheep director, the infliction seems to be a series of negative feedback loops. My participation in any field studies will ultimately cause nonblack sheep employees (hereafter referred to as normal) to take longer to accomplish field tasks [which costs the field station director (me) more money in salaries], and will result in loss or breakage of expensive equipment (which causes the same field station director to have to secure more funding to cover these mishaps).

What can a black sheep do to remedy this problem? Recognize and acknowledge the early warning signs. In my case, bringing an arctic blast and 35-degree temperatures to the Florida Keys in May, and experiencing Crater Lake in Oregon covered by clouds in a thermal inversion while on vacation are not events that occur regularly or with high probability. When a national park ranger is standing next to you at Crater Lake taking pictures and saying that he has never seen anything like this thermal inversion in his 30 years of employment at the park, "Here's your sign!"

Once the symptoms are acknowledged, there may or may not be two choices, depending on how much confidence, if any, your normal employees have in you. In short, one can, 1) remove himself from any and all field work and take the often clichéd, pointy-headed (or ivory tower) scientist's approach of sitting behind a computer, compiling field data that someone else has collected, and hoping that your curse is not aerially or tactically spread to your field workers; or 2*) slowly, yet frequently, increase your appearances in the field. Start slow and typically show up when the media are present; it is more difficult to break or lose anything when talking and acting like you know what you are doing. Next, gradually work up to giving orders like you know what you are doing when field sampling. At this stage it's important to never drive a vehicle or boat or touch any equipment that normal employees use in the field on a day-to-day basis. Lastly, over time, try to gain the confidence of your field workers so they will once again allow you to participate in field activities. Still, remember to never, ever drive a vehicle or boat. Although unknown to me at this time, listening, experience, equality, and continued participation may be the only anecdote for loosening the clutches of the black sheep plague.

Much of the overall reality, enjoyment, and pride in field studies are that every single scientist who works in the field will eventually become the "black sheep" for some unspecified amount of time. The plague is unpredictable in duration of infliction and can range from minutes to lifetimes. It also is not gender-biased. Still, some will be the black sheep more often than others. With the unpredictable nature of this plague, I preach caution. You or your normal colleagues may be a day away from contracting this affliction and suffering with it for the rest of your field career. Overall, though, field work would not be nearly as fun and rewarding (and challenging) without black sheep as they add that air of unpredictability to life on the river.

* Denotes cooperation from your normal employees to help administer treatment.

River poet.

The Illinois River . . .
Thad Cook

With interest, I watched her slowly roll by as a young boy, standing on her banks with a fishing rod in hand...

With intrigue, I ventured into her backwaters as a young man with a shotgun and decoys, eager to see what she had in store for me that season...

With excitement, I explored and researched as a young scientist what remained of a river that was once described by so many before me as being so productive...

With passion, I enjoy every day working alongside an experienced group as an established scientist dedicated to making a difference in her future...

With honor, I walk in the footsteps of renowned greats that shared the same love for her and left their prints in her backwaters for me to follow. Forbes, Kofoid, Bellrose, Starrett, Richardson, Sparks, Havera, Blodgett, the list goes on...

With love, I continue to learn and explore as a man and a scientist, with rod and gun, probe and laptop, knowing in my heart this is where I was meant to be...

Everything has changed, and nothing has changed.